MUGHAL PAINTER OF FLORA AND FAUNA
USTĀD MANṢŪR

TO THE SACRED MEMORY OF
MY TEACHER
PROFESSOR EMERITUS S. NURUL HASAN
(b. 1921; d. 1993)

MUGHAL PAINTER OF FLORA AND FAUNA *USTĀD* MANṢŪR

SOM PRAKASH VERMA

abhinav publications

First Published in India 1999

Published by
Shakti Malik
Abhinav Publications
E-37 Hauz Khas
New Delhi - 110016 (INDIA)
Phone: 6566387, 6524658
Fax: 91-11-6857009
e-mail: shakti@nde.vsnl.net.in
abhinav.abhinaf@axcess.net.in

ISBN 81-7017-365-5

Typeset in Baskerville 11pt by
Tara Chand Sons
Naraina, New Delhi

Printed at
D.K. Fine Art Press Pvt. Ltd.
Ashok Vihar, Delhi

CONTENTS

The beauty of things born before eyes and
Sufficient to itself; the heart-breaking beauty
Will remain when there is no heart to break for it.

ROBINSON JEFFERS

AUTHOR'S NOTE

The Mughals invaded, conquered and settled down to enamour Hindustan as their own. Exalted by a sense of prowess and possession they relegated the memories of their land of origin to the confines of occasional nostalgic references only. They swore by their sword, ruled by the dint of their merit, built with passion and verve massive structures of wonder and beauty, encouraged arts and crafts of the finest quality, rewarded and patronized every outstanding talent of their realm. Under their unique patronage such a philosophy of life and action flourished that with its maturity it acquired a distinct culture, so much so, that it carved for itself a permanent niche in history. Emperors Akbar, Jahāngīr and Shāh Jahān are triumvirate high peaks of this imposing range of culture. The best in anything hardly eluded their notice and recognition, notwithstanding fine art. Their meticulous historical sensibility is expressed in the records they left of their lives, times and events. They called upon their commissioned artists to illustrate the recorded descriptions with paint and brush with all exactitude, and rare beauty. Besides, they instructed the artists to paint portraits of the royalty, and all that lured them into wonderment of the strange and the beautiful. The fantastic collections of these records that they left behind, in spite of the time wrought destruction of a great many, are indelible and an infallible source of history of that great period of the Mughals. Their ateliers produced works of art that is known the world over, for its exclusiveness, originality and finesse, and later baptized as Mughal school of art by the critics.

In this wonderful throbbing age of high action, Manṣūr, the great painter of natural history, received recognition of rare excellence in Jahāngīr's atelier, and left his impress to continue through Shāh Jahān's period and later. Jahāngīr, the astute critic of art, conferred upon him the singular title of *Nādir u'l 'Aṣr* for his perfection and achievement.

Great scholars of art history, both here and abroad, have written volumes on the Mughal school of art. International collections and galleries have separate sections devoted to pictures of this school. However, in Manṣūr's case, it seems that he deserved a more detailed study than what has so far been done, in order to fill up certain, perhaps, inadvertent lacunas, and also, to re-evaluate his merit as an artist whose fame and achievement in naturalistic portraiture of a large number of species from the world of fauna and flora has remained unsurpassed till today.

Manṣūr is an artistic phenomenon, a creative event of the highest order within the imposed limitations and conventions of the Mughal atelier. He, as a keen observer of nature endowed with almost Euclidean intellect, was also capable of lending certain emotional undertones, wherever the opportunity was, to his purely objective studies, and thereby, produced an art that is at once an admiration of the zoologist, and the art lovers and critics simultaneously. He is a high priest of natural history in art, penetrating the very life of nature with supreme imagination, as well as, unflinching objectivity through the vast multiplicity of Nature's wonderful forms, he saw an inexhaustible range of individuality, variations of moods, myriad colours, and a vibrant continuity. And, the discipline of his mental faculties obliged him to reproduce those forms with the precision of a microscopic vision.

Our exploration is an attempt to enter into the very creative process of this great Mughal painter; to relive in his times and environment, in order to discover a fresh perspective for the appreciation of his work, and in the light of which, try to see those possible factors and mechanics of approach that are responsible for such astounding results. The exercise may, in some cases, involve a re-evaluation of some already existing notions and comments on Manṣūr, of course, without ever intending to be uncharitable to scholarly insights.

In view of the scanty evidential material available on the subject, and the misfortune of not being able to find any continuity in the sequence of Manṣūr's works because of the complete loss of a large number of them, the difficulties faced have not been very easy to surmount. Besides, the protracted exercise of scanning through a large number of such works which are either copies of the originals, or, pictures with faked ascriptions and forged signature, or, even those which are altogether unascribed but attributed to Manṣūr, has posed problems which could lead, for lack of alertness, into pitfalls of wrong judgement and erroneous interpretations. To avoid this, I have depended only on those authentic pictures of Manṣūr which have come out as such after a thorough process of check and recheck, and confirmed with the help of direct and indirect sources. My sole aim in this study has been to remain objective, and avoid, to the best of my efforts, all temptations to hazard interpretations and observations on hypothetical conjectures or unanalytical intuitions.

For transliteration of inscriptions used in the text, I have exclusively followed the system of spelling and diacritical marks adopted by Steingass in his *Comprehensive Persian-English Dictionary.*

The possibilities of this present work occurred to me during my preparation of the volume *Mughal Painters and Their Work — A Biographical Survey and Comprehensive Catalogue* (Oxford University Press, 1994) which includes a fair amount of information on such material as: biographical records, lists of signed, ascribed and attributed works, and notes on styles, of as many as over two hundred painters of the Mug͟hal school (16th-17th centuries). The magnitude of the problems faced in the preparation of it, demanding vigorous search and continuous scrutiny of the facts, could only be significantly mitigated with the aid of right research methods, and patient inculcation of academic discipline, the training of which I received under the guidance of Professor Irfan Habib. With the same cast of my mind I ventured to give shape and form to my study of Manṣūr. In this endeavour also, Professor Habib's encouragement and inspiration had always been coming forth ungrudgingly whenever I needed them. For all this, I owe him a deep sense of gratitude.

I am no less indebted to Professor M.A. Alvi and Professor A.J. Qaisar for their sincere and friendly support, and keen interest in my work. Their patient and enlightening discussions on research problems, and valuable suggestions throughout proved to be my mainstay in the preparation of the book.

I am thankful to Professor Shireen Moosvi; Professor Iqbal Husain and Dr. Mohammad Afzal Khan who assisted me in the interpretations of the Persian inscriptions; and to Professor S.K. Saxena and Professor Wajahat Husain of the Department of Botany, Aligarh Muslim University, and Mr. Ambar Habib, an avid bird-watcher, for their help in identifying some of the species of birds and flowers, painted by Manṣūr.

I am sincerely grateful to Mr. P.K. Ghosh for editing the text of this book, and giving many useful suggestions of highly critical nature on the aesthetic aspects, which proved to be very helpful in the evaluation of Manṣūr's paintings.

The Fulbright Fellowship, awarded to me in 1987, enabled me to visit museums and art galleries of New York, Washington and Baltimore, and to have rare pleasure of working with Dr. Milo C. Beach, and discussions on the subject with Professor S.C. Welch and Dr. Esin Atil. This work could have remained bereft of much of its originality had not the opportunity to study Mug͟hal miniatures in the cherished collections in the United States come my way.

My acknowledgements and special thanks are due to the authorities of the National Museum, New Delhi; Sawai Man Singh ll Museum, Jaipur; Indian Museum, Calcutta; State Museum, Lucknow; Prince of Wales Museum of Western India, Bombay; India Office Library, London; British Museum and Library, London; Royal Library, Windsor; Victoria and Albert Museum, London, for their cooperation.

I should like to thank Ms. Lily Kecskes, Head Librarian, Freer Gallery of Art and Arthur M. Sackler Gallery, Washington, who gave me ungrudging assistance in using these splendid libraries. Thanks are due to Mr. M.H. Razvi (Librarian), Mr. Baqar Ali Khan and Mr. Masitullah at the Maulana Azad Library, Aligarh Muslim University and Mr. Aijaz M. Khan, Arshad Ali, M. Yusuf Siddiqi and Noor Ahmad at the Research Library, Centre of Advanced Study, Department of History, Aligarh Muslim University, where most of my work was given shape and completed.

Mr. Ishrat Alam's contribution by way of checking and comparing the typescript to its final shape must need be mentioned here especially.

Last, but not the least, my gratitude is due to all the members of my family and Dr. Pushpa Prasad, my friend and colleague, and her daughter Dr. Smriti Prasad, for their patient cooperation and continuous encouragement.

Aligarh
3 February 1995

Som Prakash Verma
Professor of History
Aligarh Muslim University

LIST OF ABBREVIATIONS

AA	*Artibus Asie,* Hellerau-Dredson, subsequently Ascona
AAA	*Archives of Asian Art,* London
AAL	*Art and Letters,* Journal of Royal India, Pakistan and Ceylon Society, London
Akb.	*Akbarnāma*
Anwār	*Anwār-i Suhailī*
AOS	*Ars Orientalis,* Freer Gallery of Art, Washington, D.C.
Bāb.	*Bāburnāma*
BCA	*Bulletin of College of Arts,* Baghdad
BLO	Bodleian Library, Oxford
BM	British Museum, London
BMFA	*Bulletin of Museum of Fine Arts,* Boston
BMMA	*Bulletin of The Metropolitan Museum of Art,* New York
BUM	*Burlington Magazine,* London
CANH	Alice and Nasli Heeramaneck Collection, New York
CBL	Chester Beatty Library, Dublin
CBL (A)	Album of Separate Miniatures of the Mughal School, Chester Beatty Library, Dublin
CBMR	Baron Maurice Rothschild Collection, Paris
CBQ	Bernard Quaritch Collection, Paris
CCJ	Cowasji Jehangir Collection, Bombay
CE	Eckstein Collection
CECM	Collection of Edward Croft Murray, London
CG	Gloubew Collection, Boston
CGCNS	Collection of Geoffrey C.N. Sturt, Painswick, Gloucestershire
CHPK	Hans P. Karus Collection, New York
CHV	M. Henri Vever Collection, Paris

CMA	Cleveland Museum of Art, Cleveland
CMDu	M. Duffeuty Collection, Paris
CPCM	P.C. Manuk Collection, Bankipore, Patna
CR	Collection of Professor William Rothenstein, S.K. London
CRC	Ross-Coomaraswamy Collection (Mola Ram Series), Boston
CW	Wantage Collection, London
Dārā (A)	Dārā Shukoh Album
Dīwān (A)	*Dīwān* of Anwarī
EAQ	*Eastern Art Quarterly,* Philadelphia
EW	*East and West,* Rome
FAM	Fogg Art Museum, Harvard University, Cambridge, USA
FGA	Freer Gallery of Art, Washington, D.C.
FMC	Fitzwilliam Museum, Cambridge
Gulshan (A)	*Muraqqa'-i Gulshan (Gulshan Album)*
HL	Hermitage, Leningrad
IHR	*The Indian Historical Review,* Journal of Indian Council of Historical Research, New Delhi
IL	Imperial Library, Teheran
IM	Indian Museum, Calcutta
INI	*Indo-Iranica,* Journal of Iran Society, Calcutta
IOL	India Office Library, London
IPM (A)	*Album of Indian and Persian Miniatures of the XVI-XVII Centuries*
ISC	*Islamic Culture,* Hyderabad
Jahāngīr (A)	Jahāngīr Album
Jāmi'	*Jāmi'-ut Tawārīkh*
Johnson (A)	*Johnson Album*
JIAI	*Journal of Indian Art and Industry,* London
JIM	*Journal of Indian Museum,* Calcutta
JBNHS	*The Journal of the Bombay Natural History Society,* Madras
JWAG	*Journal of the Walters Art Gallery,* Baltimore
Kevorkian (A)	*Kevorkian Album*
KFM	Kaiser Friedrich Museum, Berlin
Khamsa (K)	*Khamsa* of Amīr Khusrau

Lalit	*Lalit Kala,* Journal of the Lalit Kala Academy, New Delhi
Marg	*Marg,* Bombay
MAU	Maulana Azad Library, Aligarh Muslim University
MduL	Musee du Louvre, Paris
MECM	Museum of Eastern Cultures, Moscow
MFA	Museum of Fine Arts, Boston
MG	Musee Guimet, Paris
Minto (A)	*Minto Album*
MMA	The Metropolitan Museum of Art, New York
Naṣīruddīn (A)	*Naṣīruddīn Album*
NM	National Museum, New Delhi
OA	*Oriental Art,* London
OIUSSR	Oriental Institute of the U.S.S.R. Academy of Science, Leningrad
OPL	Oriental Public Library, Patna (Khuda Bakhsh Library)
Phoenix	*Phoenix,* Amsterdam
PQ	*Pakistan Quarterly,* Karachi
PWM	Prince of Wales Museum of Western India, Bombay
RFM	Red Fort Museum, Delhi
RKTC	R.K. Tandon Collection
RLWC	Royal Library, Windsor Castle, Windsor
Roopa	*Roopa-Lekha,* Journal of All India Fine Arts & Crafts Society, New Delhi
Rupam	*Rupam,* Quarterly Journal of the Oriental Art, Calcutta
Studio	*Studio,* London
SLB	State Library, Berlin
SLR	State Library, Rampur (Raza Library)
SML	State Museum, Lucknow
SMS	Maharaja Sawai Man Singh II Museum, Jaipur
Tūzuk	*Tūzuk-i Jahāngīrī/Jahāngīrnāma*
VA	Victoria and Albert Museum, London
WAG	The Walters Art Gallery, Baltimore

LIST OF ILLUSTRATIONS (IN TEXT)

Fig. 14 Himalayan griffon, CBL. Unascribed. An early nineteenth century copy of Manṣūr's original. Compare with Plate XIV and Fig. 13 above.

Fig. 15 Spotted forktail, *Kevorkian (A),* MMA, no. 55.121.10.15. Painted by Abū'l Ḥasan, c. 1620. For an early nineteenth century copy forged in Manṣūr's name, see below, Fig. 16.

Fig. 16 Spotted forktail, *Kevorkian (A),* FGA, no. 39.46b.

Fig. 17 Assembly of pigeons, Private Collection. A late eighteenth century work forged in Manṣūr's name.

Fig. 18 Fantastic bird, *Kevorkian (A),* MMA, no. 55.121.10.26r. An early nineteenth century work forged in Manṣūr's name.

Fig. 19 Jungle fowl, *Kevorkian (A),* MMA, no. 55.121.10.27r. An early nineteenth century work forged in Manṣūr's name.

Fig. 20 Jungle fowl, G.C. Sturt, Esq. Collection. Unascribed. A work of late eighteenth century.

Fig. 21 Portrait of Ḥājjī Ḥusain Bukhārī, *Kevorkian (A),* MMA, no. 55.121.10.28r. An early nineteenth century work forged in Manṣūr's name.

Fig. 22 Siberian crane, IM, no. R32. Unascribed. A work of late eighteenth century.

Fig. 23 Turkey cock, SMS, no. AG839. Unascribed. An early nineteenth century copy of Manṣūr's original. Compare with Plate V.

Fig. 24 Drawing of a pair of Tibetan cranes. Unascribed. VA, IM, no. 42-1925. Compare with Plate XVII.

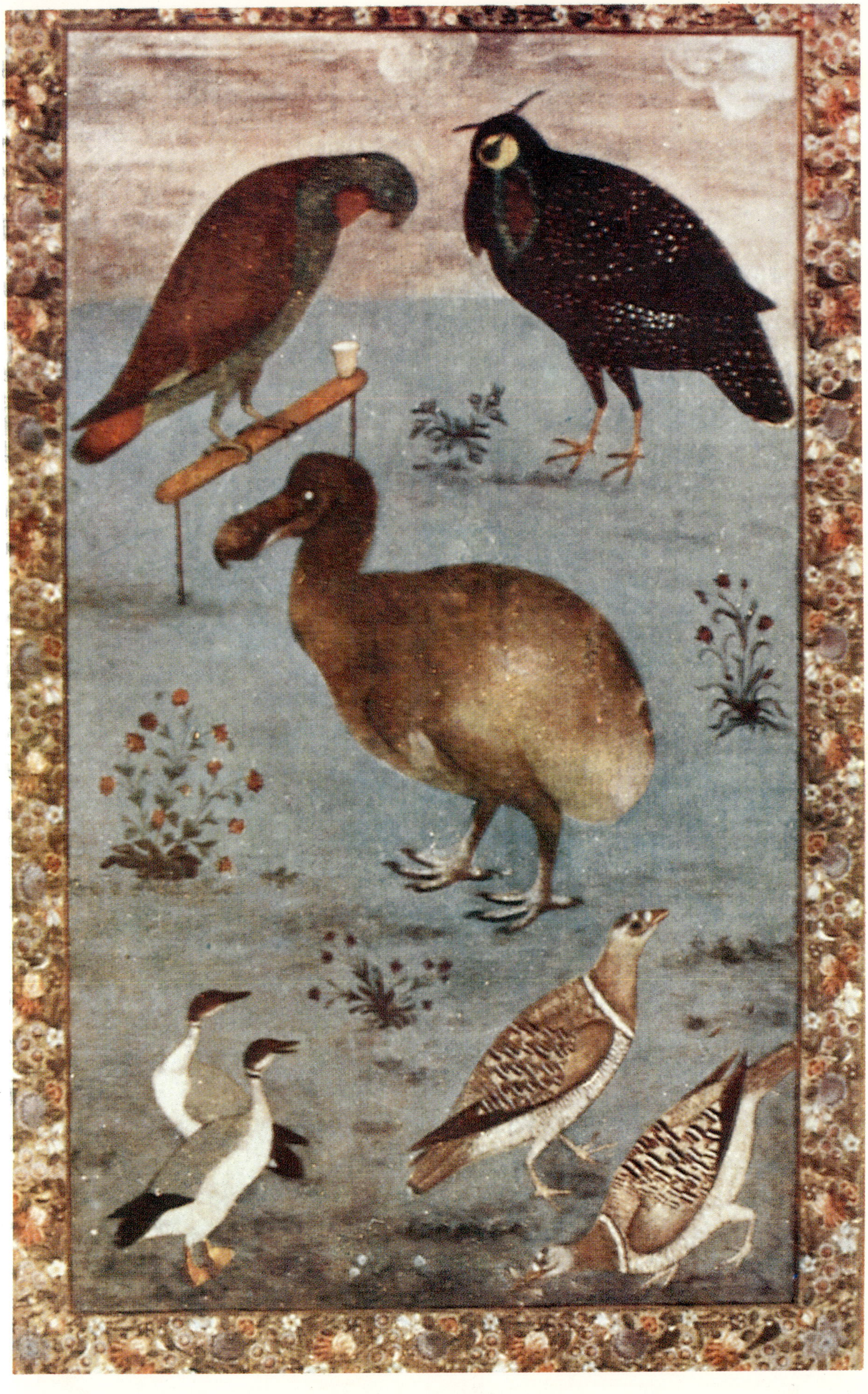

Fig. 1 Pictures of the dodo, tragopan, Sumatran loriquet, ducks and partridges, *IPM (A)*, OIUSS. Unascribed. c. 1630-50.

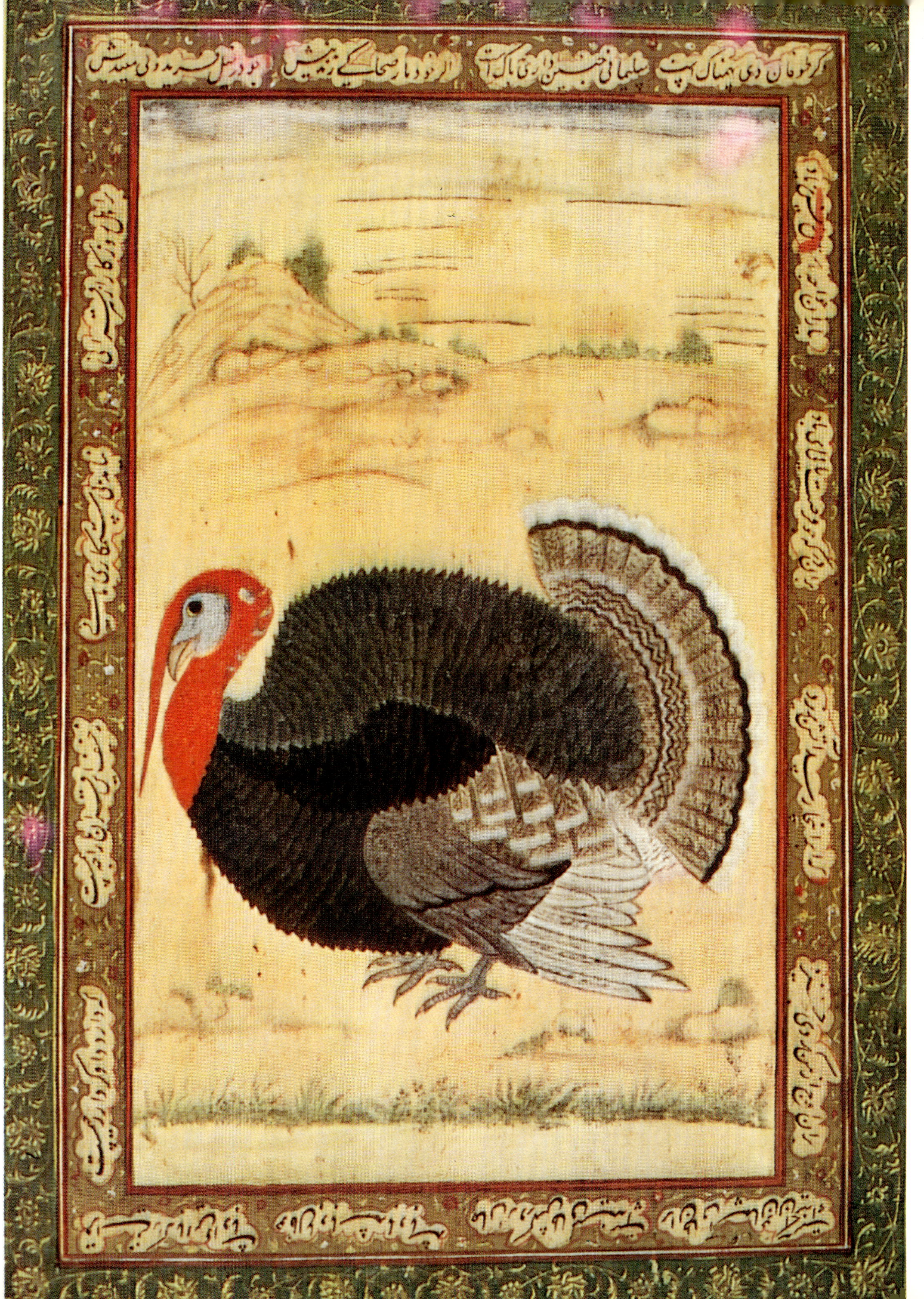

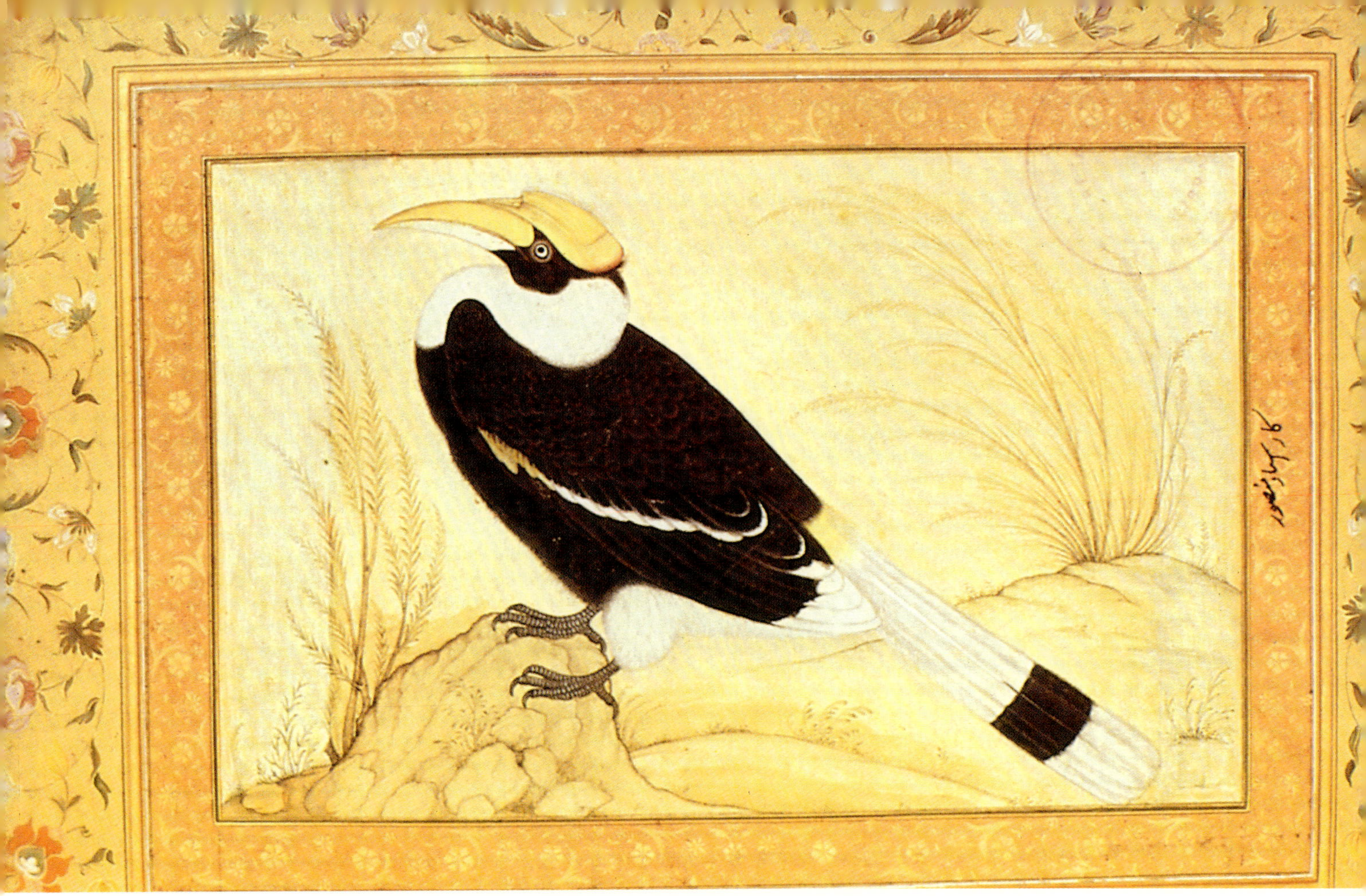

Fig. 9 Hornbill, *Kevorkian (A)*, MMA, no. 55.121.10.14v. Painted by *Ustād* Manṣūr.

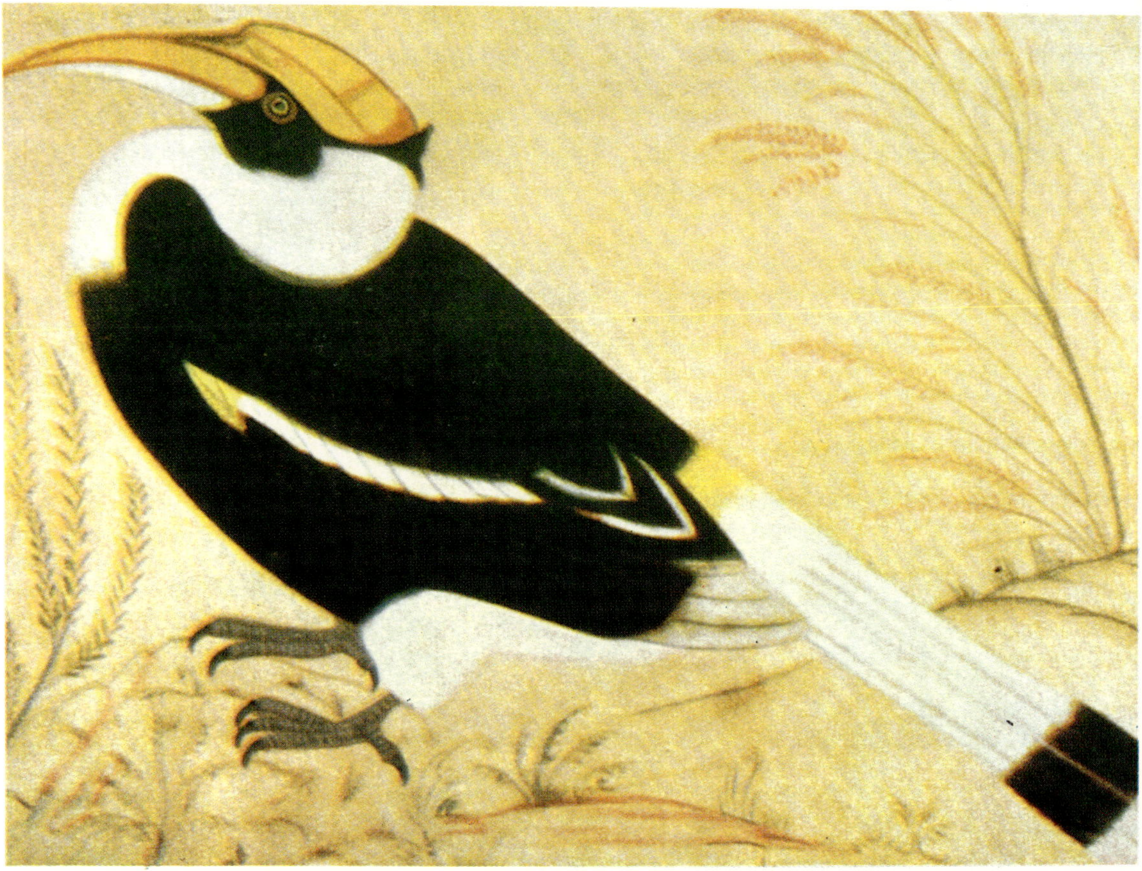

Fig.10 Hornbill, CGCNS. Unascribed. An early nineteenth century copy.

Fig. 8 Turkey cock, IM, no. R210. Unascribed. Late eighteenth century copy

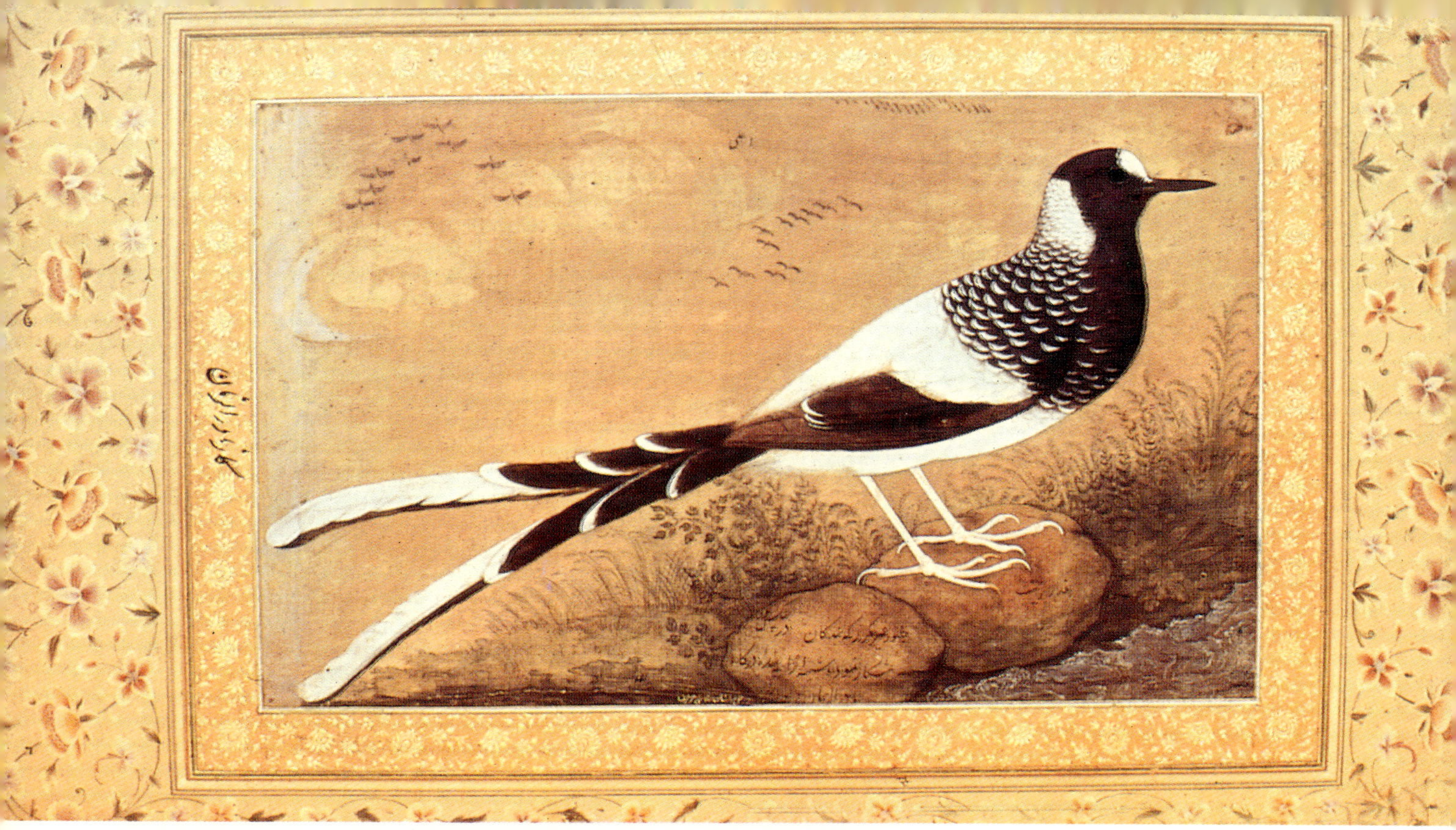

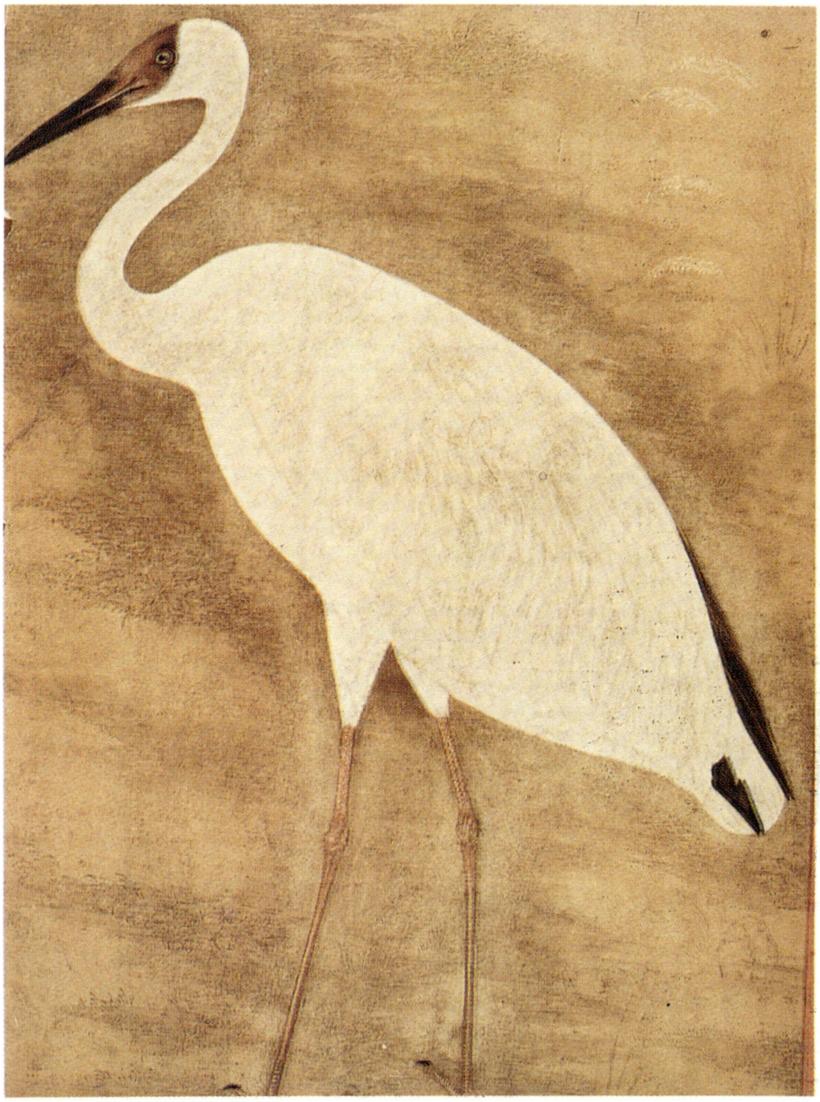

Fig. 15 Spotted forktail, *Kevorkian (A)*, MMA, no.55.121.10.15. Painted by Abū'l Ḥasan, c. 1620.

Fig. 22 Siberian crane, IM, no. R32. Unascribed. A work of late eighteenth century.

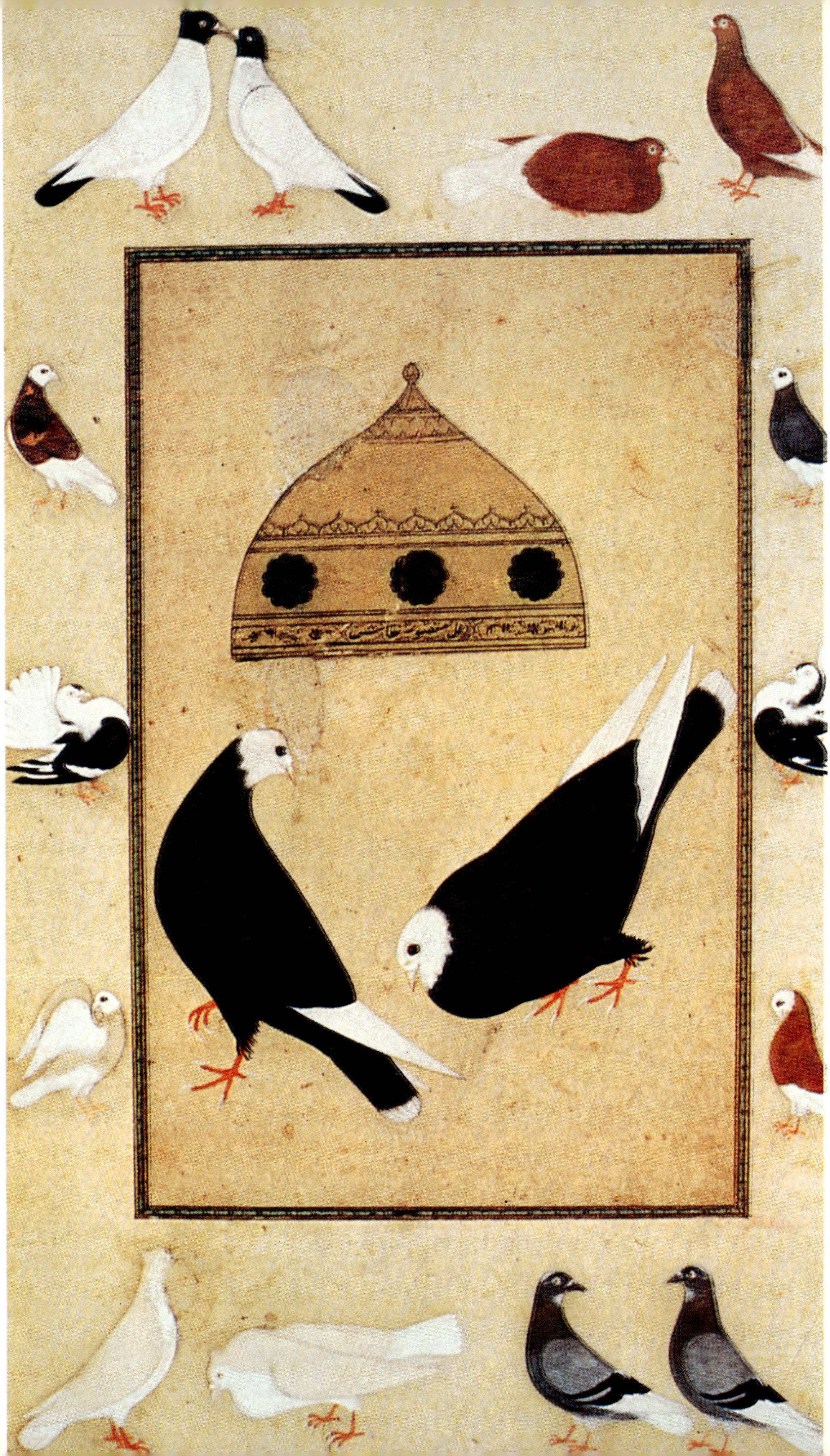

Fig. 17 Assembly of pigeons, Private Collection. A late eighteenth century work.

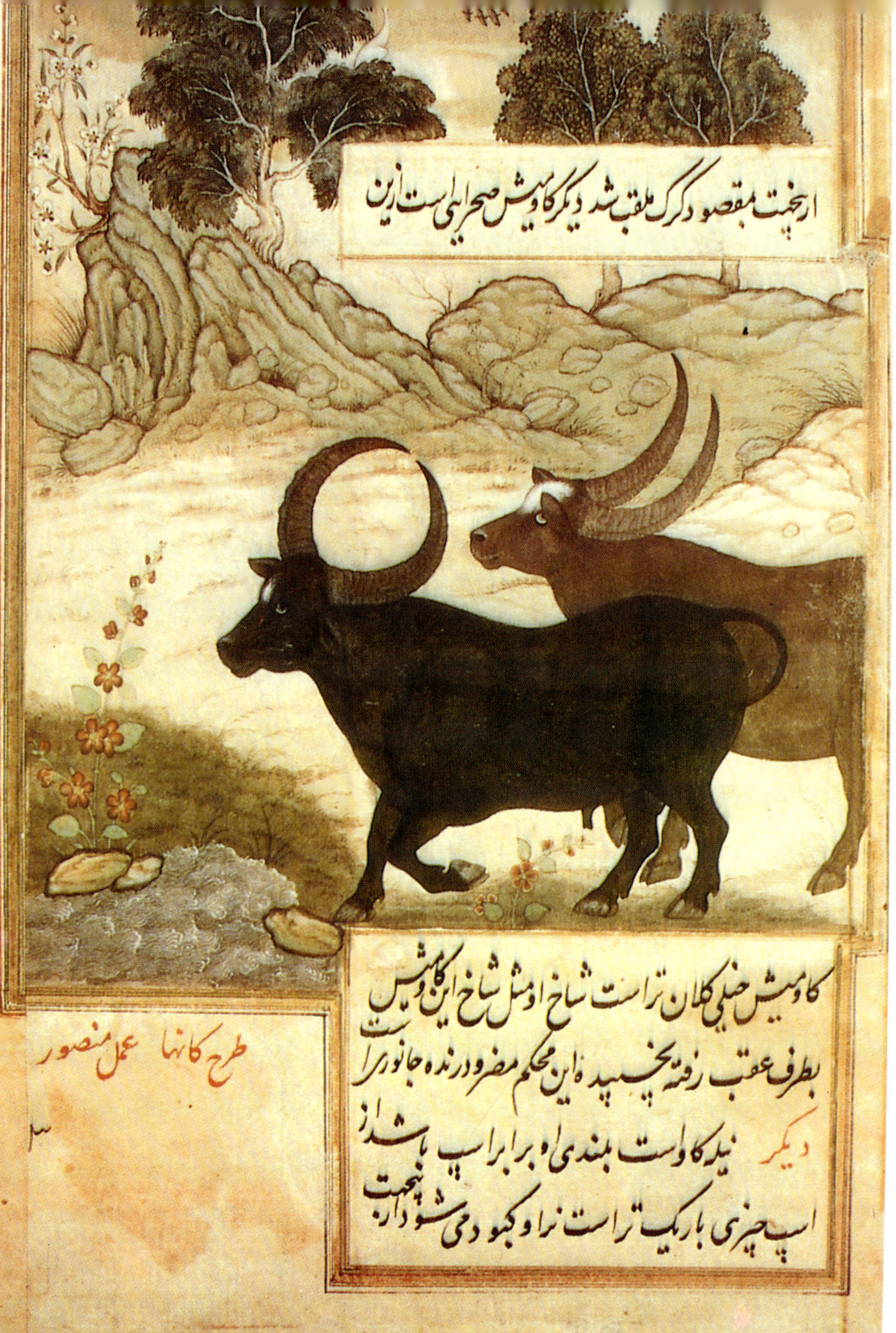
از بخت بمقصود گرگ ملقب شد دیگر گاومیش صحرایی ست ازین
گاومیش خیلی کلان تر است شاخ او مثل شاخ این گاومیش است
بطرف عقب رفته پیچیده این محکم مضر و درنده جانوری
دیگر نیله گاو است بلندی او برابر اسپ باشد از
اسپ چیزی باریک تر است نر او کبود می شود ازینجهت
طرح کانها عمل منصور

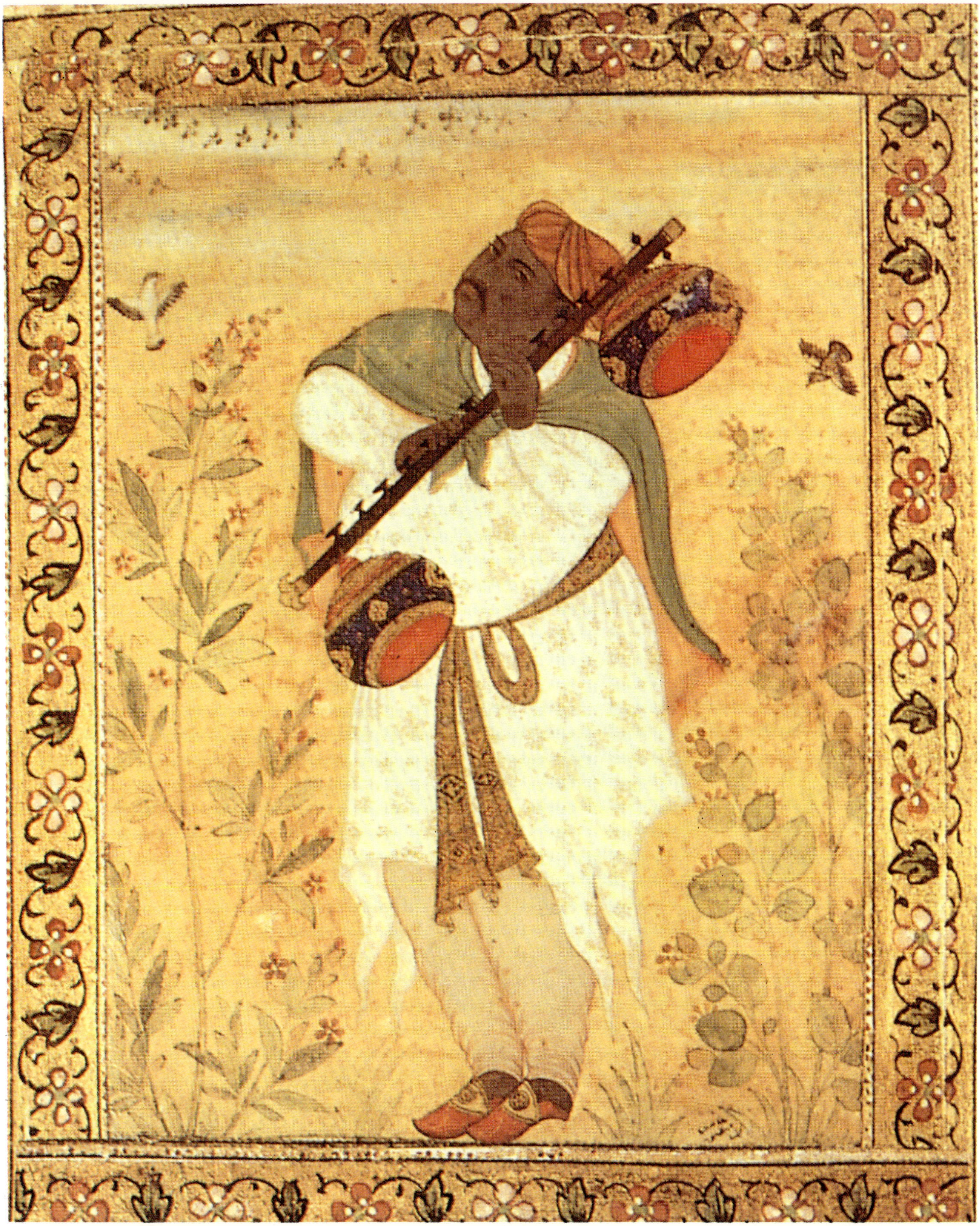

Pl. I(A) Two wild buffalo. Folio from the *Baburnama* (*c.* 1590-1600), Freer Gallery of Art, Washington. D.C.

Pl. III *Vina*-player. *C.* 1600. Collection of Edward Croft Murray, London.

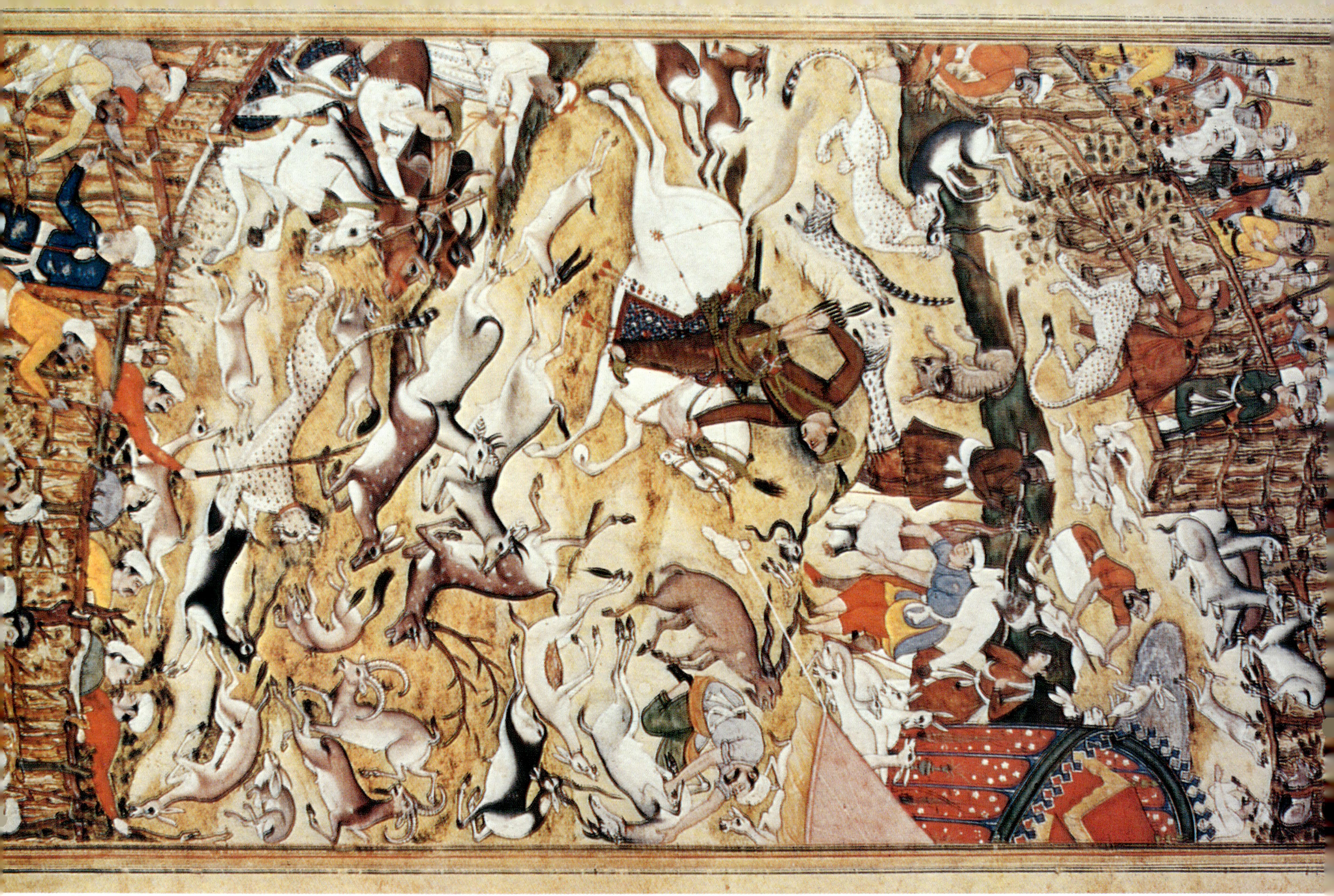

Pl. IV Akbar hunting. *Akbarnama*, Victoria & Albert Museum, London. *C.* 1602-05.

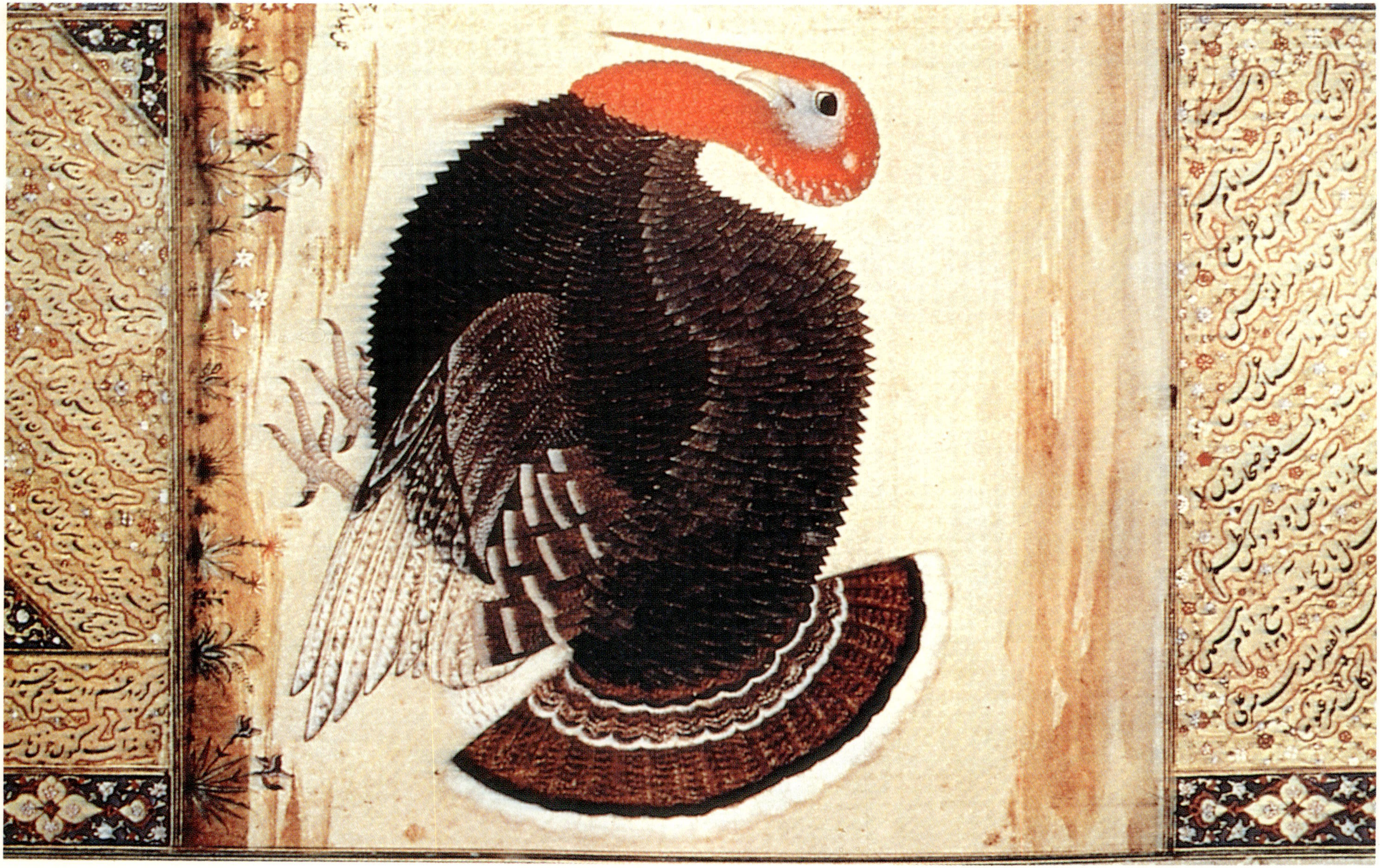

Pl. V Turkey cock. *C.* 1612. Wantage Collection, Victoria & Albert Museum, London.

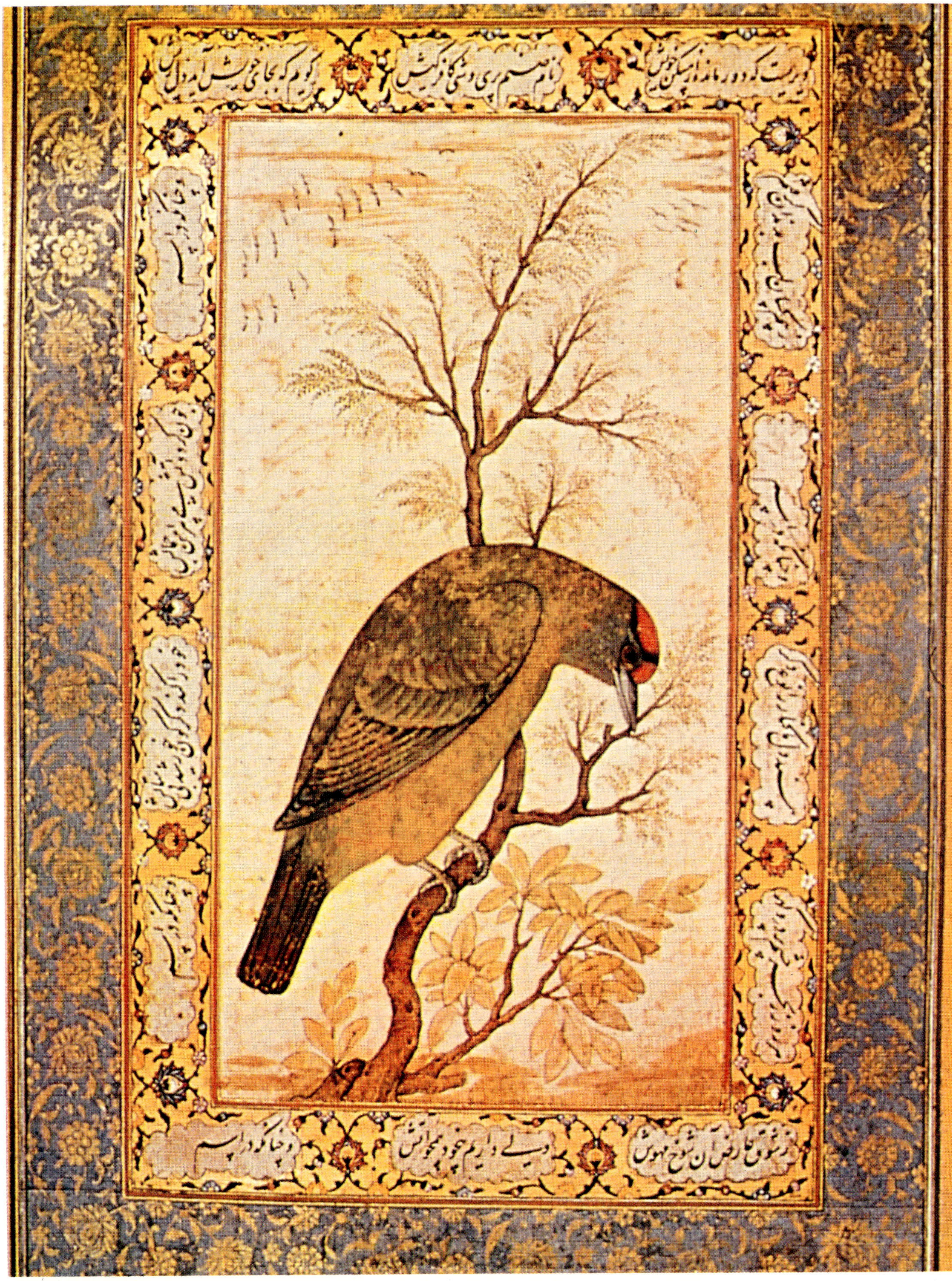

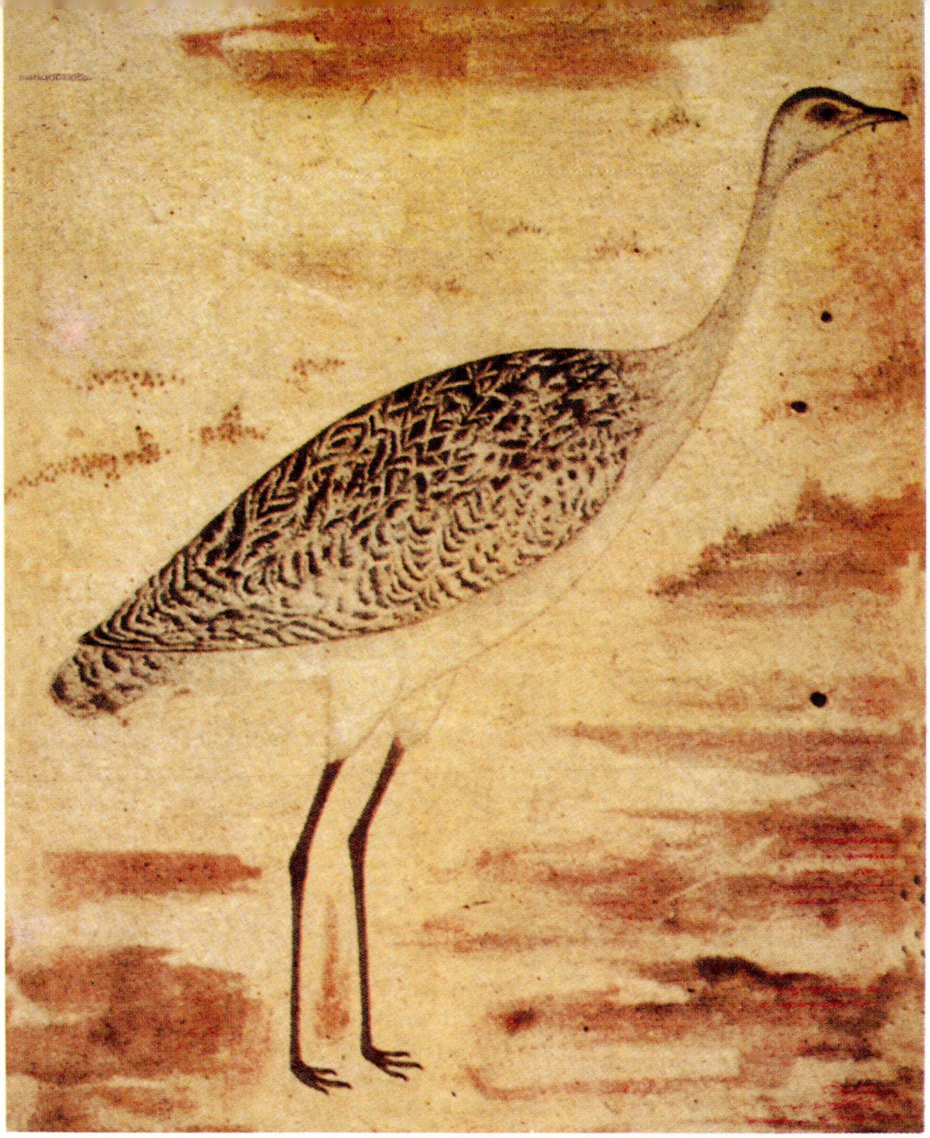

Pl. IX Indian bustard (*Charz-i bor*). 1619. Indian Museum, Calcutta.

Pl. X Chameleon on a branch. *C.* 1610-20. Royal Library, Windsor.

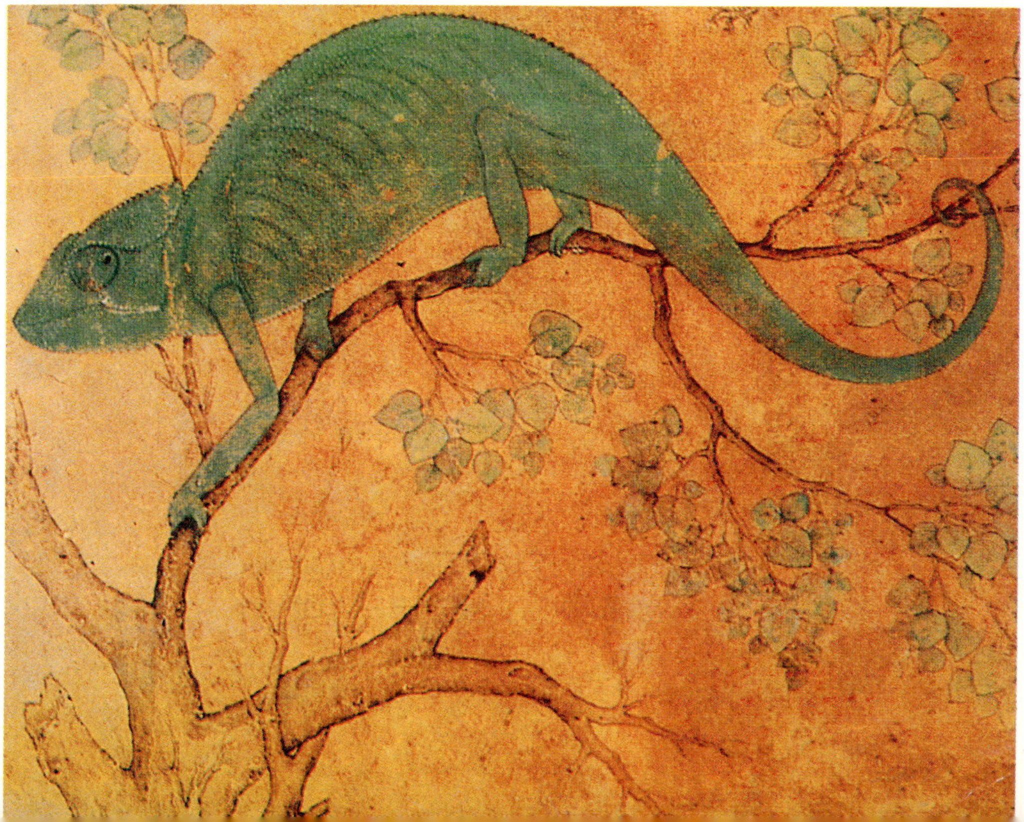

Pl. VII Himalayan blue throated barbet. *C.* 1615-20. Wantage Col lection, Victoria & Albert Museum, London.

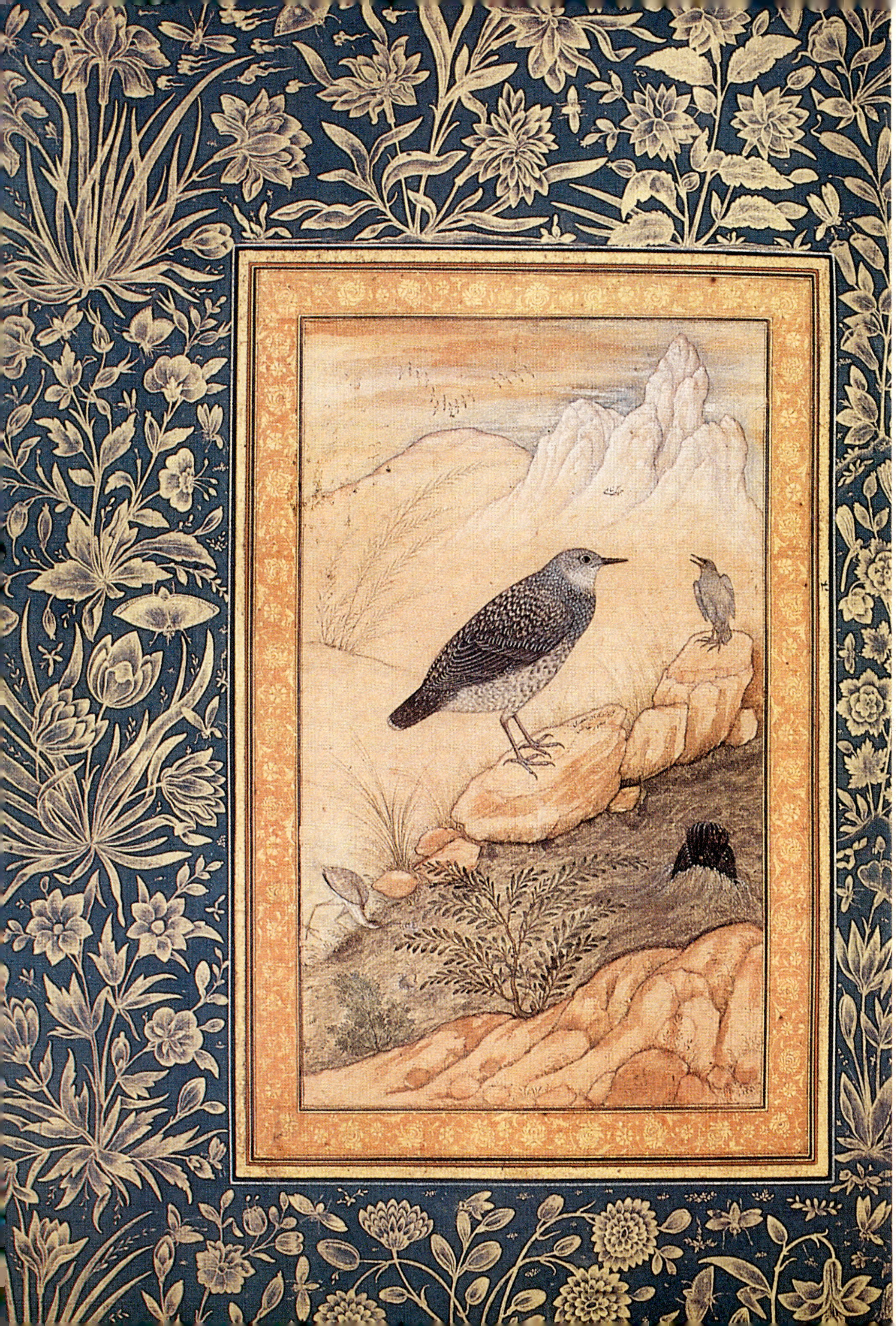

Pl. XIII Dipper (*Saj*). *C.* 1620. The Metropolitan Museum of Art, New York.

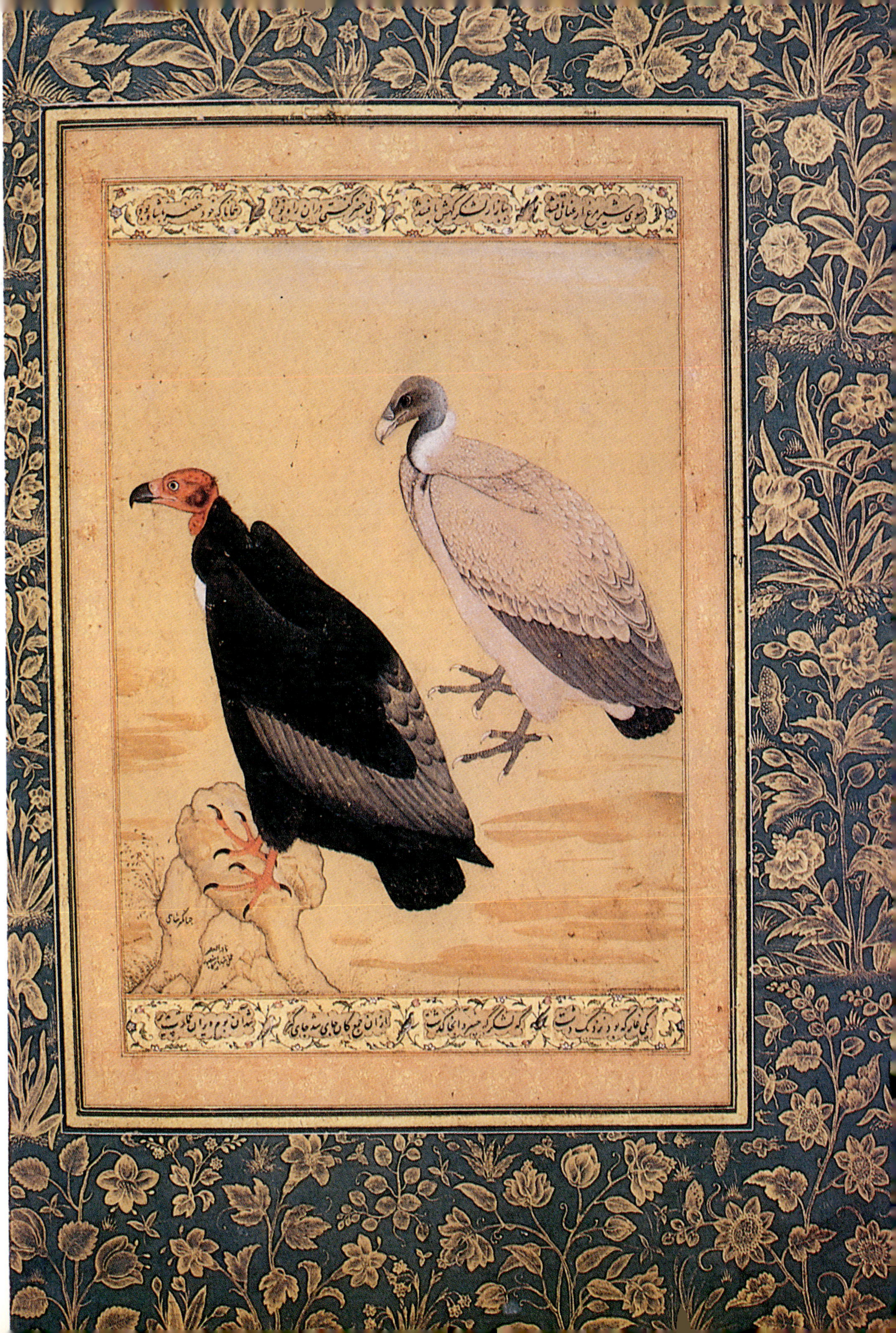

Pl. XIV King vulture and Himalayan griffon. *C.* 1620-25. The Metropolitan Museum of Art, New York.

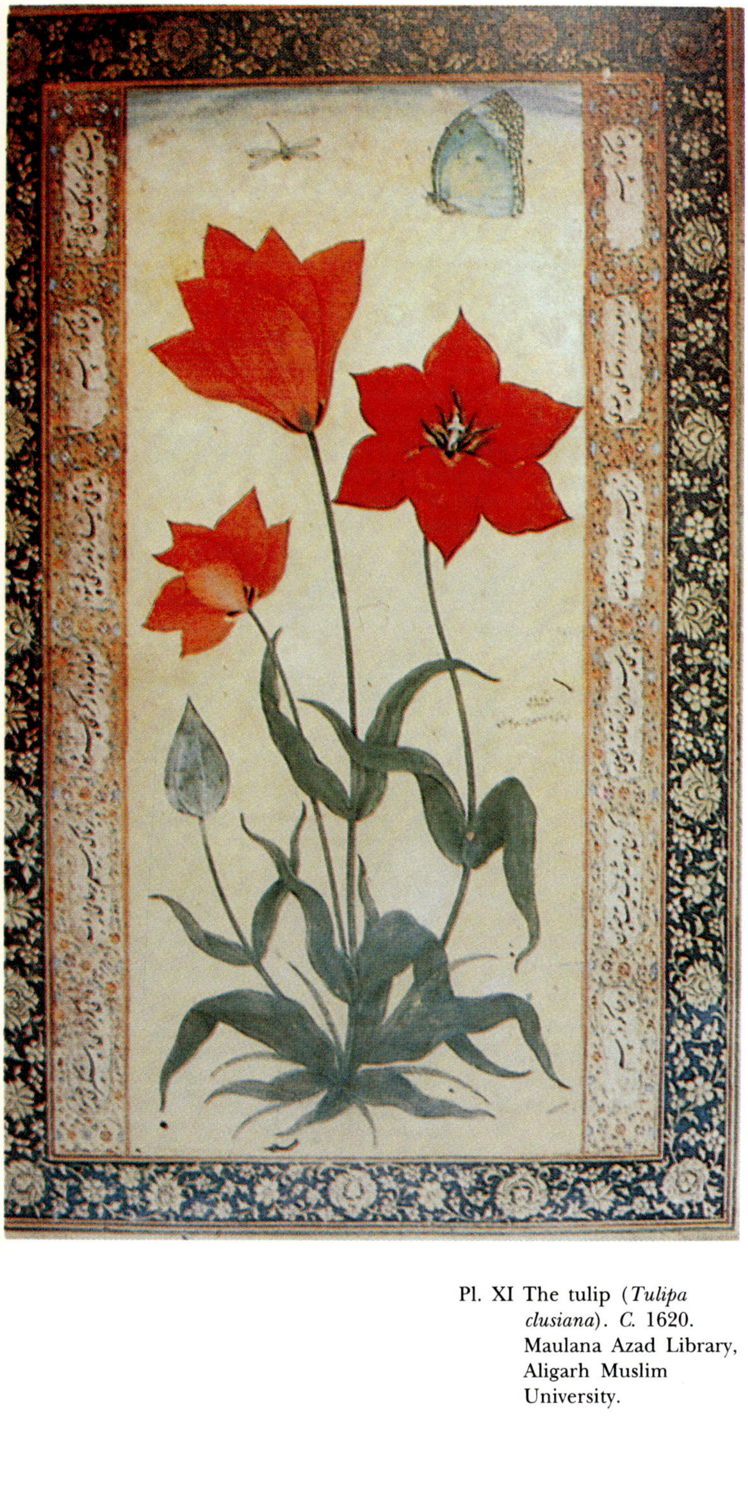

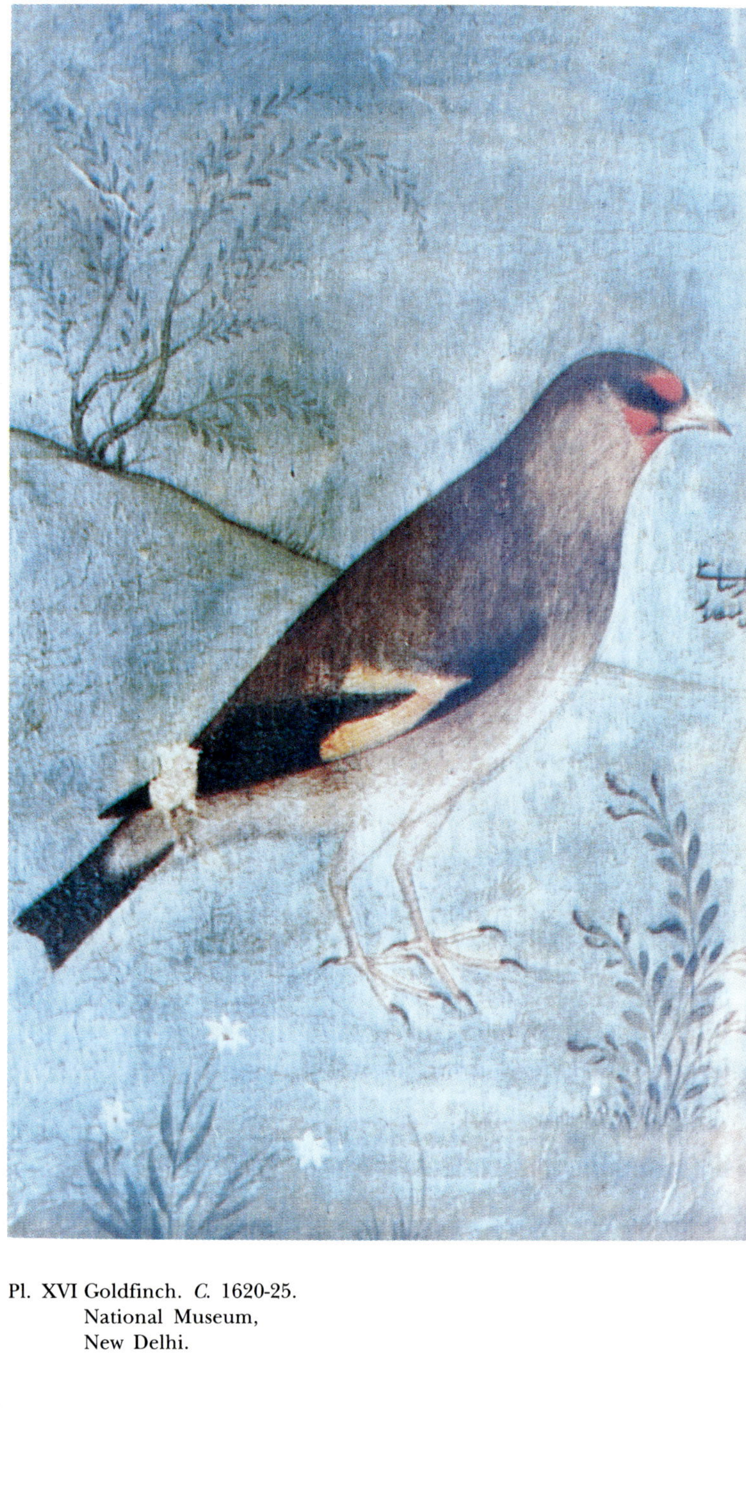

Pl. XI The tulip (*Tulipa clusiana*). *C.* 1620. Maulana Azad Library, Aligarh Muslim University.

Pl. XVI Goldfinch. *C.* 1620-25. National Museum, New Delhi.

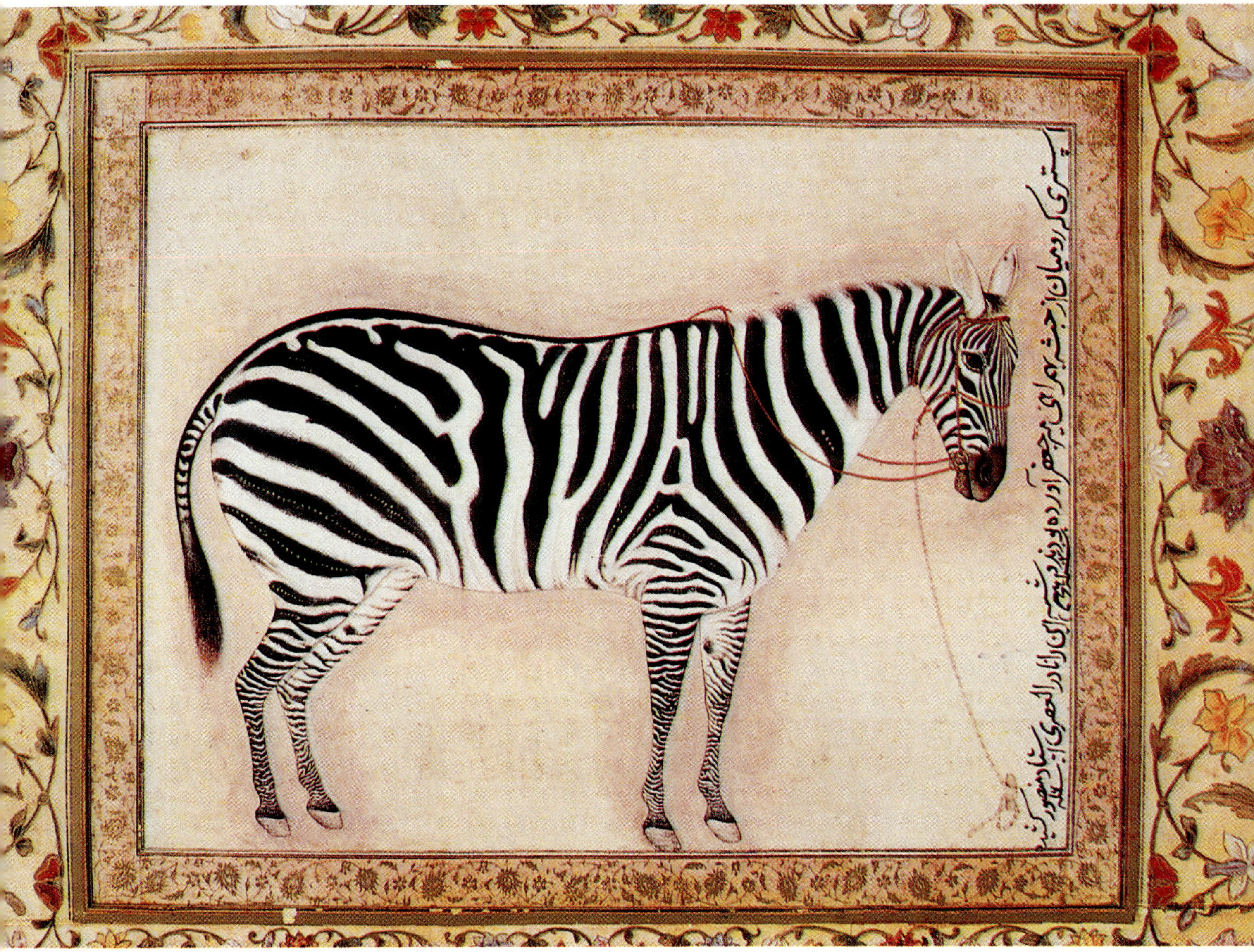

Pl. XV Zebra. 1621. Victoria & Albert Museum, London.

Pl. XVII Pair of Tibetan cranes. *C.* 1621-25. Wantage Collection, Victoria & Albert Museum, London.

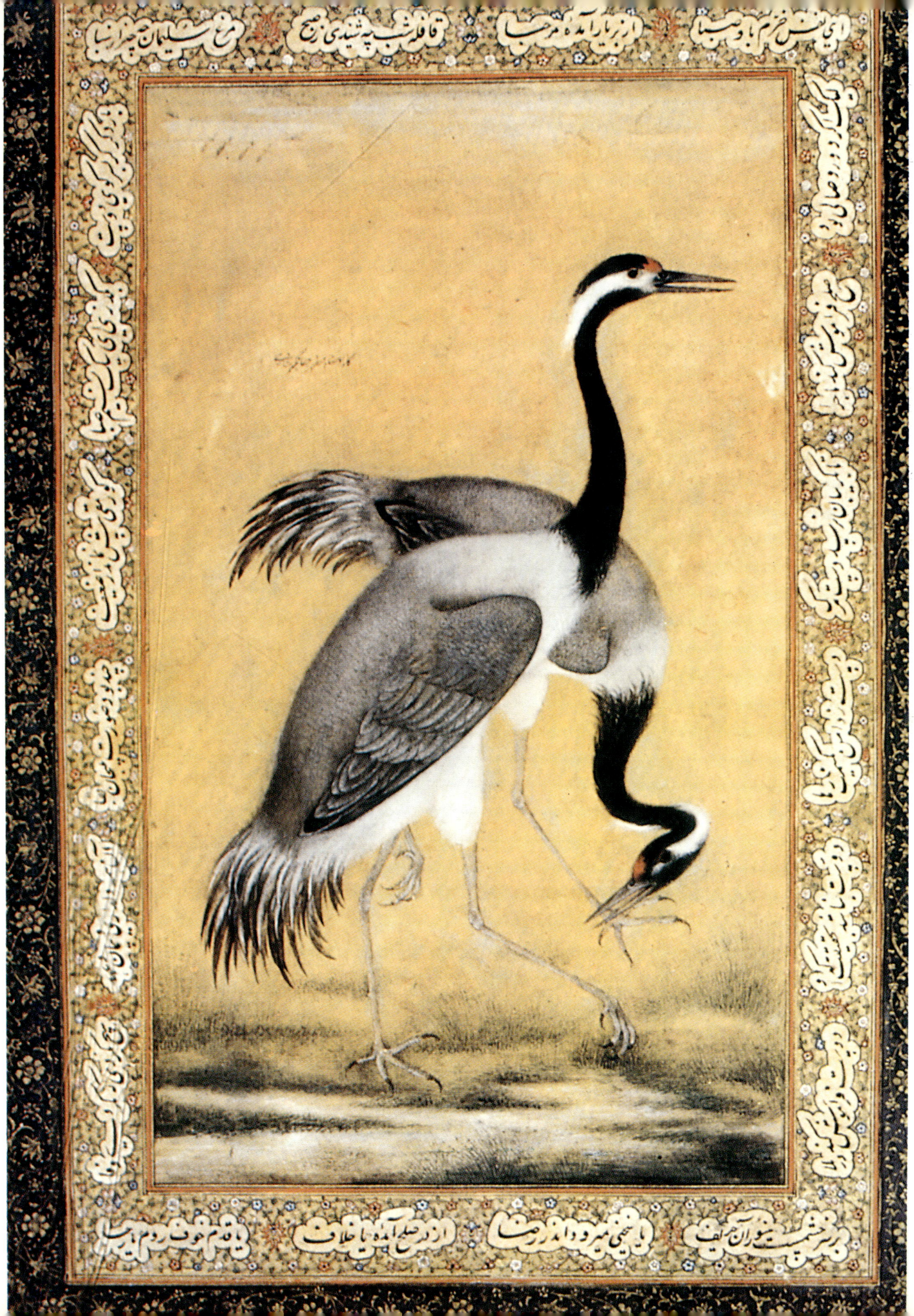
ای نفس خرم باد صبا
از بر یار آمده مرحبا
قافله شب چه شنیدی ز صبح
مرغ سلیمان چه خبر از سبا
بر سر خشم است هنوز آن حریف
یا سخنی میرود اندر رضا
از در صلح آمده یا خلاف
یا قدم خوف روم یا رجا

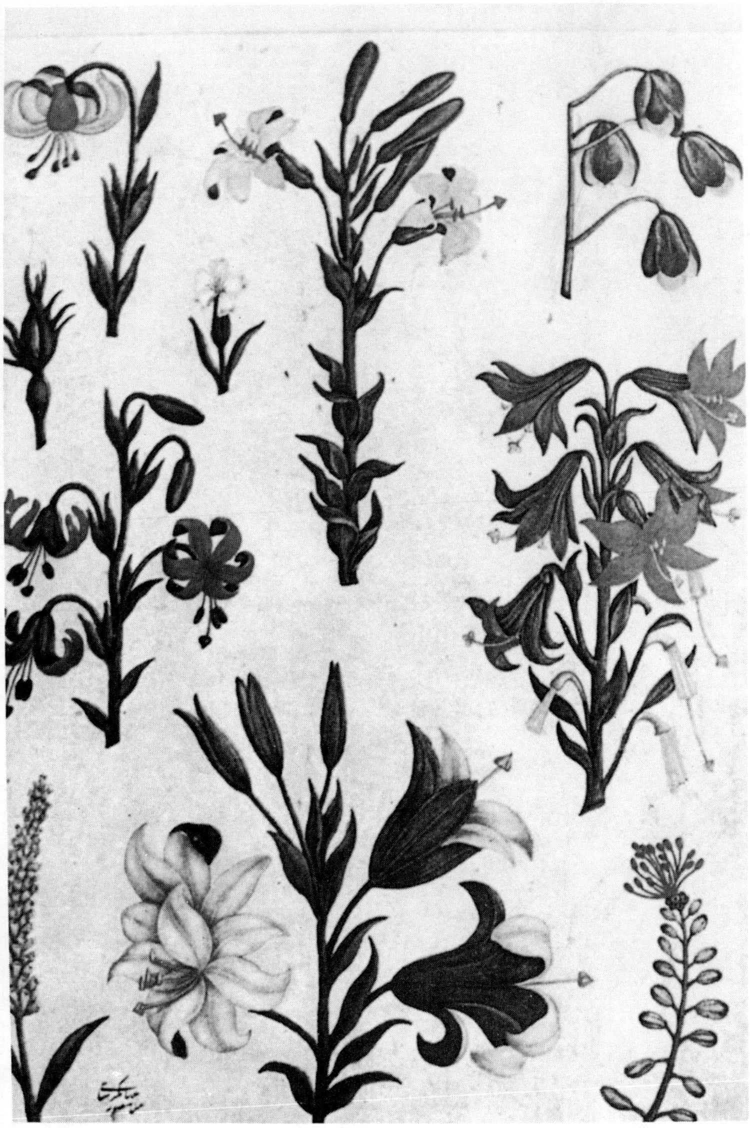

Fig. 2 Seven varieties of flowers, *Gulshan* (*A*), IL, f. 103. By Manṣūr *Jahāngīr Shāhī*.

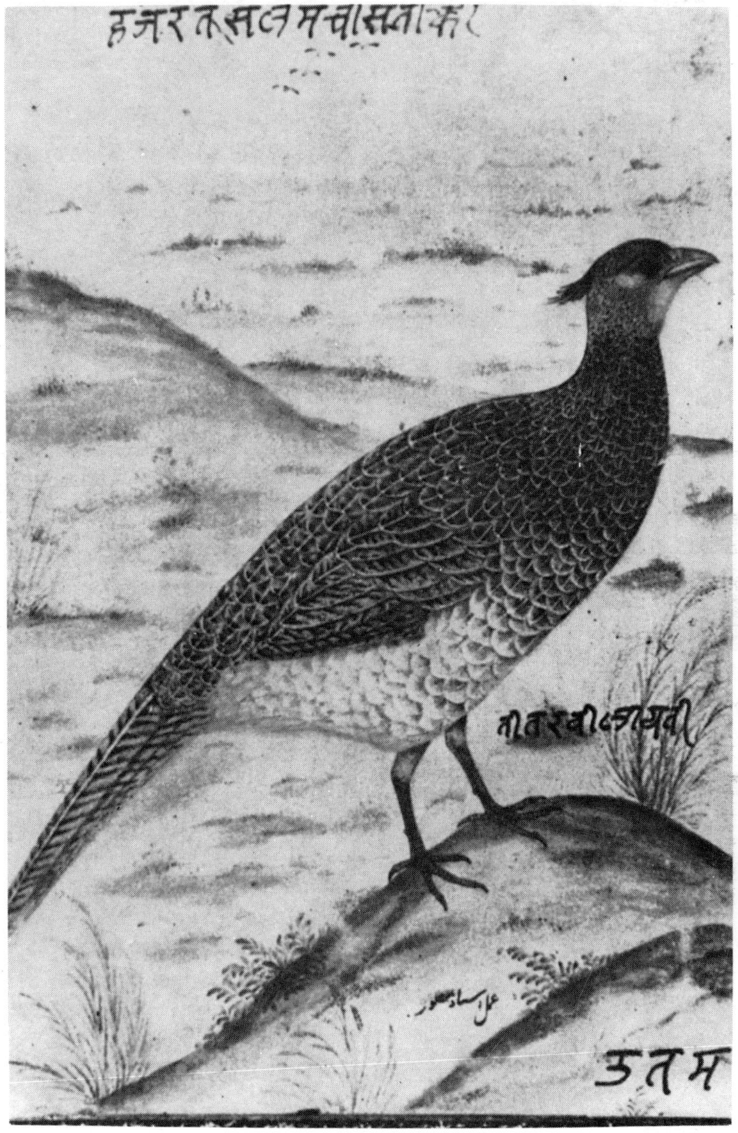

Fig. 3 Himalayan cheer pheasant, SMS, no. AG834. An early nineteenth century copy.

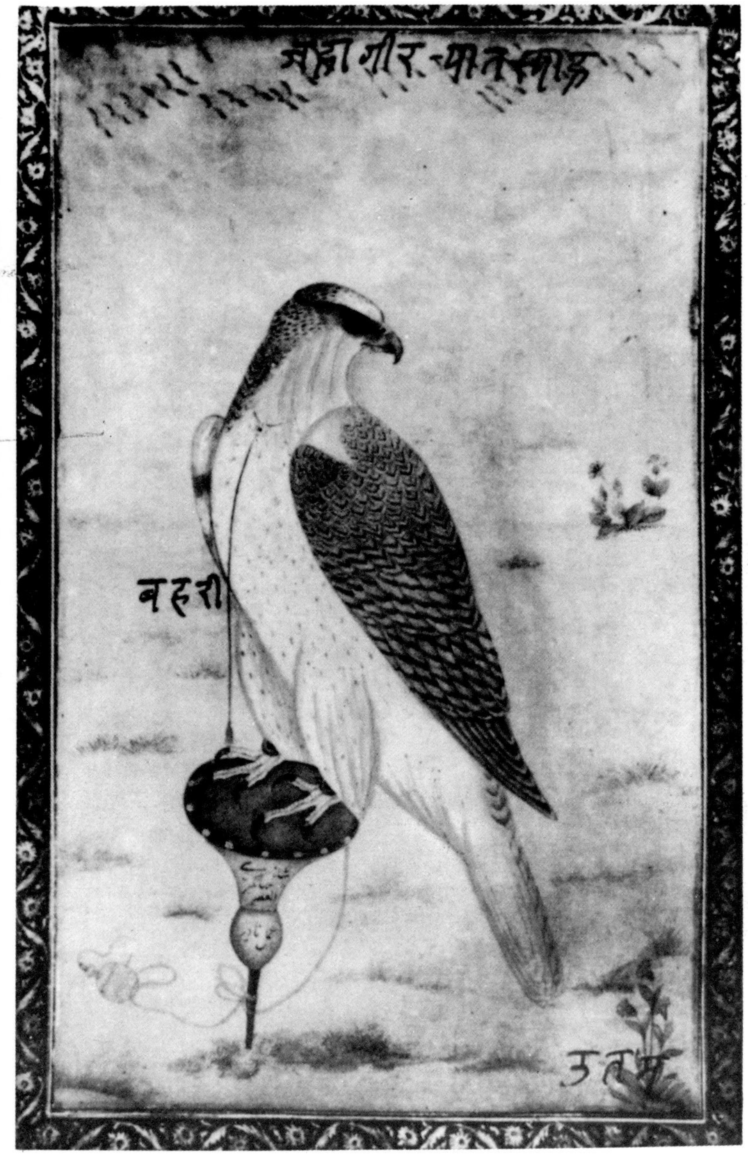

Fig. 4 Falcon on perch, SMS, no. AG824. An early nineteenth century work.

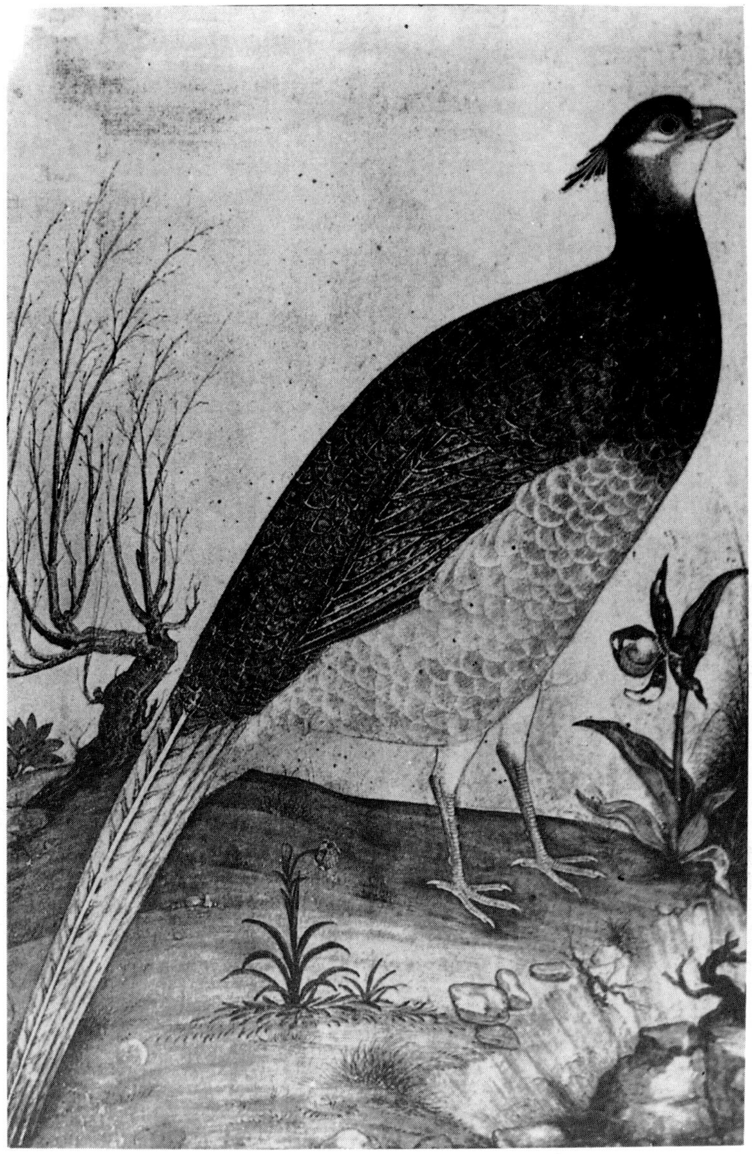

Fig. 5 Himalayan cheer pheasant, CMBR. Unascribed. An early nineteenth century copy.

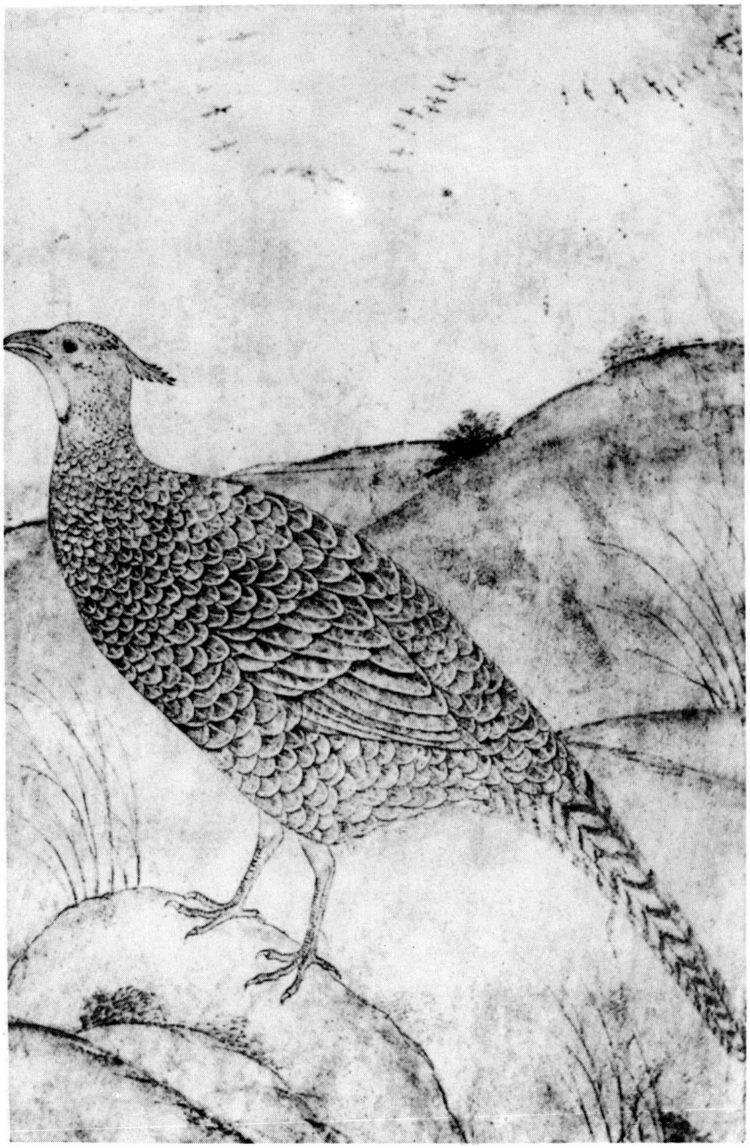

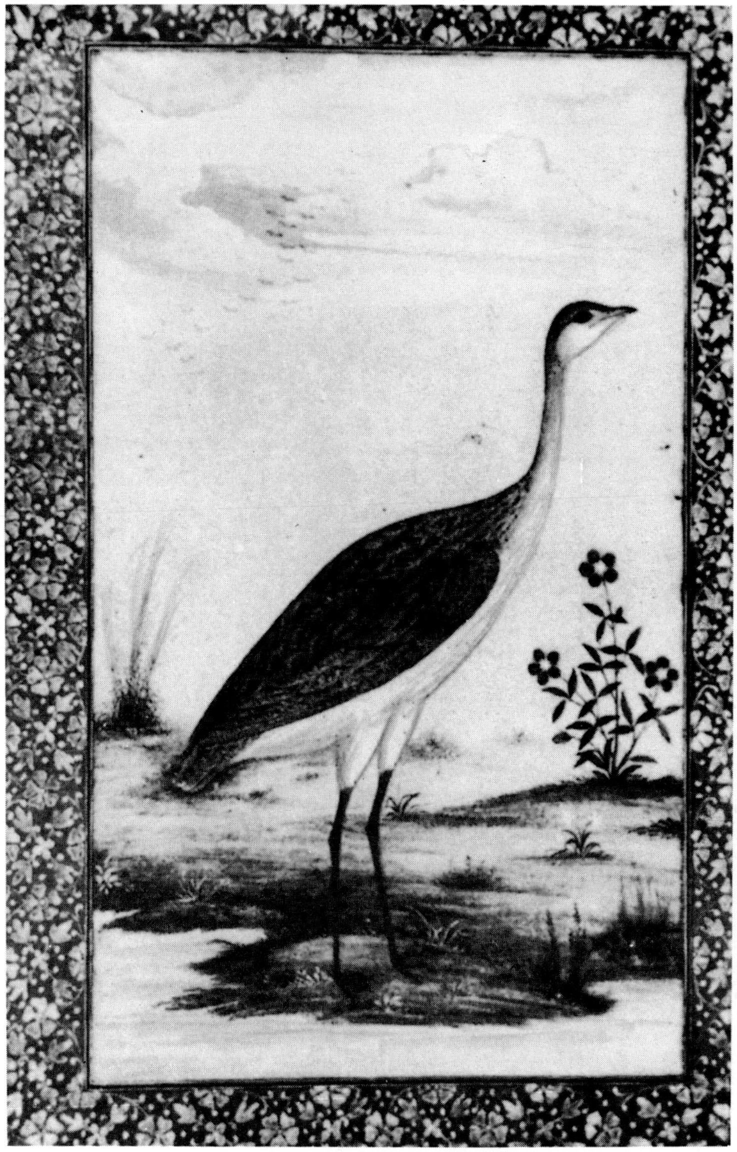

Fig. 6 Himalayan cheer pheasant, CBQ. Unascribed. An early nineteenth century copy.

Fig. 7. Indian bustard (*Charz-i bor*), *Dārā Shukoh (A)*, IOL. Unascribed. Late eighteenth century copy.

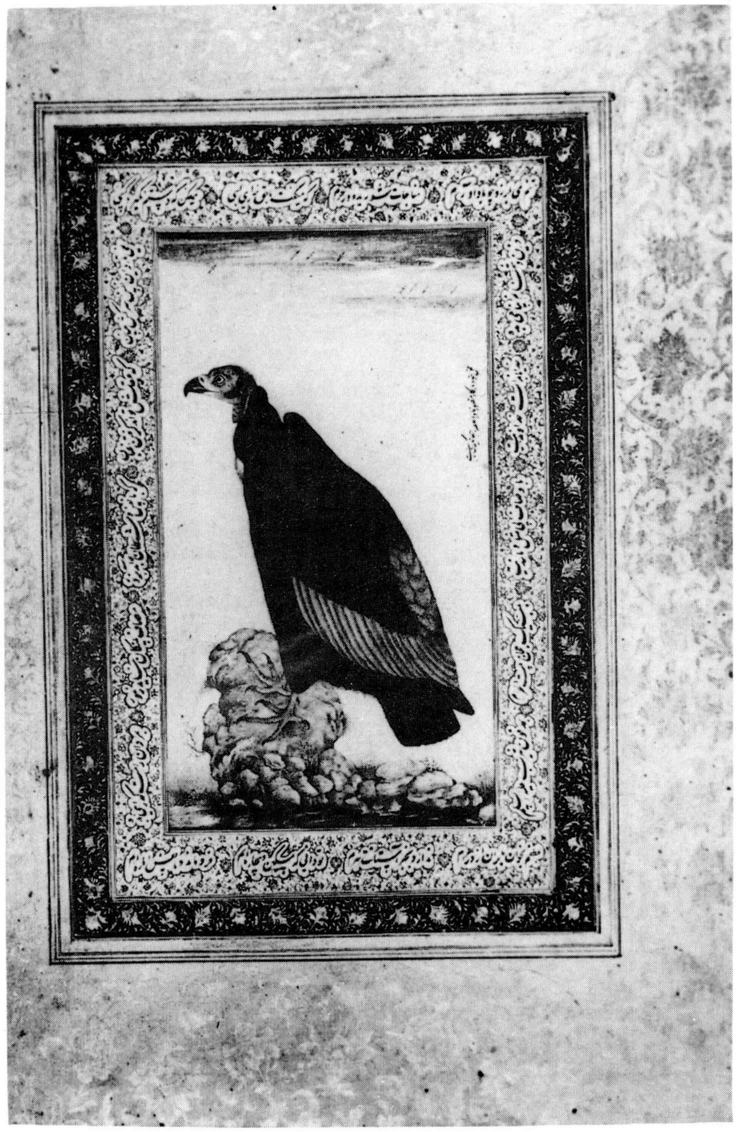

Fig. 11 King vulture, *Kevorkian (A)*, MMA, no. 55.121.10.25r. An early nineteenth century copy.

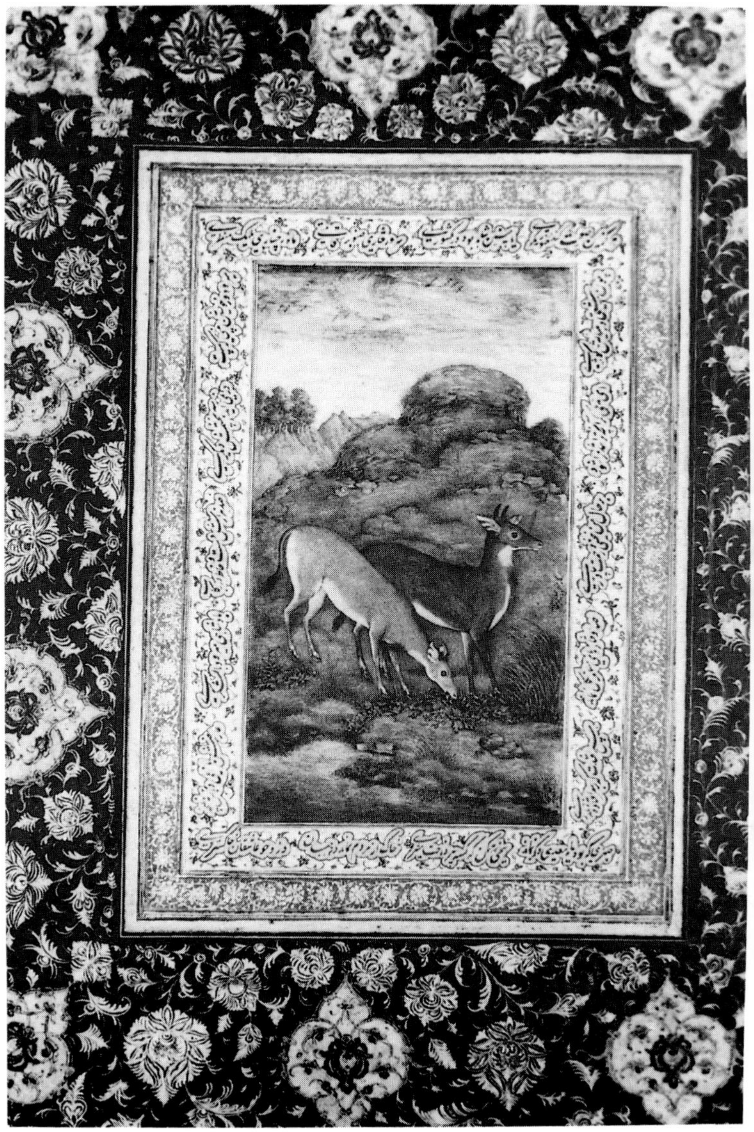

Fig. 12 Two deer in landscape, *Kevorkian (A)*, FGA, no. 39.48a. An early nineteenth century work.

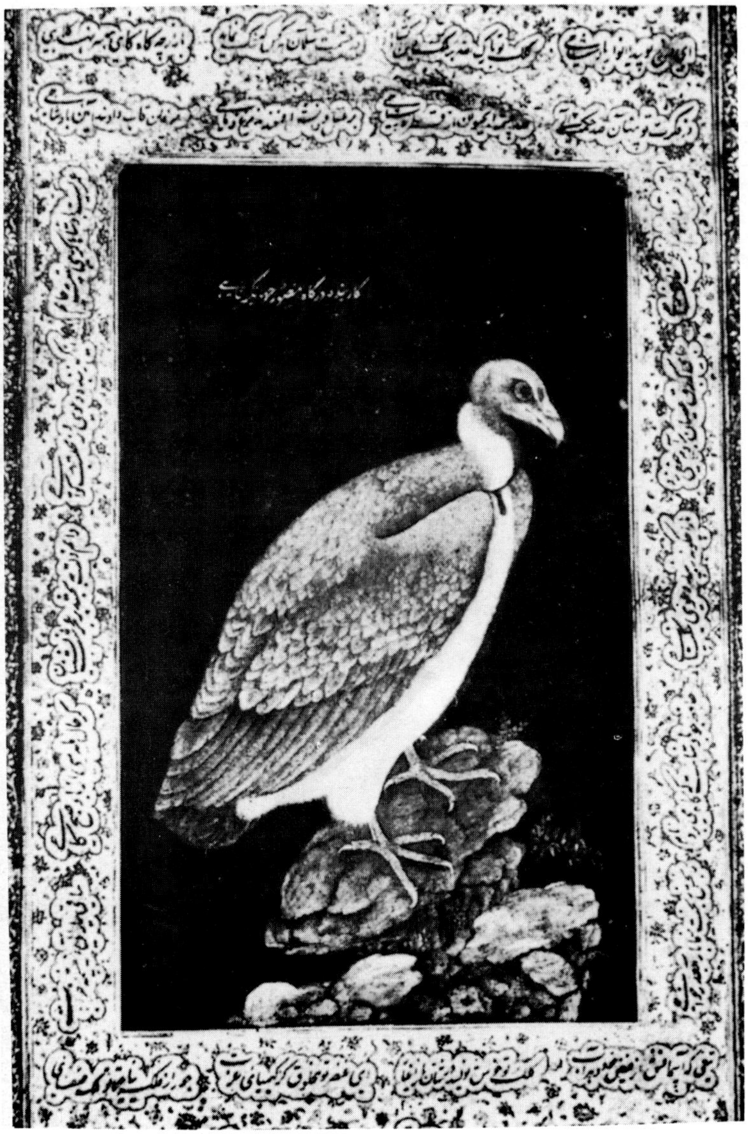

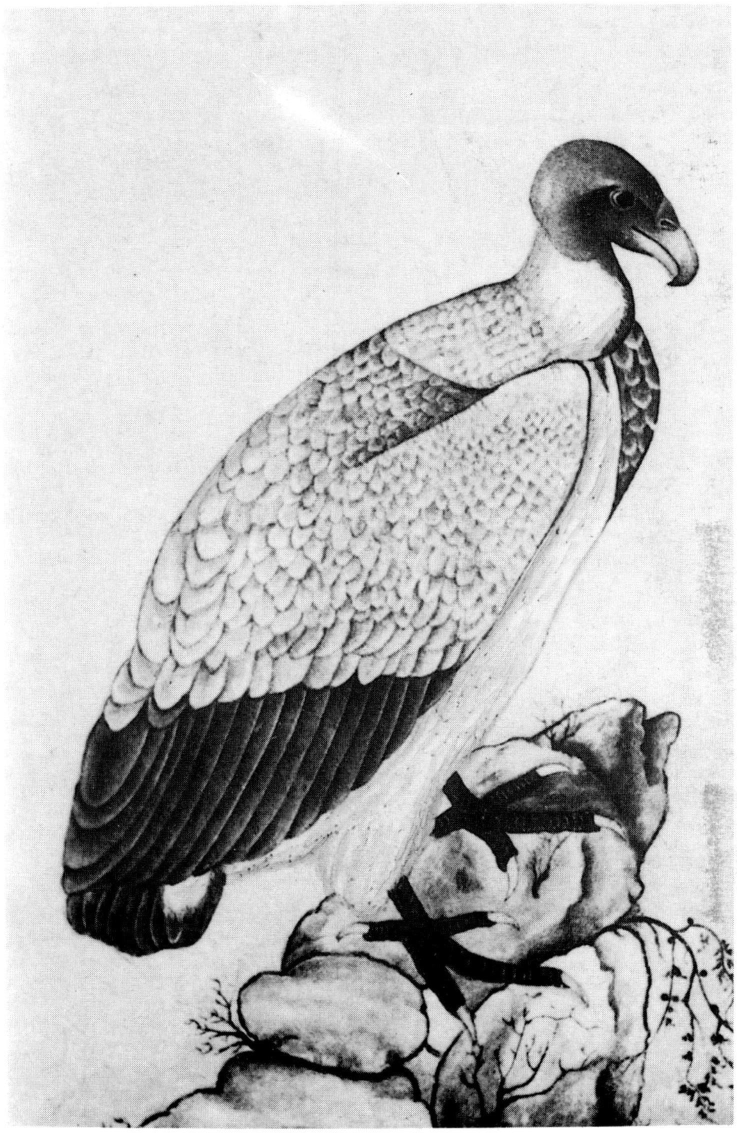

Fig. 13 Himalayan griffon, *Kevorkian (A)*, FGA, no. 48.19a. An early nineteenth century copy.

Fig. 14 Himalayan griffon, CBL, Unascribed. An early nineteenth century copy.

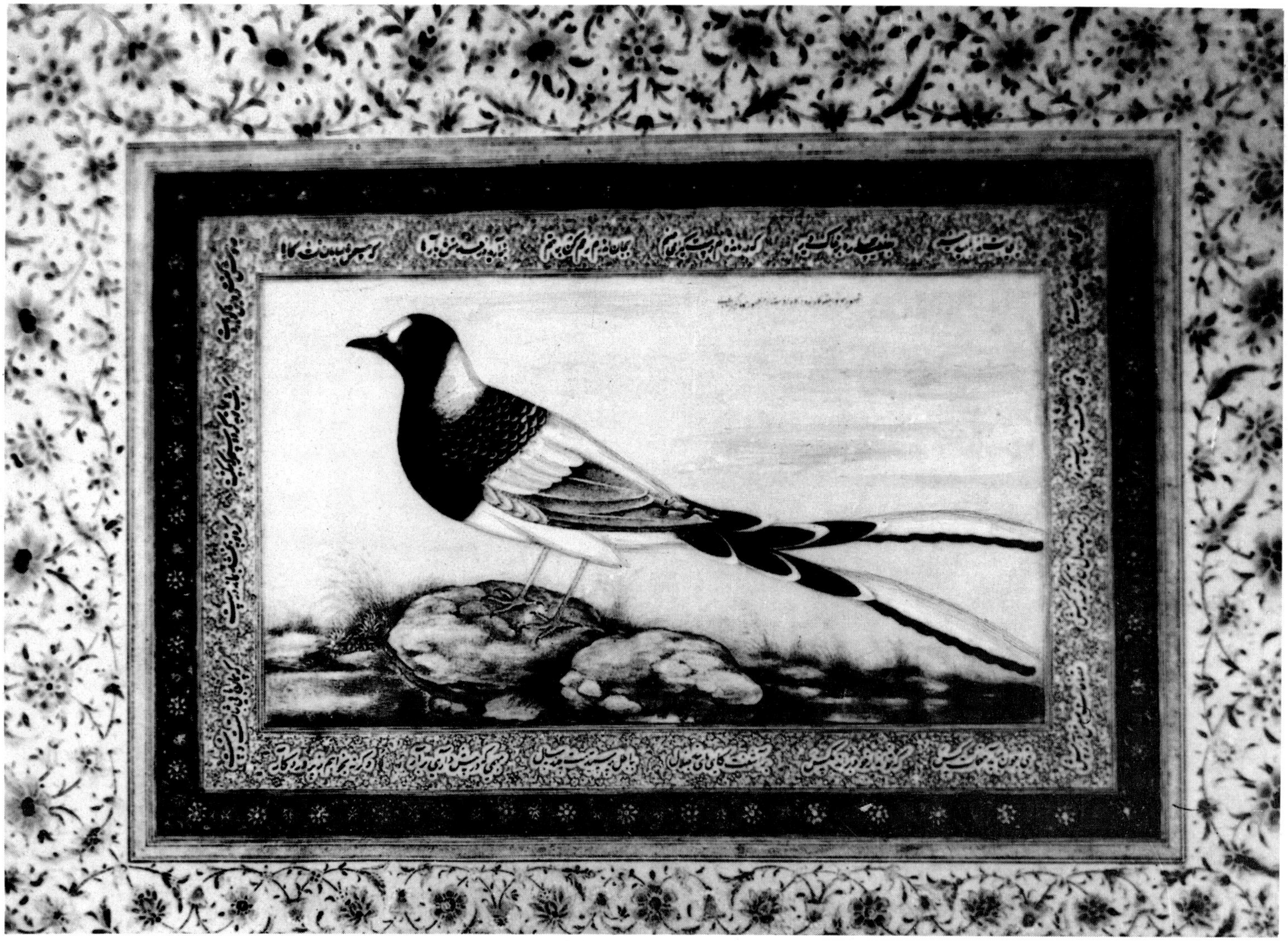

Fig. 16 Spotted forktail, *Kevorkian* (*A*), FGA, no. 39.46b.

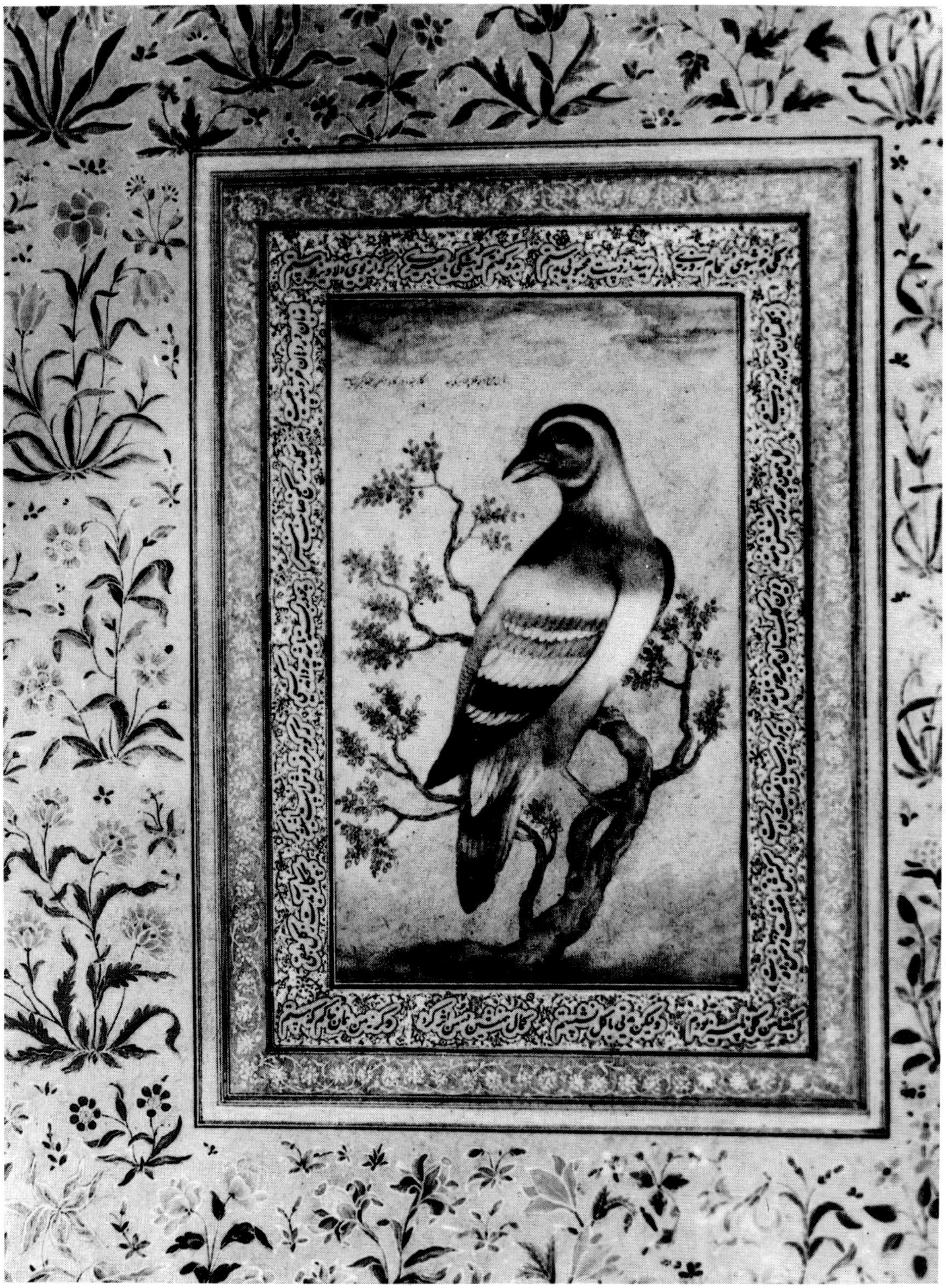

Fig. 18 Fantastic bird,
Kevorkian (*A*), MMA, no.
55.121.10.26r. An early
nineteenth century work.

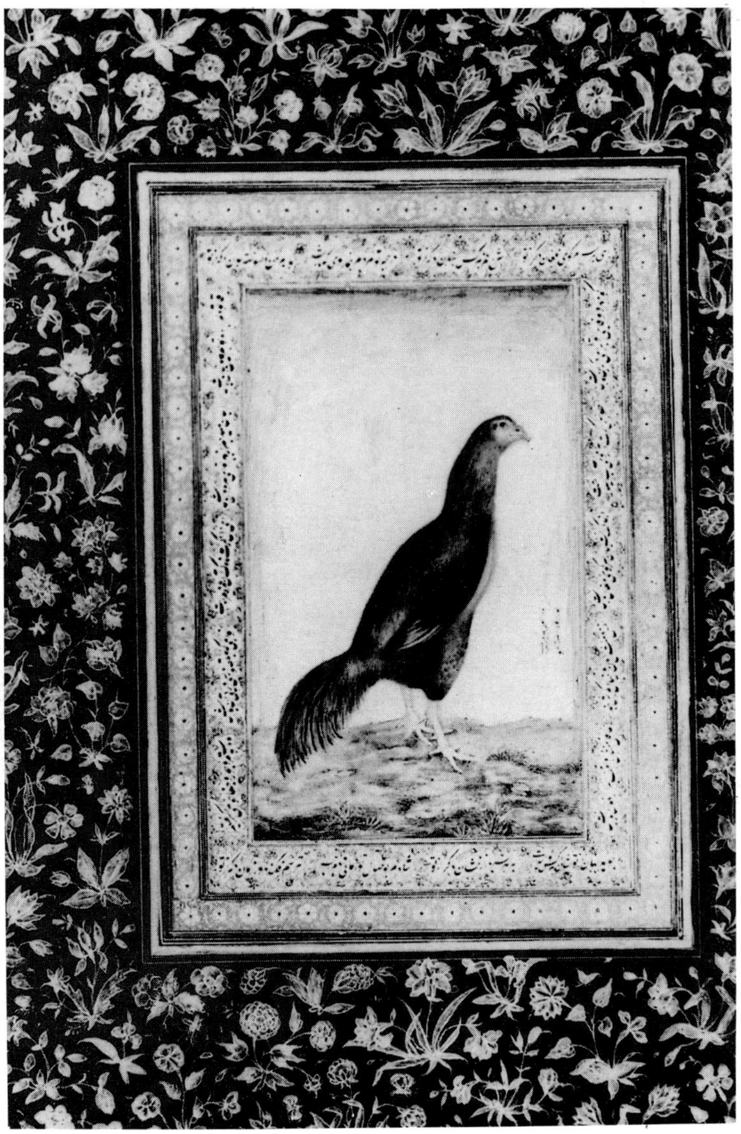

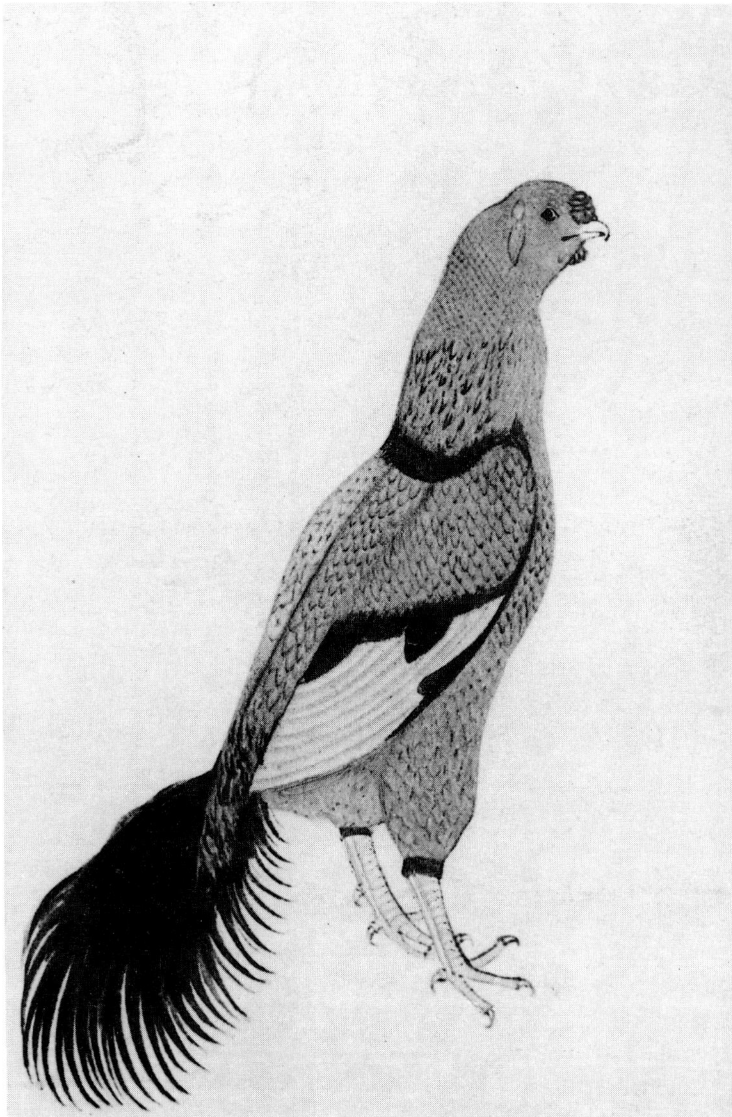

Fig. 19 Jungle fowl, *Kevorkian* (*A*), MMA, no. 55.121.10.27r. An early nineteenth century work.

Fig. 20 Jungle fowl, G.C. Sturt, Esq. Collection. Unascribed. A work of late eighteenth century.

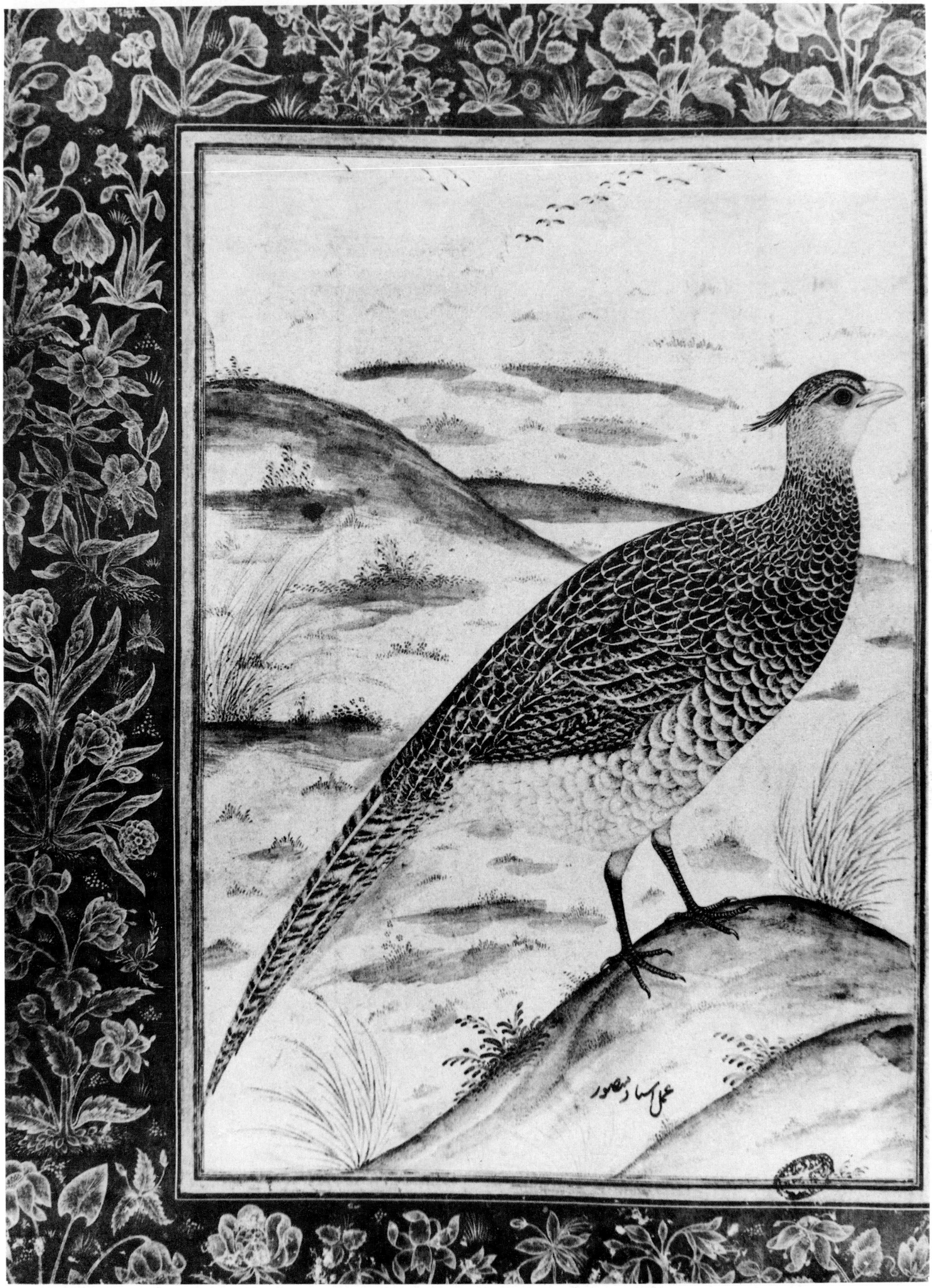

Pl. VI Himalayan cheer pheasant. *C.* 1612. Wantage Collection, Victoria & Albert Museum, London.

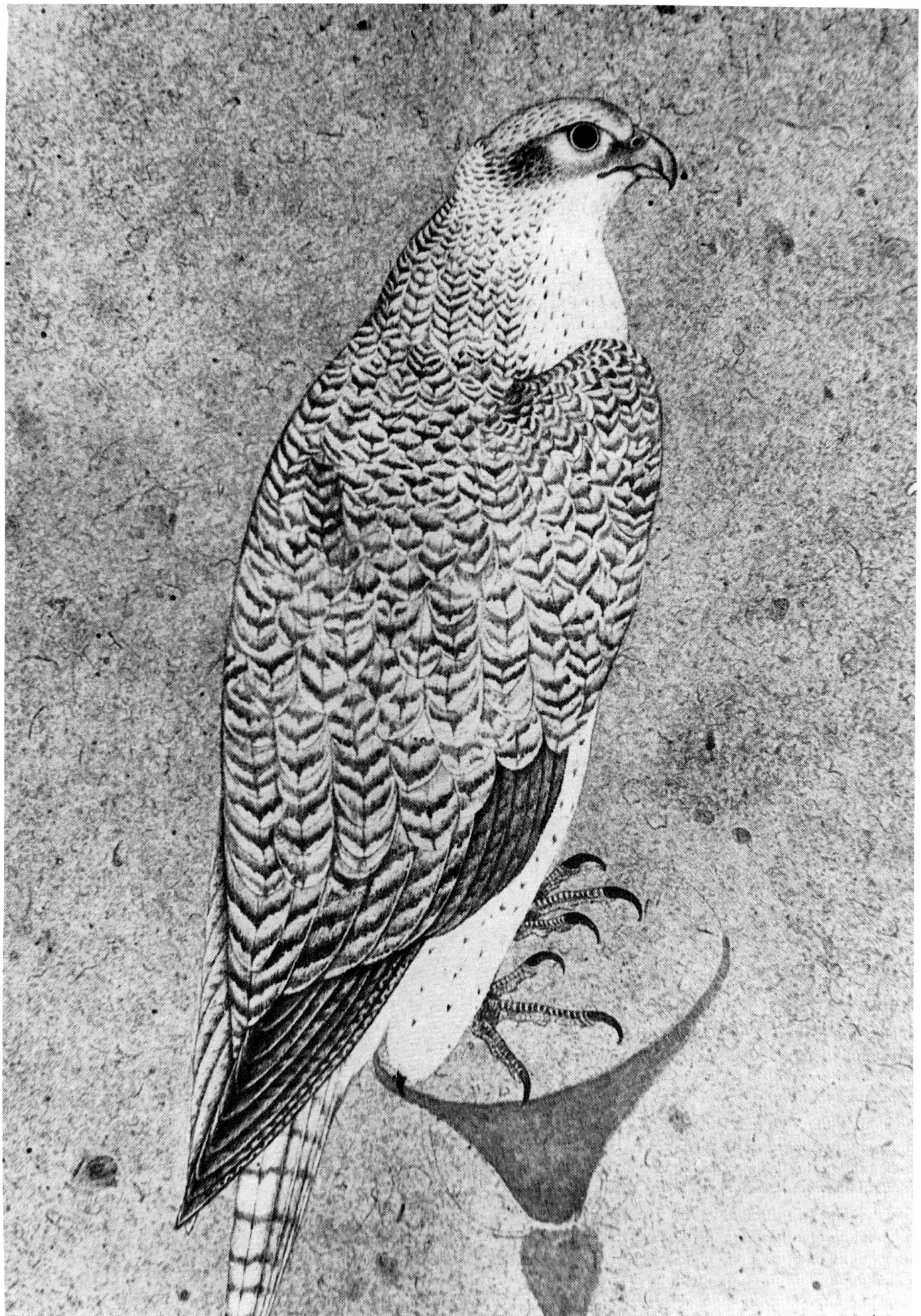

Pl.VIII Falcon. *C.* 1619. Museum of Fine Arts, Boston.

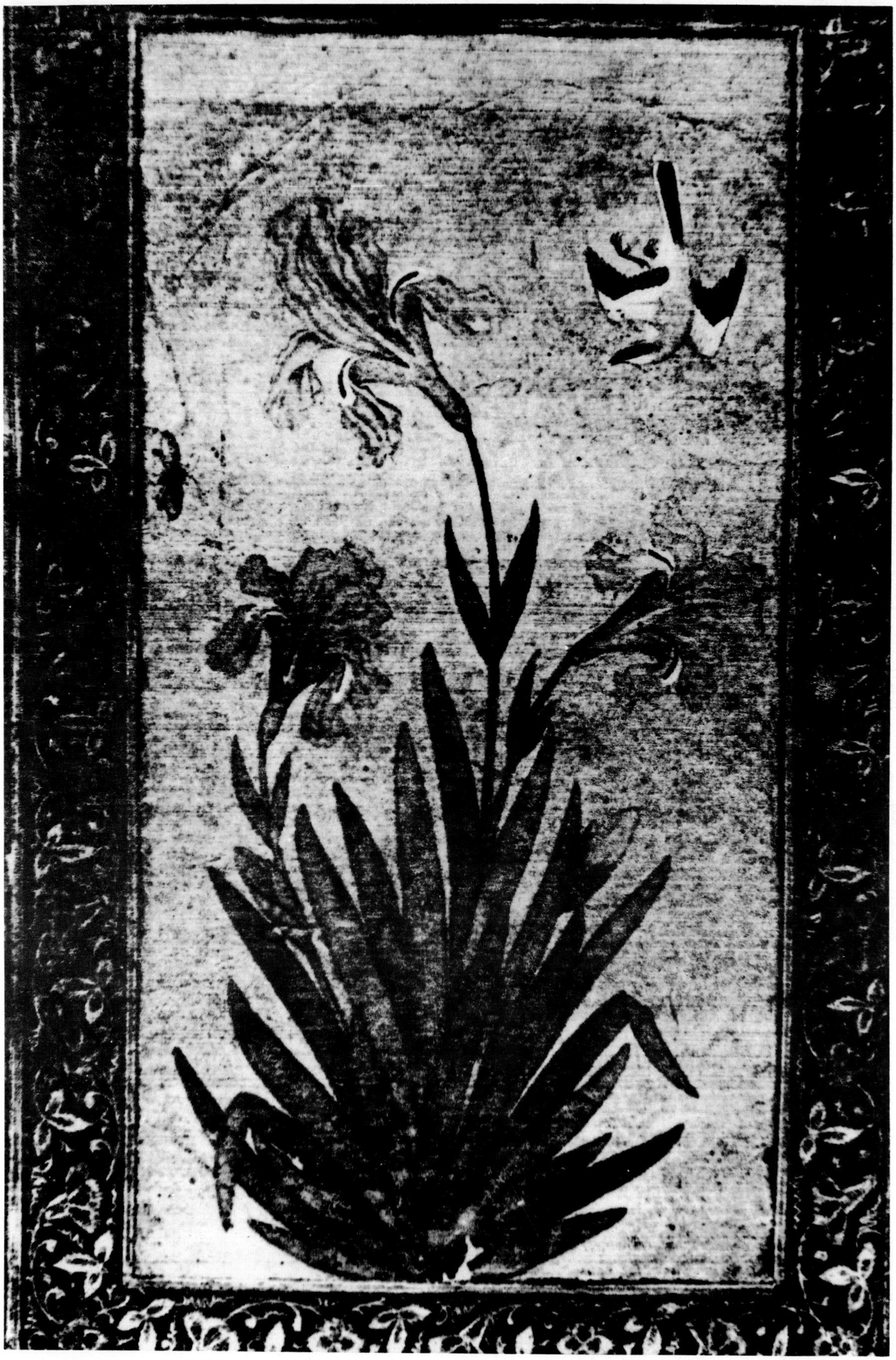

Pl. XII Iris plant with blossom. *C.* 1620. Imperial Library, Teheran.

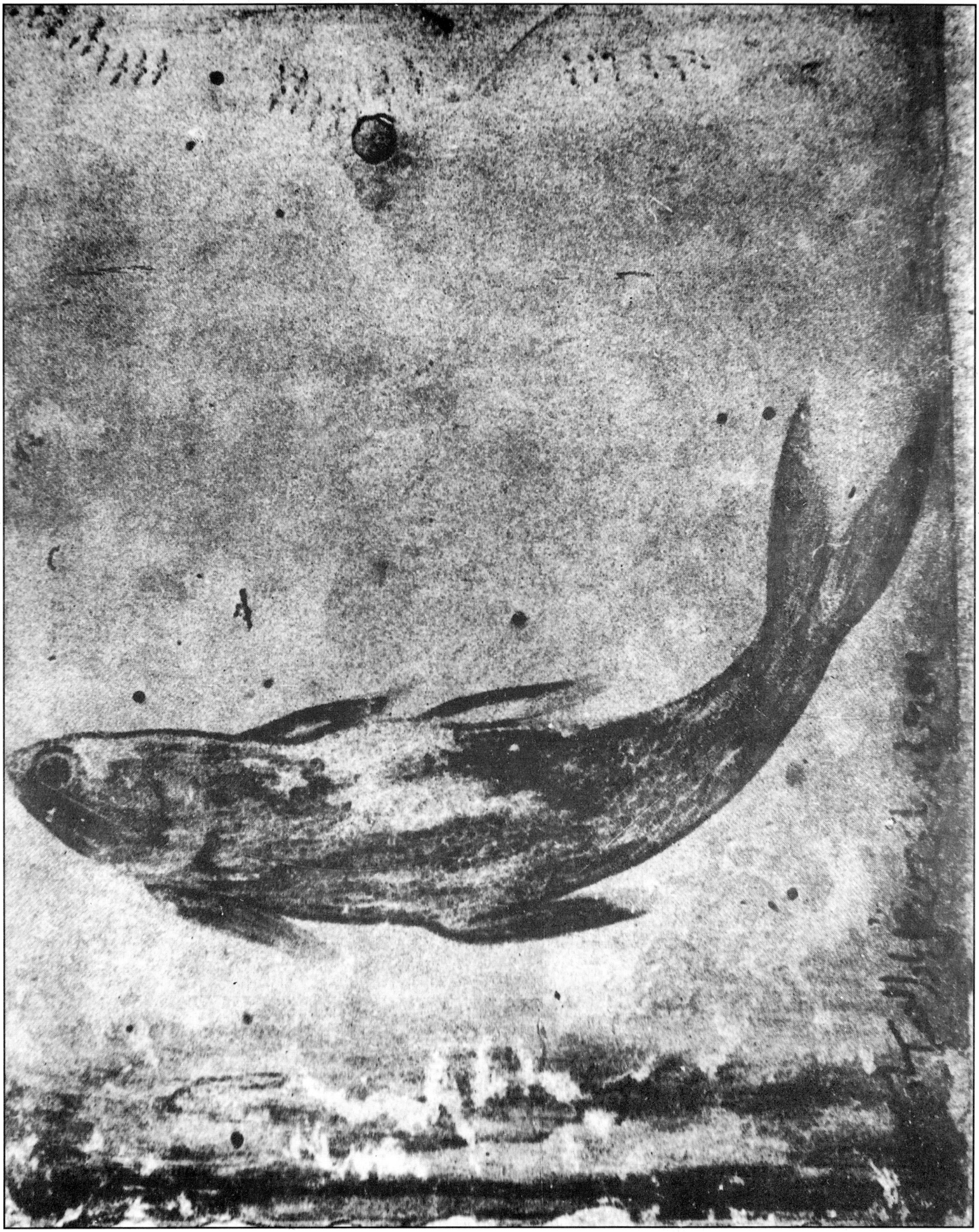

Pl. XVIII Salt-water fish. *C.* 1621-25. Red Fort Museum, Delhi.

PART I

1
INTRODUCTION

The growth of objective pictures of birds and animals, plants and flowers, etc., during the sixteenth-seventeenth century reflects the passion of the Mughal emperors for nature and wild life. Bābur, the founder of the Mughal dynasty, has given a graphic description of flora and fauna of India which bears testimony to his careful study.[1] Jahāngīr not only showed his curiosity for unique birds and animals but was also interested in their emotions as well. Long passages devoted in his Memoirs to the description of *sārus* (crane) from the moment of copulation to the time of feeding the fledglings, is the best example.[2] As an experientalist, he cross-bred *mārkhūr* and *rang* (ibex) with barbary goats. He wrote in 1619:

> "In Ahmadabad I had two male *mārkhūr* goats. As I had not a female in my establishment to pair with them, it occurred to me that if I could pair them with Barbary goats, which they bring from Arabia, especially from the port of the city of Darkhar, young of their form and qualities might be obtained. In short, I paired them with seven Barbary ewes, and after six months had elapsed each of the latter had a young one at Fathpur: there were four females and three males, very pleasing in appearance, of good shape and good colour."[3]

In the same year he further wrote:

> "Of *mārkhūr* and hill sheep I have seen many brought up in the house, but I never saw a *rang* (tame). I ordered them to keep it with the Barbary goats, in order that they might pair and produce young ones."[4]

Percy Brown has published a painting, 'Ibex with Barbary goats' (early 17th century) which is a rare pictorial record of this zoological experiment of Jahāngīr.[5] The Emperor wrote:

> In their colour, those (kids) which resembled the male were dun-coloured with black stripes on their backs. Red, indeed, appears to me a more pleasing colour than any other, and it is the mark of a better breed. Of their liveliness and laughable ways and their manner of gambolling and leaping, what can be written? Some of their ways are such that the mind derived uncontrolled pleasure from looking at them. It is notorious that painters cannot draw properly the motions of a kid. Granting that they may chance to draw the movements of an ordinary kid after a fashion, they certainly would have to acknowledge themselves at a loss how to draw the motions of these kids.[6]

However, an unascribed miniature (outline drawing) which represents *mārkhūr* goats in a variety of moods and postures, testifies to the skill of the Mughal painter in capturing varying movements of this animal with success.[7]

In another instance, Jahāngīr bred Himalayan cheer pheasant *(tadrū)* as well as cheetah in captivity:

> "Of the wild birds which they call *tadrū* (pheasant) till now it has never been heard that they breed in captivity. In the time of my revered father they made great efforts to obtain eggs and young ones but it was not managed. I ordered them to keep some of them, male and female, in one place, and by degrees they bred.... It was said that in the Wilāyat (Persia?) the people there had made efforts, but no eggs were produced and no young were obtained."[8]

About the cheetah, the Emperor notes:

> "It is an established fact that cheetahs in unaccustomed places do not pair off with a female, for my revered father once collected together 1,000 cheetahs. He was very desirous that they should pair, but this in no way came off....(Jahangir records an event of his time) It happened that a tigress became pregnant and after three months bore three cubs; it had never happened that a wild tiger after its capture had paired."[9]

His curiosity for unique and uncommon animals always encouraged his painters to observe wild life. In 1607, he ordered his painters to draw the likeness of a *mār<u>kh</u>ūr* ('a serpent eating goat'), the like of which he had never seen.[10] Of this animal he writes that it weighed 4 Hindustani maunds and its horns measured 1½ gaz.[11] Das has suggested that the picture of a mountain-goat preserved in the Minto Album (now in the Victoria and Albert Museum, London) is the most probable likeness of the animal described by Jahāngīr.[12]

In 1616, Muqarrab <u>Kh</u>ān presented Jahāngīr with a small elephant brought from Abyssinia. Jahāngīr took notice of its peculiarities. He wrote:

> "In comparison with the elephants of Hindustan, it presents some peculiarities. Its ears are larger than the ears of the elephants of this place, and its trunk and tail are longer."[13]

Here, he also takes notice of a young elephant (African) presented to his father Akbar by I'timād <u>Kh</u>ān of Gujarat in the year 1567.[14] A picture of a young African elephant preserved in the Ehrenfeld Collection, San Francisco, could possibly be taken as the likeness of the animal presented to Jahāngīr.[15] Ehnbom has attributed this miniature to Govardhan, a famous painter of Jahāngīr's court. Here, Ehnbom specially takes note of the artist's love of subtle shading and textured surfaces revealed in the delineation of the creature's hide, each wrinkle, bump, and roll of flesh—all carefully depicted.[16]

Jahāngīr's vivid and accurate graphic description of several birds and animals presents him as a keen observer of nature and his desire for a more realistic expression. But Jahāngīr not satisfied with an almost scientific textual description of rarities of nature, ordered his court painters to draw their likenesses as well so that the amazement that arose from hearing of them might be increased.[17] Obviously, he considered pictorial representation as a source of amazement and pleasure. As an aesthete, he possessed an unending urge for nature through especial studies of animals characterized by realism and executed as much as possible objectively. With Jahāngīr, then a new era in the field of art, i.e., portrayal of natural history became established.

Nevertheless, realism is apparent in Mu<u>gh</u>al painters' work from the very beginning. Barrett and Gray observe a shift from strict conventions of Persian art while describing miniatures of the *Anwār-i Suhailī* (SOAS, c. 1570): "But the animals are at once more natural and more self-possessed than the remote and exquisite animals of the Persian school. They are more deeply engaged by the action, and within the terms of the system as much realism is given to the architecture and figure drawing by shading and modelling as possible."[18] According to Eletr, with the general emergence of Indian ideals, the Persian traditions and ways were weakened.[19] This facilitated a more naturalistic rendering of birds and animals. An Indian element, i.e., sympathy with animal world, further gave rise to the emotions and feelings in their representation, though only a few painters could claim this achievement. Faithful rendering of the subject prompted the artist to rise above the imposed conventions, leading him to successfully depict animals in a naturalistic manner with the details of individual physiognomy. The realism thus achieved in the depiction of nature later got accentuated with the impact of the European technique of painting on the Mughal style.

It was this background which prompted pictures on natural history at the Mughal atelier. In addition, the long tradition of manuscript painting illustrating fables and legends, etc. — both at the Persian and the Mughal court — provided a logical basis to the artists' acquaintance with animal character and behaviour. Among such works at the Mughal atelier, the most favourite texts were the *Anwār-i Suhailī,* the *'Iyār-i Dānish* and the *'Ajā'ib-al Makhlūqāt* in which the animals are the main characters and an integral part of most of the themes. Numerous copies of these manuscripts repeatedly illustrated at the Mughal atelier during sixteenth century bear testimony to the depiction of wild-life.[20] Studies of birds as ornithological specimens are noticed by Saraswati in *'Ajā'ib-al Makhlūqāt* (c. 1595-1600),[21] which contains 16 illustrated folios representing birds.[22] Besides, to decorate the folios the Mughal painters showed a preference for the pictures of birds and animals painted in columns within the panel of the text, and often composed such figures freely between the lines of the text. Best examples of such representation are the decorated folios of *Gulistān* of Sa'dī (Persian MS. 258, Royal Asiatic Society, London, dated 1581) and the *Dīwān-i Ḥāfiẓ* (Chester Beatty Library, Dublin, MS. No. 15, dated 1582).[23] These represent a large number of bird and animal pictures. Losty has noticed that in the *Gulistān* MS. there are about two thousand animal figures.[24] These also include mythical animals, viz., *sīmurgh* and *kilin.* These figures, though small in scale, carry characteristic representations.

The scope of bird and animal figures further increased with the adaptation of their representation in margin-painting, early examples of which appear in the *Bahāristān* of Jāmī (Bodleian Library, Oxford, MS. Elliot 254, c. 1595-1600), the *Khamsa* of Niẓāmī (Walters Art Gallery, Baltimore, W.613) part of the British Museum MS. Or.12208, the *Khamsa* of Niẓāmī (British Museum, London, Or.12208, dated 1596-7), *Khamsa* of Amīr Khusrau (Walters Art Gallery, Baltimore, W.624, dated 1597-8).[25] In these instances, birds and animals are represented amidst landscape, hunting scenes, etc., and are executed in various tones of gold pigment. The Mughal painters derived this method of margin-illumination from the Safavid and Timurid traditions, and finished the drawings in gold pigment only. Outlines of the objects are invariably drawn heavy in gold pigment and the inner details are suggested through line with casual modelling and shading. A change in this technique is seen later when the animal figures executed in colour within the margin-illumination became frequent during seventeenth century. Numerous folios of Jahāngīr and Shāh Jahān's albums decorated with broad margin-painting depict exquisitely detailed bird and animal drawings which form the subject of natural history.[26]

Hunting, animal-fight, and trapping of birds and animals are other themes, illustrations of which are equally important.[27] Hunting, the royal game, is the subject of several Mughal miniatures. These exhibit a great variety of animals in one composition. Though in such compositions, the animals are drawn in groups and in diminutive scale, their drawings are finished as portrait-studies. Miniatures of the *Akbarnāma* (Victoria and Albert Museum, London), e.g., "Akbar hunting tigers near Narwar" (17-8/117), "Akbar hunting near Lahore" (65-6/117) and "Akbar hunts with trained cheetahs" (92-3/117) present vivid description of numerous species of animals and seem to have excelled other pictures on this theme.[28] Trapping of birds and animals, too, show their depiction in groups and in a variety of postures.[29] The theme of animal fight mainly illustrates combats between cocks, goats, rams, deer (especially, black buck), buffaloes, camels and ele-phants. These, as a matter of rule, show careful studies of animals engaged in violent action.

Portrait studies of animals by Govardhan, 'Ināyat, Abū'l Ḥasan, Manṣūr, Murād and Pidārath are accurate and lively. They could fuse life into their drawings and through their works many rare and unfamiliar species became more and more familiar. In such studies, the figures occupy a central place in the composition and unnecessary details are generally avoided, especially in the treatment of the background — most probably to bring the main subject under immediate focus. Sometimes, the background is left plain, which suited best for pictures on natural history.

From our point of view, the *Bāburnāma* miniatures illustrated towards the close of the sixteenth century are significant since these represent a rich variety of flora and fauna of India as described by Bābur (r. 1525-1529) in his Memoirs.[30] These may suitably be accepted as 'trend-setter' in the course of the development of independent studies of animals at Jahāngīr's atelier. Accuracy of forms and anatomical details reported through well-defined firm lines and the depiction of maximum details are the chief characteristics of them. There is always an emphasis on the representation of the typical features of the objects, and these are depicted so realistically as to enable one to distinguish their species.[31] To achieve this, the painter must have seen the object closely and many times as his creations are not merely the likenesses of external appearances of the animals but are sometimes truthful portrayal of their mood as well. In brief, these pictures of birds and animals are examples of vivid, minutely detailed realistic art.

It is important to note that the realism seen in the Mughal painters' work is confined to the artists' visual experience. In no way the animal world is the subject of "adoration" in their expression as one might experience in the art and sculpture of ancient India. The Mughal painters clearly seem to have aimed at portraying the reality of the physical world where the idealisation of the subject occupies almost no place. Spiritual and emotional matters hardly occupy a significant place in the Mughal school. Grousset has rightly remarked that the Mughal studies of wild life are frankly material, intended to give earthly pleasure.[32] Nevertheless, this aspect of the Mughal painter's aesthetic lends his creations a quality of earthly charm and pleasure. His material approach finds its expression in an emphasis on objectivity in the presentation of nature. Though this element of art best suited for the studies taken up as an ornithological specimen intended to depict maximum possible details, it constrained the creativity of the artist. As a result of which only a few works of great masters are found imbued with warmth of feeling and wealth of emotions. Kühnel and Goetz speak on the miniature "Two magpies" (c. early 17th century) that it reminds one of "the Dutch specialist painters of the 17th century, who portrayed subjects from the animal kingdom with equal knowledge, but their paintings are seldom so full of feelings as this one from India".[33] At any rate, the Emperor's combined interest in realistic-cum-ornithological portrait studies does not find a parallel in the art of Persia and pre-Mughal art in India. Of a drawing "Siberian crane" (c. early 17th century) Havell says that as an ornithological study it rivals the work of the best Japanese masters. He adds that "the delicate feathers of the white plumage and the microscopic details of bird's anatomy are drawn with infinite patience and scientific exactitude."[34]

A large number of pictures of birds and animals executed by Abū'l Ḥasan, Govardhan, 'Ināyat, Manohar, Manṣūr, Murād and Pidārath have survived. These appear as manifestation of Jahāngīr's curiosity for unusual things in nature, and of the Mughal painters' aesthetic heavily burdened with objectivity. However, such works do not seem to have been executed to decorate the copies of the *Jahāngīrnāma*; and in all probability these belonged to the tradition of album pictures. Jahāngīr did order his painters to draw the likenesses of birds and animals for the *Jahāngīrnāma* but such illustrations are not known in any copy of this MS.

Important notices of the likenesses of birds executed by Manṣūr at the command of the Emperor suggest that there was an emphasis on the delineation of actual portraits of animals taken from life. An intimate, careful observation of the object seems the basis of their characteristic and life-like pictures. In 1612, Jahāngīr ordered Manṣūr to draw the likeness of a falcon brought from Persia,[35] and in 1620, Manṣūr painted the picture of a bird, called *sāj* (dipper), while he was in the entourage of the emperor in Kashmir.[36]

It also suggests that the painters accompanied the royal entourage and were engaged in portraying rarities of nature. Jahāngīr also records that during the course of his visit to Kashmir in 1621, Manṣūr painted no less than one hundred flowers of the Kashmir Valley.[37] Later in 1623, while Jahāngīr was in *parganā* Rahimabad, he ordered his painters to draw the likeness of a tiger shot by him. Of this animal, he writes:

> "Driving the elephant forward, the tiger's flank came into view, and with one wound from my gun he fell and gave up his life. Of all the tigers I have shot from the time when I was a prince until now I never saw a tiger like this for size and majesty and the symmetry of its limbs. I ordered the artists to take its portrait according to its real form and body."[38]

In other instance, Abū'l Ḥasan "*Nādir uz Zamān*" executed the picture of spotted forktail (bird) at the command of Jahāngīr, hunted by his men in Jengespur.[39]

Independent studies of birds and animals are depicted in profile and generally single in composition, dominating the picture plane. These show simpler composition accommodating the central theme more spaciously to allow the maximum details. This effect is further enhanced in the picture where we occasionally meet with a subdued background executed in harmonious colours, or in the blending of the pigments. Birds and animals painted in isolation—in serene effect—is another quality of these works. It is important to note that these studies are characteristic of minimum (slow) action reported in them, which suited the standard of the pictures on natural history. While there are Mughal drawings filled with spirited movements and violent action, the best studies from our point of view are the drawings finished as portraits of single animals or pairs. It is not the violent action but the technical finesse presented with refined workmanship in a more restrained manner that makes the picture valuable as evidence of natural history. The figures seen sometimes static and still is the result of an emphasis on the representation of details, i.e., firm lines describing the anatomy of the animal and definite details of wings, feathers, beak, tail and talons, etc. Nevertheless, these pictures are an outcome of slow careful work imbued with realism achieved within the framework of traditional mannerism of draughtsmanship: they show a straightforward naturalism. Salim Ali writes of a Mughal picture of the bird "Himalayan cheer pheasant": "Though the picture may appear somewhat stiff and "wooden" if judged from the modern Gronvoldian standard, it leaves little doubt as regards the identity of the species."[40]

The Mughal painter tried to use the pigments that could most accurately express the actual colour of the skin or fur of the animals. One cannot fail to admire the minute observation of the artist by which he was able to paint features of the animals. But some Mughal artists went further and tried to depict the character or the particular mood of the animal.

The trend of independent studies of birds and animals continued during Shāh Jahān's reign, the best representatives of which are known in Dārā Shukoh Album, preserved in the India Office Library, London. An unascribed picture "Ducks" from the same album is considered by Hasan as unique in the zoological studies of birds.[41]

Miniatures of animals and plants produced at the courts of Akbar and Jahāngīr have received the appreciation of scholars and artists alike for accuracy of detail and force of expression. But their importance as objects of morphological interest was not realized before the middle of the present century. It was in 1958 that the attention of delegates to the XII International Ornithological Congress at Helsinki was drawn to a portrait of the now extinct Mauritian bird, dodo, supposed to be the earliest and one single existing specimen of such interest. The painting, though unfortunately unsigned, is a crucial link in the evolutionary history of the study of tropical pheasant. The creation of this portrait is credited to the school of Jahāngīr.

Jahāngīr's keen interest in the study and painting of fauna and flora is well known. Of the more than hundred artists employed in his atelier, no less than eight were commissioned to the portrayal of animals and plants.[42] Of these specialists, *Ustād* Manṣūr was undoubtedly the greatest. His virtuosity in true-to-life depiction of animals and flowers earned from the Emperor the boastful title of *Nādir u'l 'Aṣr,* i.e., "Unique of the Age".[43]

Manṣūr's miniatures belong as much to art as to natural history. Perfection in drawing, detail and colour lends photographic fidelity to his creations, because of which his figures of different species acquire in representation the full impact of objective reality, and at the same time, their individual identity in nature.

If the Helsinki Congress aroused interest in natural history paintings of the Mughal school on the international plane, Salim Ali, the doyen of Indian Ornithology, through his article published under the title of "The Moghul Emperors of India as Naturalists and Sportsmen" had drawn attention to it already thirty years before in 1926-7. Salim Ali had enthusiastically brought to light the contributions of Bābur and Jahāngīr to the knowledge of Indian fauna and flora. The next step was taken by the Indian National Science Academy, New Delhi, when in 1968 it published *Jahangir the Naturalist* authored by M.A. Alvi and A. Rahman. This book sets out to project in a more elaborate and systematic form the link between the flora and fauna paintings that occurs in the narratives of Jahāngīr's well-known memoirs *Tūzuk-i Jahāngīrī*. The incorporation in it of the significant quotations (both in original and in translation), and the reproductions of paintings by the Emperor's court artists, make the work indeed very relevant and authentic.

The artistic aspect of these paintings had for long been a favourite subject of study with scholars like A.K. Coomaraswamy, E.B. Havell, Rai Krishnadasa, Niharranjan Ray, M.S. Randhawa, Robert Skelton and S.C. Welch. Manṣūr's work came under special focus in the researches carried out by the younger generation of scholars, particularly Tasneem Ahmad, Asok Kumar Das, Milo C. Beach, Amina Okada and S.P. Verma. Without prejudice to the scholarly predilections and observations of several avid researchers and scholars, it yet remains doubtful if a more definitive study of Manṣūr's art is not called for.

Evaluation of an art work rounded off in such general terms as "minutest possible details", "thinly applied pigment", "delicate modelling", "accuracy", "lively depiction", "true to life", "characteristic representation", etc., make for such a general frame of reference that shall accommodate with slight variations of latitudes the work of any of Manṣūr's contemporaries. Such a treatment would be more in the nature of generalities testifying to certain refinements and draughtsmanship only, but would fall short as a method of correct evaluation and appreciation of works of art by individuals.

Quite a few of Jahāngīrī painters had achieved their individual distinctive styles, and amongst them, the names of Abū'l Ḥasan, Bichitr, Farrukh Beg, Govardhan, Kesavdās and Manohar are well known. Masters, of course, they were in their respective fields of specialization, but they could not have been so without their patient endurance and strenuous efforts over the years to achieve originality, especially because, from the very outset, the medieval artist had to work within an exacting set of conventions. Manṣūr could not be an exception to this situation. Though his early paintings display unflinching allegiance to traditional elements, yet, on close scrutiny, one would find in them some individual touches interspersed, which however, if seen casually, would not distinguish them from the common type in the absence of ascriptions. But Manṣūr seems to grow with time and practice, this can be understood by tracing the different phases of his development on the basis of his available works placed in a roughly chronological order. During the last phase of his career he strikes us as a conscious, though very guarded detractor from the conventions of contemporary art.

The present study, devoted exclusively to Manṣūr, is spread over the period of his creative life, which is also coincidental with the period of the growth and maturation of Mughal art. Manṣūr's versatility as a painter is reflected through his contributions to almost all the departments of art associated with the Mughal school, viz., illumination, book-illustration, human-portraiture, flower study and animal drawing. He proved himself to be a prolific artist, having to his credit the largest number of paintings of animals and plants in the whole of the Mughal India. A detailed study of Manṣūr's work could thus not only add to our knowledge of him but also be a positive supplement in the understanding of the characteristics and refinements of the Mughal school at large.

Paintings executed by Manṣūr have travelled in all directions both within and outside India. Quite a few remarkable works of this painter have survived the ravages of time, although, unfortunately, many more have been lost. The surviving ones are accessible to us as precious collections in libraries, musea and galleries. This advantage, however, is largely nullified for the students of art. Goetz has rightly observed that one has to waste much valuable time in the initial exercise of collecting working material from wherever chance or special circumstances have scattered them.[44] Goetz's suggestion that a complete survey be conducted of such material for documentation is a challenge to lovers of art. A really meaningful work in this direction is possible only through the collective coordinated efforts of a team with base camps distributed far and wide. Such a project demands institutional patronage. Individual scholars can at best contribute their mite towards a partial solution by taking up works of individual artists. This small book may be taken as a step in this direction.

Manṣūr's paintings, as available to us in the leading world collections, are in three different forms, namely, book-illustrations, illuminations and album pictures (assorted or dispersed folios). Of course, this division has only referential value, and in no case, to be taken for value judgement of the quality or style of his art. The available quantum of his creations can be listed as follows:

ILLUSTRATIONS

TITLE OF MS.	COLLECTION	NO. OF MINIATURES
Bāburnāma	Freer Gallery of Art, Washington	2
Bāburnāma	British Museum and Library, London	5
Bāburnāma	National Museum, New Delhi	1
Jāmi'-ut Tawārīkh	Imperial Library, Teheran	1
Akbarnāma	British Museum and Library, London	4
Akbarnāma	Victoria and Albert Museum, London	2

ILLUMINATIONS

Khamsa of Amīr Khusrau	Walters Art Gallery, Baltimore	1
Akbarnāma	British Museum and Library, London	1
Dīwān of Anwarī	Location not known	1

ALBUM PICTURES

COLLECTION	NO. OF MINIATURES
Cowasji Jehangir Collection, Bombay	1
Edward Croft Murray Collection, London	1
Gloubew Collection, Museum of Fine Arts, Boston	1
Habibganj Collection, Aligarh Muslim University, Aligarh	1
Indian Museum, Calcutta	1
Johnson Album, India Office Library, London	1
Kevorkian Album, Metropolitan Museum of Art, New York	5
M. Demotte Collection, Musee du Louvre, Paris	4
Minto Album, Victoria and Albert Museum, London	1
Muraqqa'-i Gulshan, Imperial Library, Teheran	1
Naṣīruddīn Album, Imperial Library, Teheran	2
National Museum, New Delhi	1
Oriental Institute of the U.S.S.R. Academy of Science, Leningrad	2
Prince of Wales Museum of Western India, Bombay	1
Red Fort Museum, Delhi	1
Royal Library, Windsor Castle, Windsor	1
State Museum, Lucknow	1
Ṣawai Man Singh II Museum, Jaipur	1

Out of the 54 miniatures ascribed to Manṣūr, 41 are reproduced in various modern studies, in black & white or in colour (see Appendix). Often enough, these reproductions fail to provide such essential information as artist's name and date. Ascriptions given on the reverse side of the original pictures are obviously not printed in the reproductions, and hence, one has to largely depend on cataloguers' readings, which may not be always beyond doubt. The present survey is based on published works. Wherever possible, the data so available has been checked and counterchecked rigorously and collated with originals, that are available in India, U.K. and U.S.A.

Establishing a workable chronological order of Manṣūr's paintings presents yet another problem, because a large number of his works have been lost. Any appreciation of his style, as it developed in all likelihood, through the various phases of his career should take into account with careful imagination and analysis the possible lacunas accruing from the gaps in continuity. For maximum safety against the risks involved in it the method of using the most relevant internal, or cross evidence has been employed, like the narrations of related subjects from Jahāngīr's memoirs. Other methods for reconstructing of the chronological gaps have been used in different particularized forms, according to the demands of the selected case studies. The application of these methods can be seen interwoven in the entire study. The result of this effort, however diligent, may appear as an approximation with tentative credibility only, but all the same invites a sympathetic indulgence from the reader.

The paintings available can be broadly classified as under:

1. Paintings bearing clearly the date and name of artist [5, 30, 35 and 47].*
2. Paintings which can be dated by inference from the date of manuscript given in the colophon or the text: [4] from *Jāmi'-ut Tawārīkh* (IL), dated AH 1004/1596.
3. Paintings without any direct evidence but can be grouped with the dated ones on the basis of conceptual characteristics, techniques of style and colouration: [1-10] from *Bāburnāma,* datable 1590-1600; [13-14] from *Akbarnāma* (VA), datable 1602-5.

The dispersed folio of *Bāburnāma* [1-2] presents a good example of doubtful information creeping in catalogues. In his earlier work, *The Grand*

*The numbers shown within the square brackets refer to the miniatures listed in the Appendix: Paintings by Manṣūr.

Mogul, Imperial Painting in India (1600-60), Beach suggests that the probable date of production of the two paintings is 1590-95,[45] but changes it in his subsequent publication, *The Imperial Image, Paintings for the Mughal Court,* to "1589 or even earlier".[46] Since we know that the Persian translation of the *Bāburnāma* from original Turkish version was presented to Akbar in 1590,[47] the paintings in question for illustration purpose could not have been made earlier. Hence, the revised date is difficult to accept. The folio 116 of the National Museum *Bāburnāma* is dated 1598,[48] and the presentation copy of the Persian translation is dated 1590, therefore, *Bāburnāma* paintings could not be dated earlier than 1590. They could rather be safely put between 1590-1600.

For the miniatures [15-19] contained in the British Museum MS. of the *Akbarnāma,* it has been found reasonably acceptable to date them in 1604 on the grounds that the same date occurs on one of its illustrated folios.[49]

The miniatures [13-14] belonging to another copy of this manuscript preserved in the Victoria and Albert Museum, London, are datable in 1602-5 on grounds of style. Bearing in the mind the uncertainties that creep into this kind of dating exercise, maximum precaution and restraint have been applied before arriving at any conclusion. It has been resorted to as only alternative left because of the total absence of direct evidence, or even supplementary evidence.

The album pictures are still more difficult to date because they are loose and scattered, unlike the manuscript paintings. In fact, only two of Manṣūr's pictures 'Indian bustard' [35] and 'Zebra' [47] are dated in the whole lot of it. In such a situation, indirect evidence has often proved to be reliable, such as, the facts of a particular picture could be corroborated from a contemporary historical source describing the same subject or event. *Tūzuk-i Jahāngīrī* is one such source. Mostly Jahāngīr made a note in his memoirs whenever he ordered a court painter to draw the likeness of an animal. The pictures of 'Falcon' [34][50] and 'Dipper' [45][51] may be quoted here as two such instances. Consequently, these have been dated as the records in the manuscript show.

The remaining album pictures are approximated and tentatively dated on grounds of style and a few other internal evidences. This method is adapted in the absence of any other reliable source as in the case of undated manuscript paintings. It is true that style is an evolving process and the changes do not necessarily lend themselves to a correct sequential tracing, yet, it has been found in Manṣūr's case that certain brush strokes and colouration techniques, besides his lyrical effects, do grow in intensity and spontaneity with his growing maturity and mastery of the medium, fairly clear from the dated miniatures of the early and the later periods.

The list appended at the end of the book (Appendix) is a humble attempt to present Manṣūr's miniatures chronologically, notwithstanding the aforesaid limitations.

Complications of an intricate nature are faced in cases where two identical or near identical pictures on the same subject are found ascribed to Manṣūr. Copying of the works of masters outside the royal atelier was not uncommon, therefore, the mind is quite riddled as to the genuineness of such versions, some of which are even ascribed as originals. Problem of identification of some pictures, which have no duplicates, and done in the nineteenth century, but bearing inscriptions purported to be Manṣūr's, calls to action such methods of analysis that can confirm forgery. It becomes essential to distinguish the genuine work from the fake through a greater dependency on the internal evidence, or, through a more penetrative insight into the available material, than by indulging in generalizations merely on the basis of subject and theme. Some critics have slipped in this sense, though, may be quite unwittingly!

It would not be out of place to mention here that some of the unascribed pictures attributed to Manṣūr are not to be relied upon as his work because their grounds of attribution are more subjective than analytical. The problem is further accentuated because of self-contradictions present in the statement of some scholars. For instance, an unascribed painting 'Wounded buck' [78] was first attributed to Abū'l Ḥasan by Welch and Beach in 1965,[52] but later in 1973, Welch revised his opinion and attributed it to Manṣūr.[53] Such inconsistencies apart, disputations and controversies make a legion for a student to be able to arrive at any conclusion with regard to the authenticity and dates of the miniatures. The miniature 'Himalayan cheer pheasant' [57] described as a probable work of Manṣūr by Brown[54] is disputed by Beach, who considers it to be a contemporary copy of Manṣūr's original,[55] and Edwin Binney 3rd attributes it to Payāg (a painter of Shāh Jahān's atelier).[56] Such conclusions are liable to be suspected as speculative rather than scientific, and could hardly help in tracing the authenticity of the attributions. Miniatures of such doubtful nature included in the Appendix are numbered from 55-93.

An effort has been made in this study to trace the authenticity and re-evaluate afresh the paintings of the great master Manṣūr on the basis of the available information about his career and works, and their technical excellences and peculiarities from artistic point of view. Since no genuine step so far has been taken to discover Manṣūr's expansive expressiveness, variations of style, his signatures, etc., or to trace the painter's originality, the present author is very keen to discover the real artist in him. On the side of seeking actual identification of signatures, the genuine ones have been sifted from the 'third-person inscriptions' given on the paintings. In-depth study of miniatures containing authentic signatures has been helpful in singling out the fake ascriptions, attributions and copies. It is hoped that this study will initiate and greatly facilitate further analysis and criticism of not only the work of Manṣūr, but of other individual painters of the Mughal school as well.

2
HISTORICAL BACKGROUND

What has come to be known as Mughal school in art parlance, flourished under the patronage of the Mughal emperors during sixteenth and seventeenth centuries. It was under Akbar (1556-1605) that the Mughal school with a distinct style became established. Akbar's liberal attitude and patronage to works of art and painting was a great boost to the artists of his time, which is well accounted in the description of Abū'l Faẓl in the *Ā'īn-i Akbarī*:

> "His Majesty from his earliest youth has shown a great predilection for this art, and gives it every encouragement, as he looks upon it as a means, both of study and amusement. Hence the art flourishes, and many painters have obtained great reputation. The works of all painters are weekly laid before His Majesty by the Dāroghas and the clerks; he then confers rewards according to excellence of workmanship, or increases the monthly salaries. Much progress was made in the commodities required by painters, and the correct prices of such articles were carefully ascertained."[1]

Akbar's keen interest in painting was exposed not only in his favourable disposition towards painters and their paintings, against the censorship of the conservative elements in Islam, but also in his mystical attitude towards the art of painting. A significant work of art, for him, was a source of revelation of divine wisdom:

> "One day" says Abū'l Faẓl "at a private party of friends, His Majesty, who had conferred on several the pleasure of drawing near him, remarked: "There are many that hate painting; but such men I dislike. It appears to me as if a painter had quite peculiar means of recognizing God; for a painter in sketching anything that has life,

> and in devising its limbs, one after the other, must come to feel that he cannot bestow individuality upon his work, and is thus forced to think of God, the giver of life, and will thus increase in knowledge." "[2]

Imperial patronage drew a large number of artists from different regions to the royal studio. Only a few are mentioned in the historical works of the period.[3] All those who came under the royal aegis brought along with them their own regional traits as well, and helped in evolving a compact, unified and homogeneous form and style of painting, and they could be mostly identified from the ascriptions given on the miniatures.[4] Such a unified result was achieved through a practice of 'joint-work' in the royal atelier, a system of work that was most ingeniously recommended by Emperor Akbar. In joint-work system the making of a picture was generally divided into two successive stages, i.e., sketching or drawing (*ṭarḥ*) and colouring (*'amal* or *rangāmezī*). While one painter sketched, another did the colouring. Sometimes, a third painter finished the main figures (*ṣūrat*) or portraits (*chihra* or *chihra nāmī*). Line drawing seems to have held the first place at the Mughal atelier. This task was usually assigned to master painters. Collaboration in painting between the master painters and the lesser skilled painters at the atelier proved indispensable in forming an independent style (*qalam*), though within the limits of the composite style, of the Mughal school. Manṣūr, too, is known to have collaborated with the master painters, viz., Basāwan, Kānhā and Miskīnā during the early phase of his career at the imperial atelier. Manṣūr did the colouring only in the drawing executed by these painters [1-2, 4, 13-14]. In one instance, Nānhā finished the portraits of august personalities in a miniature executed by him [17].

Jahāngīr who inherited an established atelier well groomed in definite style, further encouraged painters with specialized skills. The large number of painters who either painted or apprenticed during Akbar's time had to go through a screening process due to the demands of specialization. As a result the best could survive and the rest slowly declined and disintegrated. The much reduced number of painters who were left, formed an assembly of master painters at the royal atelier. Foremost amongst these painters are: Abū'l Ḥasan, Bālchand, Bichitr, Bishandās, Govardhan, Manohar, Manṣūr and Muḥammad Nādir.

Keen interest of the Mughal emperors in the study of flora and fauna gave a special impetus to the artists to portray wild life and pictures on natural history, a phenomenon that never occurred before in Indian art. Bābur, the founder of the Mughal empire, has given a penetrative description of birds, animals, flowers and trees of India.[5] It shows that the living natural history of India afforded both the excitement of discovery and novelty to the emperor. His close and precise observations about the wild life served as a logical basis for the representation of bird and animal drawings as studies in character.[6]

In the Mughal school, next to human portraiture, the important subject of representation in painting is the study of birds, animals and flowers. An event from *Tezkereh al Vākiāt* would show Humāyūn's interest in the portrayal of wild life:

> "Soon after the Rana had retired the King undressed, and ordered clothes to be washed, and in the meanwhile he wore his dressing gown; while thus sitting, a beautiful bird flew into the tent, the doors of which were immediately closed, and the bird caught; His Majesty then took a pair of scissors and cut some of the feathers of the animal; he then sent for a painter, and had a picture taken of the bird, and afterwards ordered it to be released."[7]

Jahāngīr's curiosity in natural history was perhaps intenser, and he wanted to see in the depicted representations of wild life greater likeness. Emperor Jahāngīr's enthusiasm for knowledge of natural history was further sharpened by his almost scientific curiosity, which was enough reason for his foremost preference for specialization in art, and then, precision in recapturing the exact likeness of the living objects of nature in line and colour. Most exclusive pictures of wild life executed under his patronage clearly show that the Mughal school owes its highest achievement to this aesthete Emperor. And, its continuity is well maintained in a large number of bird, animal and flower studies done during the succeeding years of post-Jahāngīr period.

Another factor responsible for the interest of the painters in wild life may be ascribed to the fact that they were called upon to paint animals and birds for illustrating fables and legends, like *Ṭūṭīnāma, Anwār-i Suhailī, 'Iyār-i Dānish* and *'Ajā'ib-al Makhlūqāt.*[8] Subsequently, the Mughal painters became intimately acquainted with the character and behaviour of the birds and animals, and their drawings aided by such an extra dimension did not remain merely confined to the externals of the animals, but became warm and sincere depictions of their moods, habits and emotions as well. In illustrating the legends involving animal characters, painters not only resorted to direct approach to the subject, but they could also exercise some amount of freedom and imagination.

Bāburnāma miniatures are the earliest depictions of natural history. The best known three copies of this manuscript, preserved in the British Museum, London (Or.4615), National Museum, New Delhi (No. 07.271) and Museum of Eastern Cultures, Moscow, contain 120 illustrations of flora and fauna of India,[9] which closely follow the descriptions of Bābur in his Memoirs.[10] In the British Museum copy the miniatures contributed by Manṣūr can be seen.[11] *Bāburnāma* paintings, in general, show the animals drawn either in pairs or groups or in singles. But, in compositional scenes of hunting or bird trapping various species of birds and animals are clustered together. Emphasis on the exact delineation of individual character of the subject is noticeable in these miniatures. One cannot fail to admire the presence of minute details of the characteristic features of the various animals in them; nothing eludes the artist's eye, whether it is the texture of the hair, or peculiarities of the horns and the ears, the mane and the tail, or the fur and the plumage. They are so realistically depicted and distinguished that each species is clearly individualized and separated from the others.[12]

Naturalistic treatment of birds and animals becomes more and more apparent by the close of Akbar's reign. Purely linear, pictorial and decorative representation of the Persian school seems to have been pushed to the background at this juncture of development of the Mughal school. Sympathy coupled with scientific orientation to the study of animals in the paintings seems to be the cause of such transition. The sympathetic attitude for the animal world incidentally comes in line with the pre-Mughal Indian tradition,[13] only with a difference that the Mughal artists by the very fact of their purpose, i.e., naturalistic portraiture, were not required to inspire the same intensity of adoration and reverence.

No less than forty names of artists from Akbar's atelier appear on the miniatures depicting animal life.[14] A greater number of these illustrations are ascribed to Basāwan, Bhawānī, Dhannu, Farrukh *Chela,* Ḥusain *Naqqāsh,* Kānhā, La'l, Manohar, Manṣūr, Miskīnā, Sarwan, Shankar Gujarātī, and Tārā, while Anant, 'Āṣī, Bāndī, Fattū, Jagannāth, Lachhman, Lumānka, Pāras, Payāg, Rāmdās and Shivdās have to their credit only a piece each.[15]

During Akbar's era a distinct *qalam* had come into existence as has already been said, but specialization in various branches of art had to wait till Jahāngīr's advent on the firmament of royal art patronage. Manohar and Manṣūr from Akbar's atelier were recognized as the two most distinct specialists in painting animal portraits in the succeeding era. They were found compatible to Emperor Jahāngīr's measures of excellence.

Jahāngīr added to the already existing importance of the art of painting by treating it as a major source of historical documentation of events:

> "Although King Bābur has described in his Memoirs the appearance and shapes of several animals, he had never ordered the painters to make pictures of them. As these animals appeared to me to be very strange, I both described them and ordered that painters should draw them in the Jahāngīr-nāma, so that the amazement that arose from hearing of them might be increased."[16]

Numerous references to the portrayal of events done at the command of the emperor may be found in the *Tūzuk-i Jahāngīrī,* which further affirm Jahāngīr's this particular attitude towards painting. In the year 1618, Jahāngīr ordered his painters to make the portrait of 'Ināyat Khān who, due to his long illness, had emaciated so much that his condition appeared to him to be an extraordinary horrifying spectre of death. Jahāngīr writes:

> "I ordered him to come into my presence and obtain leave. They put him into a palanquin and brought him. He appeared so low and weak that I was astonished.
>
> "He was skin drawn over bones."
>
> Or rather his bones, too, had dissolved. Though painters have striven much in drawing an emaciated face, yet I have never seen anything like this, nor even approaching to it. Good God, can a son of a man come to such a shape and fashion?...
>
> As it was a very extraordinary case I directed painters to take his portrait."[17]

Jahāngīr always felt concerned for great accuracy and naturalism in portrait painting of both men and animals. He sent his master painter Bishandās to Persia to take the likenesses of Shāh 'Abbās and his courtiers.[18] Obviously, Jahāngīr preferred, above all, that portraits be executed after an intimate and personal observation of the subject. This principle was adhered to unfailingly by the painters accompanying the emperor's train whenever he took an outing. An interesting event which throws light on Manṣūr's career is, when he was visiting Kashmir as a member of the emperor's train in 1620. There, not only he painted more than a hundred varieties of flowers blossoming in that exotic valley,[19] but he also painted a picture of a bird called *sāj* (dipper), seen at Sukh Nag, at the emperor's bidding.[20] Jahāngīr's scientific curiosity and innate desire for documentation of rarities gave a tremendous impetus to 'zoological portraits' of immense value and quality.

Jahāngīr had an uncanny insight to discern as much the real and rare qualities in paintings, as to recognize talent. When pleased with a work he did not fall short in his magnanimity. For the good portraits executed by Bishandās, Jahāngīr honoured him with the gift of an elephant, which was a sign of high recognition in those days.[21] Another master painter Farrukh Beg received a largesse of two thousand rupees (Akbar's rupee) from Jahāngīr in 1609.[22] Abū'l Ḥasan and Manṣūr were bestowed with the titles of *Nādir uz Zamān* (Wonder of the Age) and *Nādir u'l 'Aṣr* (Unequalled of the Age) respectively.[23] These most exalted titles would probably suggest that these two painters enjoyed the most honoured position at the royal atelier.

Among the contemporaries of Manṣūr at Jahāngīr's atelier who also portrayed wild life were Abū'l Ḥasan, Farrukh Beg, Govardhan, 'Ināyat, Manohar, Muḥammad Nādir, Murād (or Mirār) and Pidārath. One is quite wonder-struck to discover that the total number of animal paintings ascribed to these artists is far less than what Manṣūr painted alone.[24] Added to that, are his flower studies [38-42]. Manṣūr's towering command in this branch of painting can well be judged from the fact that Emperor Jahāngīr could trust no one else more than him for doing bird and animal paintings.[25] This in itself is an indubitable proof of Manṣūr being the most leading exponent of natural history painting in the atelier of Jahāngīr. The extraordinary qualities of this artist is a positive inspiration to explore further into his art as it promises very many possibilities of not only historical, but also, of aesthetic and artistic significance, and which may have escaped the critical eye so far.

3
MANṢŪR

Earliest reference to Manṣūr is found in the dispersed miniatures of *Bāburnāma* at the Freer Gallery of Art, Washington, and is datable between 1590-95. But his actual *tour de force* as a painter comes to be recognized in the *Tūzuk-i Jahāngīrī* in the account of the 13th regnal year, i.e., AH 1027/1618, wherein Jahāngīr writes:

> "Also, Ustād Manṣūr had become such a master in painting that he has the title of Nādiru-l-'Aṣr, and in the art of drawing is unique in his generation. In the time of my father's [Akbar's] reign and my own these two [Abū'l Ḥasan and Manṣūr] have had no third."[1]

Nevertheless, Manṣūr had attained this reputation earlier than 1618, which can be inferred from his signed ascription given on the miniature 'Turkey cock' [27], executed by him in about 1612, which reads: ' *'Amal-i banda-i dargāh Manṣūr Nādir u'l 'Aṣr, Jahāngīr Shāhī*' ('Work of the slave of the court Manṣūr *Nādir u'l 'Aṣr* (Unequalled of the Age), [servant] of the King Jahāngīr'). Turkey cock, one of nature's rarities, brought by Muqarrab Khān from Goa was presented to Jahāngīr in the year 1612.[2] Jahāngīr, who had not seen such a strange and wonderful bird ever before, described it in detail in his Memoirs,[3] and in all probability, required that a painting be made in its exact likeness for the purpose of visual illustration.[4] Since Jahāngīr had confidence in Manṣūr's ability for exactness in painting, it is very likely that he commissioned this artist to do the turkey cock for him. There are instances on record when Jahāngīr ordered Manṣūr to paint the animals and birds that fascinated him. In 1619, Jahāngīr ordered Manṣūr to take the portrait of the falcon sent to him by the Shah of Persia.[5] In the following year, 1620, when Jahāngīr visited Kashmir, Manṣūr, who was in his train, had yet another assignment to fulfil, that of painting the exotic flora of the valley.[6] Thus, Manṣūr's genius was recognized in flower studies as well. During this visit itself his royal patron asked him to portray a bird called *sāj*.[7]

An inscription on the miniature 'Zebra' [47] provides an additional information on our artist's career, which is in the handwriting of Jahāngīr.

It reads: *"Astrī kī Rūmīān az Ḥabsha bā hamrāhī-e-Mīr Ja'far āwurda būdand. San 1030 Hijrī. Shabīh-i īn rā Nādir u'l 'Aṣrī Ustād Manṣūr kashīdah. San 16"* ('A zebra [lit. mule] which the Turks who came in company with Mir Jafar had brought from Abyssinia. Year 1030 of the Hijra. Painted by *Nādir u'l 'Aṣrī Ustād* Manṣūr, 16th regnal year, i.e., 1621'). Jahāngīr gives a vivid description of this animal in his Memoirs, in the account of the same year, while he was at Agra — the capital town. He writes:

> "At this time I saw a wild ass (*gūr-khār*), exceedingly strange in appearance, exactly like a lion. From the tip of the nose to the end of the tail, and from the point of the ear to the top of the hoof, black markings, large or small, suitable to their position, were seen on it. Round the eyes there was an exceedingly fine black line. One might say the painter of fate, with a strange brush, had left it on the page of the world. As it was strange, some people imagined that it had been coloured. After minute inquiry into the truth, it became known that the Lord of the world was the Creator thereof. As it was a rarity, it was included among the royal gifts sent to my brother Shāh 'Abbās."[8]

The year of the description of the animal coincides with the year of the execution of the portrait, as we have observed. It can be inferred that Manṣūr portrayed the zebra immediately after it was presented to the emperor in 1621, and that, after his return from Kashmir, Manṣūr continued to work in the imperial atelier at Agra.

Since no miniature of Manṣūr bearing date after 1621 is known, the active period of this painter, historically speaking, may clearly be said to have lasted at least till 1621. This does not necessarily mean that the zebra would have been the last one executed by Manṣūr in a strictly chronological order. His active period, without being much speculative, may be said to have extended to a few more years, perhaps, upto 1627. The miniatures of these years, related to him after careful screening, clearly possess the distinct style and technique of the master at his best. There is obvious evidence of continuity, and marked ascendancy to greater freedom and spontaneity of expression. However, there is no concrete proof left to us to stretch his career beyond this date, and it seems to have ended with Jahāngīr's reign, in 1627. No miniature ascribed to Manṣūr is datable during Shāh Jahān's reign. Asok Kumar Das's view that Manṣūr worked during the early reign of Shāh Jahān is based on an unascribed miniature [89] 'the picture of dodo, pasted on a folio along with other pictures showing a tragopan, a Sumatran loriquet, ducks and a pair of partridges'.[9] His method does not seem to be logically conclusive, and may be termed as rather a sort of conditional suggestion unsupported by either historical or internal evidence. The dating of it by Salim Ali[10] and A.J. Qaisar[11] between 1624-7 is in contradiction to Das's. Therefore, perhaps, it is safer to consider, for historical study, only the ascribed paintings.

The suffix *Naqqāsh* (lit. a painter, engraver, sculptor, carver, gilder, limner) with Manṣūr's name in some of the ascriptions on the miniatures [6-8, 12, 16, 25, 30-1, 38, 45] would probably suggest that Manṣūr belonged to a family which was engaged in some sort of a profession as connoted by the word *naqqāsh,* or, may be, he had also practised some form of art other than painting, which left no record. The term *naqqāsh* does not seem to have been employed in the ascriptions given on the Mughal miniatures to refer to a painter, in general. This term is suffixed as exception with the names of only four painters, viz., Manṣūr *Naqqāsh,* Ḥusain *Naqqāsh,* Iqbāl *Naqqāsh* and Maulānā Ibrāhīm *Naqqāsh.* The restricted use of this term suggests that possibly it denoted an individual's affiliation to some kind of art profession other than painting. Manṣūr[12] and Ḥusain[13] are known to have done the work of illuminating the manuscripts; Maulānā Ibrāhīm is known to have worked for 'Abdu'r Raḥīm Khān-i Khānān, but nothing of it has survived.[14] However, the relevance of the term *naqqāsh* with painter's name remains ambiguous, and since several other painters who also illuminated margins, *'unwāns,* etc. are not referred to with the suffix *naqqāsh.*[15]

3.1 EARLY PHASE

The earliest surviving work of Manṣūr are the illustrations from the *Bāburnāma.* These illustrations are datable 1590-1600. A dispersed folio of the *Bāburnāma* (c. 1590-5) preserved at the Freer Gallery of Art, Washington, shows that Manṣūr started his career as an assistant collaborator of Kānhā, a leading painter of Akbar's atelier.[1] Here, Manṣūr has done the colouring (*'amal*) only in the drawing (*ṭarḥ*) made by Kānhā [1-2]. Beach holds that this folio shows basic elements of Manṣūr's style fully formed, which continue throughout the rest of his career.[2] Though in joint works individuality of painters is hard to discern but Beach thinks that "the slow, careful drawings and thinly applied paint, however, seem especially distinctive of Manṣūr."[3] As most of the stylistic features of the painting also appear rather commonly in the works of many other Mughal painters, therefore, they do not necessarily individualize Manṣūr for originality. As such, we have to look for some other finer points in the painting to locate Manṣūr, like the particular formation of bird flights, the treatment of the sky and vegetation, aspects where Manṣūr is clearly different from others. His special way of handling them could be traced to his other independent works as well.

Manṣūr's solo work in the British Museum copy of the *Bāburnāma* (c. 1590-1600) would probably lend a fairer view of the formative stage of Manṣūr's style. Miniatures executed on folio nos. 387a-b, 388a-b and 389a show different birds, painted in single or in groups of two, amidst landscape, with every object treated in elaborate details and with equal emphasis—a trait so characteristic of the sixteenth century Mughal landscape painting. It was later discarded by Manṣūr in favour of total emphasis on the central theme. Such a centrally concentrated focusing of attention makes his bird studies excellent examples of minute observation and objectification. The details of pictures in *Bāburnāma,* viz., the pictures of birds pulpaiker species (f. 387b) and *charz* (f. 389a) do seem to have achieved greater precision, superior drawing and colouration, yet his real talents are still dormant.

Again, the National Museum copy of the *Bāburnāma* (1598) which contains 43 folio drawings of flora and fauna, shows that Manṣūr was not entrusted with the task of portraying them. However, only one miniature, folio 8, which represents 'Bābur meeting his sister' [3] is ascribed to Manṣūr. It almost suggests that, at least till this date, Manṣūr had not achieved such distinction and that remarkable specialization in the art of portraying wild life for which he was uniquely acclaimed during Jahāngīr's time.

Manṣūr's works, in the National Museum and British Museum copies, when compared in terms of former's fixed dating and the latter's dating of somewhat tentative nature, as also, that he was entrusted to do just one folio painting only of human figures in indoor set-up, in National Museum MS, it all strongly implies that Manṣūr painted the birds and animals of the British Museum copy only after 1598.

Manṣūr, in his early phase, also collaborated with the master painters, like Basāwan, Miskīnā and Nānhā on the folios of the manuscripts: *Jāmi'-ut Tawārīkh* (IL, 1596), *Akbarnāma* (VA, c. 1602-5) [4, 13-4]. In these joint works Manṣūr was only assigned to 'colour'. Nevertheless, by the time we reach the end of Akbar's reign (1605), Manṣūr had already carved out a distinct niche for himself among the top-notchers of the royal atelier, as is evident from his solo paintings in the British Museum copy of *Akbarnāma* (1604; ff. 35, 110a-b, and 112a), and the ascriptions given on them along with the prefixed epithet *'ustād'* [17-8]. The term *ustād* (lit. master) was an honorific title denoting an individual's excellence in his profession. For sure, when Manṣūr was addressed by this epithet in Akbar's royal atelier it meant a rare and lofty recognition of his calibre. Other master painters referred to with this title are Bābū, Basāwan, Ḥusain, La'l and Miskīn only, out of more than two hundred painters who are known to have worked in Akbar's atelier.[4] Basāwan, La'l and Miskīn are again qualified as the three of the top seventeen painters recorded by Abū'l Fazl.[5] Omission of Manṣūr's name by Abū'l Fazl in his list of the leading painters is understandable in the light of the completion date of this chronicle, i.e., 1596-7; the date which corroborated with what has already been said about the point in reference to the National Museum copy of *Bāburnāma,* that is, Manṣūr had yet to establish his skill in painting par excellence. Manṣūr's progression from this early phase to his perfection in painting natural history, passes through a phase of his interest in the twin activities of illumination work and painting. Then, he moves on to painting only, and that too, in the exactness of the living objects of nature, the sphere in which he left no equal.

Manṣūr was entrusted the work of illuminating *'unwān* of the manuscript of *Khamsa* of Amīr Khusrau (WAG, W.624).[6] Later he illuminated *sar-i lauḥ* of the *Akbarnāma* (CBL, c. 1604-5)[7] and *shamsa* of the *Dīwān* of Anwarī (location not known).[8] These are examples of Manṣūr's aptitude for design work, which continued simultaneously along with his concentration in painting. The latter comes to its excellent flowering in due course. Akbar's atelier, besides a host of painters, also included a large number of unchronicled limners (*naqqāshān*), gilders (*muzaḥḥibān*), line-drawers (*jadwal ārāyān*) and bookbinders (*ṣaḥḥāfān*).[9] However, only some illuminators, other than Manṣūr, namely, Ḥusain *Naqqāsh,* Khwāja Jān Shirāzī and Luṭf Ullāh *Muzaḥḥib* are known from the inscriptions given on the illuminated folios.[10] Manṣūr[11] and Ḥusain *Naqqāsh*[12] were the two exceptions who were assigned to do illumination work and painting both. An illumination work shows the painter's skill in the execution of intricate patterns, repeatedly drawn with uniformity, accuracy and clarity of fine details. Though no definite evidence of illumination work done by Manṣūr after Akbar's reign has so far come to light, Skelton suggests that floral borders found on Shāh Jahān's album pages may have been executed by Manṣūr.[13] Skelton does not specify these pages so as to enable us to examine them, and his statement, thus, suffers from the same type of error of judgement as has already been seen earlier in the case of Asok Kumar Das in reference to the dodo's picture. Skelton's contention is most unconvincing, because Manṣūr, according to inscriptions given on his works, never indulged in any other type of illumination work other than *sar-i lauḥ* and *'unwān* illumination done at the beginning of the folio chapters, least of all floral borders, and that too, at a much later date, i.e., during Shāh Jahān's reign.

Miniatures executed by Manṣūr in the *Akbarnāma* (BM, Or.12988), imbued with the characteristics of the Mughal *qalam* of late sixteenth century, apparently project him as a conventional painter. One of the conventions adopted by Manṣūr and seen on folio 110b, is clearly an attempt, like others, to accommodate the European style of creating distance perspective; it is characterized by an in-set placed at a remote end of the landscape with blurred effect. The in-set of this folio shows a man pulling at horses in training action in a hazing away manner.[14] This idea and theme of the in-set could easily have been picked from his senior collaborator Miskīnā's composition in a miniature 'Unfaithful wife' (c. 1595-1600).[15] Manṣūr's association with Miskīnā is clear since he worked as his collaborator, at least on one folio painting of *Akbarnāma* (VA, c. 1602-5).[16] In the present example, although Manṣūr is quite conventional and unoriginal in selecting the subject and style, yet, his forms of galloping horses become very live in vigour and strength by the touch of his skilful brush, so much so, that he appears to have equalled his senior Miskīnā.

Manṣūr never lacked special felicity in painting, is evident from the beginning, be it illumination, book-illustration, bird and animal drawings, or human-portraits (only one has survived from his early phase). His genius seems to have gained a rare maturity even at his early phase, and is vivid in the portrait of a '*Vīnā*-player' (c. 1605). Welch has noticed that the rhythmic flutter of birds and flowers lends it a distinct lyrical quality, which was a step further taken by Manṣūr in the art of portraiture. According to him, "Although no horizon line is drawn, the clouds and birds imply space and provide the drama of tempting quarry... Here, the rhythmic flutter of birds and flowers goes beyond physical description in a successful attempt to interpret music in paint."[17] This extra embellishment of lyrical stylization of Manṣūr can again be witnessed in the flower studies executed by him later, where birds, butterflies and other insects are shown hovering over the blossoms, which creates an extraordinary rhythmic quality to an otherwise naturalistic still life.

The plants with blossoms drawn almost arcading the portrait of the musician *Vīnā*-player strongly reflects Manṣūr's innate love for nature even at this stage of his development. In the present picture, Manṣūr's masterly touch is again seen in employing appropriate rhythmic lines in the drawing of the main figure suggesting the musician's mood. Manṣūr showed a distinct progress in the art of portrait painting in a span of few years. Manṣūr was not considered deft enough to paint portraits at least as late as 1604. For example, in a miniature [4] from *Jāmi'-ut Tawārīkh* (IL, 1598), where he had the assignment of colouring only, Mādhav, a prolific painter of Akbar's court, finished the human figures.[18] An inscription given on this folio reads: *"Ṭarḥ-i Nānhā, 'amal-i Manṣūr, ṣūrat Mādhav"* ('Sketch by Nānhā, colouring by Manṣūr and figures by Mādhav'). In another instance, late in 1604, in the miniature [17] from the *Akbarnāma* (BM, f. 110a) Narsingh finished the portrait of the august. Inscription on it reads: "*Ustād Manṣūr, chihra nāmī Narsing[h]*" ('Painted by *Ustād* Manṣūr, august portrait by Narsingh').[19]

'Coronation (?) portrait of Jahāngīr' (c. 1605),[20] a yet another portrait study, is a joint work of Manṣūr and Manohar [20]. Ornate in style, it represents Jahāngīr, the royal personage possessing grandeur. Firm lines representing restricted movement is another distinctive quality, which is rarely seen in other royal portraits from the Mughal school. Wild life depicted in the panel of imperial throne, embellished with intricate patterns all over, appears in contrast with the flat background which effectively isolates the central subject. It is hard to distinguish in this portrait as to how much portion of it was executed by Manohar and how much by Manṣūr, because, as we will later see, Manṣūr's typical style of portrait drawing has something in common with this.

In the portrait of Khwāja Kalān Beg [33], executed by Manṣūr alone a little later, the main figure is shown perched against dark background. Here the space is dealt with an introduction of clouds and flight of birds in the high margin, and the horizon line is done away with unlike the portrait of the '*Vīnā*-player'. This method of handling the space has been employed by Manṣūr afterwards also in the portrayal of birds and animals. Clarke considers this work of Manṣūr as "...unmistakably a work of the second stage of the transition period of Mogul painting".[21] According to him it "serves as an admirable record of his [Manṣūr's] rapid progress in brush drawing, colouring and shading" and "affords evidence of the advance and the onward trend from Persian to Indian" notwithstanding, as Clarke alleges, the latter's "coquetting with European influence".[22]

So far we have seen in our journey with Manṣūr that he did not simply move from mere illustration and colouring assignments to human portraiture, but he stamped the latter with his originality of approach to space treatment in a very unique way, so as to highlight the central subject, and to lend the whole a lyrical quality. And, all this he does while still remaining within the conventions of Mughal art of the period.

3.2 SPECIALIZATION

With this profound background, Manṣūr obviously earned privileged patronage of Jahāngīr — an exceptionally discerning connoisseur of art. Jahāngīr's love for art supplemented by his scientific curiosity and wonderment at natural objects, gave special impetus to painting of pictures on natural history. By

1618, Manṣūr had undoubtedly attained such a perfection and refinement that his position as a portrait painter of birds and animals had become unsurpassable. This is confirmed from Jahāngīr's account of him of the same year, "in the art of drawing he is unique in his generation",[1] and also, from his subsequent references to Manṣūr in his Memoirs. In 1619, Jahāngīr ordered Manṣūr to paint the likeness of a falcon brought as a gift from Shāh 'Abbās of Persia. Jahāngīr writes:

> "At this time the king of Persia had sent with Parī Beg Mīr Shikār (chief huntsman) one falcon (shunqār) of good colour. There was another which had been given to the Khān 'Ālam. This one was sent along with the Shāhī falcon (i.e., the one intended for Jahāngīr), and it died on the road. The Shāhī falcon, too, got mauled by a cat owing to the carelessness of Mīr Shikār. Though it was brought to Court, it did not live more than a week... As it was something out of the common, I ordered Ustād Manṣūr, who has the title of *Nādiru-l-'Aṣr* (wonder of the age) to paint and preserve its likeness."[2]

Two drawings of the falcon nos. 34 and 55 ascribed to Manṣūr are known. Miniature no. 34, preserved in the Fogg Art Museum, Boston, is described by Coomaraswamy as the possible drawing of the one referred to by Jahāngīr above.[3] It is a perched isolated figure of the bird, and is thinly coloured with detailed markings on each wing, on its back, and sides. It bears an inscription on the right hand corner (below): "*'Amal-i Nādir u'l 'Aṣr Ustād Manṣūr*" ('Work of *Nādir u'l 'Aṣr Ustād* Manṣūr'). However, Das doubts the ascription and considers it to be a copy of an earlier work.[4] According to him, a picture of this bird [55], preserved in the Sawai Man Singh II Museum, Jaipur, is the genuine likeness of the falcon referred to by Jahāngīr, and is an authentic work of Manṣūr (it is controversial, and has been discussed later).

As we already know that Jahāngīr, during his sojourn in Kashmir (1620), had commissioned Manṣūr to do a lot of paintings, which included a portrait of bird *sāj* (dipper). About it he records:

> "In this stream I saw a bird like a *sāj*. A *sāj* is of black colour and has white spots, while this bird is of the same colour as a *bulbul* with white spots, and it dives and remains for a long time underneath, and then comes up from a different place. I ordered them to catch and bring two or three of these birds, that I might ascertain whether they are waterfowl and were web-footed, or

> had open feet like land birds. They caught two and brought them. One died immediately, and the other lived for a day. Its feet were not webbed like a duck's. I ordered *Nādiru-l-'aṣr* Ustād Manṣūr to draw its likeness."[5]

Miniature no. 45, a rare picture of the *sāj* bearing Manṣūr's signatures, is well identified. Here the depiction of the *sāj* bird in a rocky landscape with a gushing stream, and one of them diving deep into the water, fully corresponds with the above graphic description.

Earlier to this event in the same year, as has already been said in passing reference, Manṣūr painted flowers of Kashmir. Jahāngīr notes:

> "The flowers that are seen in the territories of Kashmir are beyond all calculation. Those that *Nādiru-l-'asrī* Ustād Manṣūr has painted are more than 100."[6]

Although Jahāngīr mentions more than hundred flower studies of Manṣūr, only five out of them [38-42] are extant, and they are qualitatively sufficient proof why Jahāngīr had so much preference for Manṣūr.

It may permit here a conjecture in view of Jahāngīr's passion for natural history and a very dependable preference for Manṣūr alone to paint it, that birds and animals which are described in the Memoirs, but not mentioned to have been done as a result of royal command as such, were, perhaps, in reality actuated by some form of the Emperor's expressed wish or curiosity for a particular object: in those days it could easily have been taken as an implicit way of commissioning. Manṣūr's pictures in this category are 'Turkey cock' [27] and 'Himalayan cheer pheasant' [28].

The turkey cock and Himalayan cheer pheasant were presented to Jahāngīr in 1612.[7] These were part of the rarities brought by Muqarrab Khān from Goa. Jahāngīr's impassioned naturalistic description of these is worthwhile, to evaluate by comparison their immaculate reproduction in drawing and colour by Manṣūr:

> "One of these animals in body is larger than a peahen and smaller than a peacock. When it is in heat and displays itself, it spreads out its feathers like the peacock and dances about. Its beak and legs are like those of a cock. Its head and neck and the part under the throat are every minute of a different colour. When it is in heat

it is quite red—one might say it had adorned itself with red coral—and after a while it becomes white in the same places, and looks like cotton. It sometimes looks of a turquoise colour. Like a chameleon it constantly changes colour. Two pieces of flesh it has on its head look like the comb of a cock. A strange thing is this, that when it is in heat the aforesaid piece of flesh hangs down to the length of a span from the top of its head like an elephant's trunk, and again when he raises it up it appears on its head like the horn of a rhinoceros, to the extent of two finger-breadths. Round its eyes it is always of a turquoise colour, and does not change. Its feathers appear to be of various colours, differing from the colours of the peacock's feathers. He also brought a monkey of a strange and wonderful form. Its hands, feet, ears, and head are like those of a monkey, and its face like that of a fox. The colour of its eyes is like that of a hawk's eye, but the eyes are larger than those of a hawk. From its head to the end of its tail it is an ordinary cubit in length. It is lower than a monkey and taller than a fox. Its hair is like the wool of a sheep and its colour like that of ashes. From the lobe of its ear to its chin it is red and of the colour of wine. Its tail is two or three finger-breadths longer than half a cubit, quite different from that of other monkeys. The tail of this animal hangs down like the tail of a cat. Sometimes it makes a sound like a young antelope. On the whole it is a very strange beast. Of the wild birds which they call *tadrū* (pheasant) till now it has never been heard that they breed in captivity. In the time of my revered father they made great efforts to obtain eggs and young ones but it was not managed. I ordered them to keep some of them, male and female, in one place, and by degrees they bred. I ordered them to place the eggs under hens, and in a space of two years sixty or seventy young were produced and fifty or sixty grew up. Whoever heard of this matter was astonished. It was said that in the Wilāyat (Persia?) the people there had made great efforts, but no eggs were produced and no young were obtained."[8]

The picture of the strange monkey in the description is, however, not traceable, but the pictures of turkey cock and Himalayan cheer pheasant ascribed to Manṣūr are very much preserved. Several versions of them are available, but indeed that in itself poses before us the problem of authenticity, the discussion of which we may defer here, to be taken up in the separate section devoted to it exclusively.

Jahāngīr's autographed and dated pictures of birds and animals by Manṣūr is another category. These were, most probably, done at the instance of his royal patron. (A slight digression may be allowed here; the category of pictures with dated autographs has helped make a chronological arrangement and that has facilitated our study of Manṣūr's development at this stage.) Pictures of *Charz-i bor* [35], 'Zebra' [47] and 'Salt water fish' [52] come in this category.

The date given in the inscription (Jahāngīr's autograph) of the painting that is the likeness of the Indian bustard (*charz-i bor*) corresponds to the date of Jahāngīr's account of it in his Memoirs; he spotted this bird in 1619 on his way from Delhi to Agra in the *pargana* Kairana while hawking:

> "In these few days I was delighted with hawking the *jarz* (bustard or florican) and *tūgh-dārī* (also a kind of bustard). I ordered the *jarz-i būr* (the red bustard?) to be weighed. It came 2¼ Jahāngīrī sirs and the variegated (*ablaq*) one to $2^1/_8$ sirs. The large *tūgh-dārī* was 1/4 sir heavier than the *jarz-i būr*."[9]

The inscription on the miniature '*Charz-i bor*' [35] reads: *"Shabīh-i charz-i bor. 'Amal-i Nādir u'l 'Aṣrī Ustād Manṣūr hurrarah-i Jahāngīr Akbar Shāh, san 14"* ('Picture of the red bustard. Work of *Nādir u'l 'Aṣrī Ustād* Manṣūr, written by Jahāngīr, son of Emperor Akbar, the 14th (regnal) year, i.e. 1619'). The correspondence between the two dates of the description and the inscription suggests that Jahāngīr ordered Manṣūr to take the likeness of this bird immediately after some of the same species were captured. It indicates that there were painters also accompanying the Emperor's train during the expedition, as on many other occasions. Jahāngīr, through his inscription on this picture, gave to posterity an opportunity to recognize it as Manṣūr's authentic work.

It never occurred to anyone earlier that the *charz-i bor* of the miniature under discussion is the picture of a female bird particularly. This identification is confirmed from the description of this bird given in the emperor's Memoirs (account of the year 1623), which clearly draws a line, after thorough physical scrutiny, between the male and female sexes of the bird, based on the difference in their colour scheme. He describes:

> "The *jarz* or *charz* (bustard) is of two kinds: one is a mottled black and other *būr* (a kind of dun colour). I now discovered that there are not two kinds, but that which is a mottled black is the male, and that which is dun-coloured is the female. The proof of it is this, that in the piebald there are testicles and in the dun one there are eggs; this has been repeatedly found on examination."[10]

An unsigned copy [67] of the same '*Charz-i bor*' picture, preserved in Dārā Shukoh Album (lOL), executed in the early nineteenth century, but which Smith thinks to have possibly been painted by Manṣūr,[11] is a controversy which has been dealt with later along with other similar cases.

The picture of 'Zebra' [47] is another such instance of Manṣūr's work which carries the dated autograph of Jahāngīr and also corresponds with the date of the animal's description in the Memoirs.[12]

These two instances fairly suggest that, as in the cases of falcon and *sāj*, the 'rarities' presented to the emperor may have aroused his curiosity and wonder so much that he desired their portraits to be made immediately. Could it be said, then, that Manṣūr's drawings of birds and animals which have also been described in the *Tūzuk-i Jahāngīrī* bear correspondences of details and point toward proximity of time between the event of seeing and the date of painting. It is perhaps quite convincing as a method to date these paintings on the basis of such correspondences.

Thus, pictures of 'Turkey cock' [27] and 'Himalayan cheer pheasant' [28], though undated, could be concluded to have been painted in 1612, as their appreciation is also entered in the Memoirs in the same year.[13] It could also be taken that the picturization of these birds came about in the same fashion as the autographed ones, that is as a consequence of Jahāngīr's first encounter of seeing them in live form, and his wonderment at their uniqueness in nature.

The miniature 'Salt water fish' [52] is conspicuous in the sense that, though it is autographed, but is undated, and no clear mention of this fish is found in the *Tūzuk-i Jahāngīrī*. It is undated indeed, but on considerations of Manṣūr's style, it is a specimen in which the artist is at his most brilliant form. It appears to belong to the same group of paintings, i.e. 'Turkey cock', 'Himalayan cheer pheasant' and '*Charz-i bor*' [27-8, 35] but of course not in terms of date. A total survey of Manṣūr's paintings does bring forth the fact that this single work possesses his artistic qualities in the same genre; and in its execution, the artist's fantastic freedom and boldness of strokes, and maturity of confidence achieve a culmination of all the experiments that he did with his brush and paint over the years. Therefore, it may be pertinent to suggest that this work was done by Manṣūr somewhere during the last phase of his career, though in a roundabout fashion: that is, looking back to the 'Turkey cock', 'Himalayan cheer pheasant' and '*Charz-i bor'* of the earlier period, and then, drawing on them to do the 'Salt water fish'.

In several cases, Jahāngīr does not mention the names of artists while ordering portraits in the 'likenesses' of the nobles, birds and animals, such as, in 1608, he ordered his artists to portray a strange animal called *deonak*:

> "At the same time a dervish from Ceylon came and brought a strange animal called *deonak* (or *devnag*). Its face was exactly like a large bat, and the whole shape was like that of a monkey, but it had no tail. Its movements were like those of the black tailless monkey which they call *ban mānush* (jungle man) in the Hindi language. Its body was like that of a young monkey two or three months old. It had been with the dervish for five years. It appeared that the animal would never grow larger. Its food is milk and it also eats plantains. As the creature appeared very strange, I ordered the artists to take the likeness of it in various kinds of movements. It looked very ugly."[14]

Later, in the year 1618, Jahāngīr wanted his painters to draw the portrait of 'Ināyat Khān.[15] In 1623, he called upon his artists to draw the portrait of a tiger shot by him:

> "Driving the elephant forward, the tiger's flank came into view, and with one wound from my gun he fell and gave up his life. Of all the tigers I have shot from the time when I was a prince until now I never saw a tiger like this for size and majesty and the symmetry of its limbs. I ordered the artists to take its portrait according to its real form and body."[16]

Jahāngīr's use of the word 'artists' (*muṣauwirān*) in plural in the three instances, quoted above, certainly cannot assure us that Manṣūr alone was in view of the emperor. Besides, neither any stylistic device, nor internal evidence, nor any available opinion of a critic, can be banked upon in isolating Manṣūr's work from among them with any amount of credibility. Sufficient ground is there to believe, on the basis of the surviving drawings of birds and animals by Abū'l Ḥasan, 'Ināyat, Manohar, Pidārath and others,[17] as well as Jahāngīr's use of the word 'artist' in plural, that besides Manṣūr, there were other artists too who followed the vocation of Manṣūr's specialization.

Like the bird and animal portraits, flower portraits, though few, also occupy the place of pride in the art of this period, though their precursors, plants and trees along with blossoms, and not as individualized studies, had come into existence in the form of illustration, as may be seen in the *Bāburnāma* (c. 1590-1600).[18] These, of the illustration, possess deficient conscious form of naturalism in representation.

However, keeping in view the fact that a relatively smaller number of flower studies, as compared to human, and birds and animals, were done during seventeenth century (not forgetting the loss of many flower studies), it may be surmised that this subject was given less importance for portrait purpose. The only painters of this period who indulged in it are Manṣūr[19] and Muḥammad Nādir of Samarqand.[20] Although, the margin paintings in vogue during Jahāngīr's reign contain various favourite embellishments of blossoming plant motifs, which were done in the verisimilitude of their beautiful natural forms (in repetitive blocks),[21] yet, one wonders why the subject received so scant interest of the painters for independent portrait study. From whatever is available to view (the survivors out of the number recorded in the Memoirs and ascribed to Manṣūr), it seems that they were painted, though beautifully, but more for the purpose of visual recording of Jahāngīr's exotic thrill and excitement at the sight of these flowers in the wonder valley of Kashmir, rather than his casual naturalistic informations as in case of live animals. His racy and graphic description of the beauty of the flowers is more of an exclamatory expression:

> "The red rose, the violet, and the narcissus grow of themselves; in the fields, there are all kinds of flowers and all sorts of sweet-scented herbs more than can be calculated. In the soul-enchanting spring the hills and plains are filled with blossoms; the gates, the walls, the courts, the roofs, are lighted up by the torches of banquet-adorning tulips... There are many blue jessamines in the gardens, and the white jessamines that the people

> of India call *chambīlī* are sweet-scented. Another kind is of the colour of sandal-wood, and this is also very sweet-scented. This is special to Kashmir. I saw several sorts of red roses: one is specially sweet-scented, and another is a flower of the colour of sandal (light yellow), with an exceedingly delicate scent. It (the scent?) is of the nature of (that of) the red rose, and its stem is like that of the red rose. There are two kinds of lilies. That which is grown in gardens is vigorous (*bālīda*) and fresh (lit. green) coloured, the other is a wild kind. Although the latter has less colour it is very sweet-scented. The flower of the *Ja'farī* (a yellow flower) is large and sweet-scented; its stem is above a man's height, but in some years, when it has grown large and has flowered, a worm is produced, and spreads over the flower a kind of spider's web, and destroys it and dries up its stem. This year it has so happened."[22]

In spite of less emphasis on flower studies during this period, what little Manṣūr left for us could possibly form an album of rare botanical drawings of exquisite beauty. Seven varieties of flowers, independently composed on one folio [39], are a testimony to Manṣūr's indelible note on natural history; for their sheer accuracy of details and colours, these studies of flowers in isolation have no parallel. The meticulously drawn stems with leaves, buds and flowers, etc. in a variety of arrangements are flawless in depiction. Here the plain background is treated in 'light 'buff' shade' that seems most appropriate. Studies of seven different flowers on a single folio raises a doubt, if the artist did not mean them to be his first version to be converted into individual studies in magnified form later.

The 'Tulip' and 'Iris plant' [38, 42] are the best flower studies from Manṣūr's brush. In them also, the background is mostly treated plain except a slight suggestion of aerial perspective with the help of a fine slick strip across the top, without defining the horizon line. The total focus is laid on the main subject which suggests the artist's inclination to project it in all its genuine objective form. In such paintings, in order to enliven the surroundings and capture a certain rhythm of movement, as well as, to manage the compositional aspects, Manṣūr prefers to depict birds, butterflies and other insects hovering over the blossoms. This trait of his can be seen in his earlier works as well, particularly '*Vīnā*-player' (c. 1600-5), and it continues in Manṣūr throughout. Perhaps, he does it to achieve a greater impact of naturalistic environment through a kind of relational placement of the main object and the other minor living things (flying) in nature, and besides, he introduces through the hovering objects a sort of freedom of movement in the space around a still life exposure of the main object. This stylistic device of Manṣūr influenced the works of other painters as well. One could see a similar approach in the work of Muḥammad Nādir's 'Yellow narcissus' (c. 1625).[23] The influence is also apparent in the broad margin paintings embellished with naturalistic flower plant motifs.[24]

Manṣūr's study of floricans amidst a landscape comprising of a plant of pea family with blossom also exhibits butterflies fluttering around the flowers [40]. Similarly, in his study of chameleon [37], insects (butterfly, etc.) are shown hovering around the animal.

This device of creating a surrounding with insects, etc. had also developed in contemporary European drawings, which, as a matter of coincidence, did find their way to India in the seventeenth century. This probably is the reason why Skelton compares Manṣūr's drawing of 'Tulip' with the Martagon Lily from Pierre Vallet's *Le Jardin du tres Chrestian Henry IV* 1608, p. 11) where too a butterfly is shown poised above flowers.[25] In the late seventeenth century Mughal copy of the Martagon Lily, the butterfly, however, has been omitted.[26] Skelton's comparison suggesting a European influence in Manṣūr's this device is doubtful in the light of the fact that such a thing was employed in the Indian art since long before, the best example of which are the illustrations from the *Vasant Vilāsa* (dated 1451). A folio published by Beach from this manuscript shows bees fluttering over the *champaka* flowers.[27] Further, Manṣūr has applied this style not only in the flower portraits but even in human and animal portraits; the '*Vīnā*-player' already has this feature which is earlier than the example quoted by Skelton. One may agree that actually it was Manṣūr's naturalistic instinct which prompted him to opt for this style in his portraits. Had this particular device of style been confined to his flower studies only, he could be close to being suspected for imitating. The various ways in which he exploited the artistic dimensions of this device in human, floral, bird and animal portraits, to achieve control, rhythms, environmental and relational aspects in living nature, establish beyond doubt Manṣūr's creative originality in this respect. However, it is relevant to point out here that if Manṣūr may not be the first in the country to introduce such a device, he certainly has the credit of being the trend setter of it in the Mug͟hal school.

We have found enough evidence in support of the view that the main subject and the insects, etc. in combination was only a continuation of the Indian tradition and not an imitation of the West altogether. In addition, it is worth noting in this context that, in the seventeenth century, the adaptation of such a device becomes only more frequent because of the royal patron's special preference for naturalism in art, so much so, that even on Emperor Akbar's mausoleum at Sikandra, near Agra, completed in 1612, we can see hovering insects in the floral embellishments in low relief.[28]

Composition in both the paintings, the 'Tulip' and 'Iris plant', is almost on similar lines. The centrally composed plant emerges from the very base line of the picture frame, and the flowers are drawn in varying delicate angles in a fine and soft rhythmic order; bird/butterfly and insects are shown to hover around; the background is plain, without any suggestion of the horizon line. The extra charm of these studies, apart from their objective realism, is their compositional rhythm. We have already seen how Welch is impressed by this lyrical quality of his early work, '*Vīnā*-player' (c. 1600-5).[29]

4
ASCRIPTIONS: ARTIST'S SIGNATURES AND EMPEROR'S AUTOGRAPHS

Indeed, only the signed works of art are important for historical purposes, but painters of the Mughal school, it seems, did not follow the practice of signing their works with any careful attention. Examples of it are far too many. Quite a few painters are known to have signed only some of their works and left the others unsigned. At least six of Manṣūr's miniatures [27, 33, 38, 45-6, 48] are duly signed, but there are others which bear 'third person ascriptions', that is, inscriptions written by the scribe or the patron (including the Emperor). We encounter a serious problem with regard to the identification of artist's signature. Some of the modern scholars, in their observation, have made no distinction between ascriptions written by the scribe and the artist himself, i.e. the 'third person ascriptions' and 'signature'. It is further intriguing that some miniatures, even the unascribed ones, have been straightaway attributed to Manṣūr on very facile grounds of style. An attempt, therefore, has been made here to identify the artist's signature with greater care, with the help of the well-known Persian and Indo-Persian terms then in vogue, whereby a person writing his name in his own hand invariably used a word or phrase in self-abasement, which no third person is likely to do. In his signatures, Manṣūr invariably designates himself as "*banda-i dargāh*" ('slave of the court'). His signatures at different places are written as follows: [27] "*'Amal-i banda-i dargāh Manṣūr Jahāngīr Shāhī*" ('Work of the slave of the court, Manṣūr [servant] of the King Jahāngīr'); [33] "*Shabīh-i Khwāja Kalān Beg Wazīr, kār-i banda-i dargāh Manṣūr*" ('Likeness of Khwāja Kalān Beg *Wazīr*, work of the slave of the court Manṣūr'); [38] "*'Amal-i banda-i dargāh Nādir u'l 'Aṣr Manṣūr Naqqāsh Jahāngīr Shāhī*" ('Work of the slave of the court *Nādir u'l 'Aṣr* Manṣūr *Naqqāsh* [servant] of the King Jahāngīr'); [45] "*'Amal-i banda-i dargāh Nādir u'l 'Aṣrī Manṣūr Naqqāsh Jahāngīr Shāhī*"; [46] "*'Amal-i banda-i dargāh Manṣūr Nādir u'l 'Aṣr Jahāngīr Shāhī*"; [48] "the same as noticed in [46]".

Manṣūr's signatures are written in firm hand in standard *nasta'līq*. These are written very minutely on the ground of the picture, mostly close to the bottom of the main subject [27, 45-6]. One exception, however, is noticed in miniature [33], where he records his signature sideways. This, incidentally, is also a fine specimen of very bold signature. Though the signatures are made in clear handwriting, these do not appear to attract notice at the first glance. In some cases, signatures are partly hidden, being put on some unimportant object of the painting; for example, it may be on a rock-contour or a secondary article [45-6]. Among other painters from Jahāngīr's atelier, Āqā Riẓā',[1] Abū'l Ḥasan,[2] Bichitr,[3] Daulat[4] and Kesavdās[5] often do the same thing. The typical unobtrusive presence of the signature in the painting could be due to the artist's desire to restrict any distraction of view from the central theme of composition.

In some signatures, Manṣūr's name is found in association with the patron, viz., "*'Amal-i banda-i dargāh Manṣūr Jahāngīr Shāhī*" [27].[6] The practice of artist's name appearing with that of the Emperor is a typical feature which started in Jahāngīr's reign. It may be pointed out here that the term "*Jahāngīr Shāhī*" was actually used by the Mughal *umarās* or *manṣabdārs*,[7] but if some painters also followed the practice, it is likely that these painters also enjoyed the privilege of holding some sort of *manṣab*, however low in order it might have been. The fact that Manṣūr, Āqā Riẓā'[8] and Abū'l Ḥasan[9] sometimes included the name of Jahāngīr (*Jahāngīr Shāhī*) in association with their own signatures, amply proves that they occupied the highest place of distinction among the royal artists, and their special stature as artists may have earned them *manṣabs*.

It may be noted that on some of the ascribed miniatures of Manṣūr, ascriptions contain only his conferred title, "*Nādir u'l 'Aṣr*".[10] It seems that the painter's title had become so familiar that the scribe simply found it sufficient to write his title only. In the same way, some ascriptions on the works of Abū'l Ḥasan also contain only his title, "*Nādir uz Zamān*" ('Wonder of the Age'),[11] which was bestowed upon him by Jahāngīr.[12] Perhaps, it is fairly convincing to think that, because the titles *Nādir u'l 'Aṣr* and *Nādir uz Zamān* were officially conferred on only these painters respectively and none else, the scribe's mention of just these titles without the actual names of the artists in ascriptions was considered enough for identification.

In some cases, the identity of Manṣūr's work can be ascertained by the presence of Emperor's autograph on them, though it is very infrequent. Such autographs of either Jahāngīr or Shāh Jahān accompanied with notes in their own hand could only be seen on the works of major painters like Abū'l Ḥasan,[13] Bichitr,[14] Bishandās,[15] Manṣūr[16] and Nānhā.[17] These records testify to the interest of the emperors in recording the events with the details which included the painter's name, the subject of painting, and sometimes, the date as well. These details are important in placing the miniatures in a chronological order, or, in tracing the painter's affiliation to a particular Emperor's atelier. The implicit significance of Emperor's autograph in relation to the recognition and worth of a work can also not be ruled out. Out of 54 miniatures ascribed to Manṣūr, only three bear Jahāngīr's autograph, two of which are dated 14th regnal year/1619, and AH 1030/1621.[18]

5
MAJOR CHARACTERISTICS OF MANṢŪR'S ART

The subtle nuances that emerge from the meticulous details of Manṣūr's objective art could be a long list. There are some very obvious aspects which are at once noticeable, one may generally observe a very plain backdrop showing a receding landscape merge with the low and blurred horizon of a flat sky (the contiguity of the two is almost indistinguishable), which is occasionally interspersed with a few small birds, almost as signs, or with a few casual but bold horizontal strokes. The sky or the landscape, individually, does not make any character as such in the pictures, but that would be a naive expectation in Manṣūr's case. In a painting, parts must be integrated into a whole, and not treated as separate entities. Manṣūr never falls short in this sense. He always achieves a total harmony between the background treatment (in whatever style) and the naturalistic foreground figure. Again, the casual growth of flowering plants or weeds and shrubs, or rock contours, etc. in the landscape portion, on the surface of it, shows that Manṣūr, perhaps, is just satisfied with covering the spaces in various styles without meaning much. However, it may not be so casual and purposeless, as there are many instances where Manṣūr's treatment of space in the landscape portion with these objects lends to the whole certain definite rhythms and moods that match the captured moment of the main object of his painting.

When we come to the main object we see that it covers the maximum space inside the frame, with every detail drawn most meticulously, even so laboriously as to produce an exact replica, almost in the same precision as that of a camera lens. His birds and animals are vivid particularization and individualization of the categorically specified species of nature. The figures marvellously impose on the domain of the frame with singular majesty. In drawing such portraits Manṣūr does not brook any interference by his own subjectivity. The domination of the main figure is achieved through minimization of the other details. This quality of Manṣūr's work is best suited to paintings of natural history. His constant endeavour to assimilate maximum details called for more and more refinement in style, and Manṣūr never got tired of it, and as such, his bird and animal drawings remain unsurpassed almost till this date.

Manṣūr's preference for subdued background in a harmonious blend of thin colour, results in relating the natural surrounding with the main figure,[1] and simultaneously, producing relief effect. There is a wonderful quality of transparency in his treatment of background. According to Beach, Manṣūr never allows the line or colour in his drawings to become purely decorative,[2] which also implies as its corollary that Manṣūr had a keen aptitude for precise use of line and colour.

The strikingly exclusive and superb achievement of Manṣūr is the horizontal and bold sweeps of brush, which he employs in building up the landscape. Though distinctly contrasted with the minute details and delicate fine lines of the main drawing, yet, it is executed in an extremely subdued and delicately balanced manner so as to create a serene harmony of its own. Handling of the pigments with such great frankness and boldness could be located in Manṣūr's expression as early as 1612,[3] and, not altogether absent even in his earliest works either [1-2]. This characteristic of his is particularly prominent in quite a few masterpieces laterly done [27-8, 31, 35, 45-6, 48, 50, 52].

Niharranjan Ray was the first scholar who noticed it while describing his picture '*Charz-i bor*' [35], executed in 1619. He observes:

> "Manṣūr's acute observation and detailed and refined draughtsmanship are noticeable in this study as well, as much as in his numerous other bird-studies. But what is more striking is the seemingly casual but well-measured and balanced, flat and broad sweeps of the brush in a colour tone which is deeper than that of the light background. These flat, broad sweeps throw the bird in relief to the fore, and despite its light and subtle colour scheme, give it a vivid naturalness."[4]

Talking about his method of throwing the figures in relief, a quick review of the pictures 'Falcon' [34] and 'Zebra' [47] would be relevant. The isolated figures are shown perched against the flat plane. This is an implied condition for painting natural history. If we look at the picture of 'Falcon', an early work of Manṣūr, the artist's expression seems confined to the execution of the most refined linear details. In this case, the role of the background in projecting the object in relief is altogether absent. Manṣūr seems to have improved upon this style through stages of his development, and finally, in his 'Zebra' picture, executed towards the last phase of his career in 1621, he employs delicate shading deeper in tone than that of the background all along the outline of the figure, to throw it up in relief.

In another instance, in the picture of '*Nīlgāī*' [48] quick horizontal sweeps of brush have been employed mostly along the borders in the heavier tone than the rest of the background to bring out the central figure in relief. Manṣūr's technique of creating relief effect through such brush strokes in monochrome tones reaches spontaneity and striking maturity in '*Charz-i bor*' [35].

Manṣūr's art of representing a variety of natural vegetation growing wild, in the animal portraits, is very characteristic; it functions to accentuate the relief effect; it provides depth and controls scale perspective in the pictures; its stylized form with soft pliant movement in combination with variations of monochrome colouring of the background make largely for the lyrical quality of his paintings; its extremely subdued nature far from interfering with the concentration on the main object, also, effects a smooth stretching out of the expansiveness of the landscape; it is mostly drawn with opposite leaves along coyly bent stems, infuses enlivening impulses to the otherwise somewhat stiff figures of natural history. Their repeated appearances may be called a sort of mannerism,[5] but functionally, it ceases to be so, in the light of the role it plays in the whole picture, as we have already seen. However, it does not altogether obliterate from our mind the question, why an artist of Manṣūr's calibre could not employ other alternatives for such functions. The answer to it may be found in the fact that in spite of his urge for greater freedom as an artist, he was constricted by the very demands of true-to-nature objective animal portrayal, and the conventions and practices of the Mughal atelier. It is worthwhile to note here that the particular convention of placing willy-nilly spreads of shrubs, sprigs, tufts of grass or blossoms in the picture made in Mughal atelier was inspired by the Persian tradition of fifteenth-sixteenth century Timurid and Safavid schools.

Beach's appreciation of this particular feature of Manṣūr as a tool to test the authenticity of 'Two deer in landscape' [72] and subsequent rejection of it as a forged work in Manṣūr's name,[6] provided one of the useful clues in this study also, to discard 'Hornbill' [71] as Manṣūr's work (discussed later).

He does not always seem particular about the depiction of surface levels, i.e., planes: horizontal and vertical in any conventional sense. But the method by which he incorporates in his paintings suggestions of these, is his ingenious originality. It is clearly marked in the process of the horizontal plane vanishing into the vertical plane through colouration in graded harmonious tones of a single pigment. There is an upward moving quality in them. The eventual receding movement of the pigment tone is supplemented mostly by bird clusters in formation on top, or cloud bars, again, in the same pigment but of a little darker hue, suggestive of the sky. This method of colouration not only creates a contiguity of planes merging into each other, but also establishes aesthetic relationship among the various components of the picture. This results in holding the onlooker's eye with an illusive impression of scale perspective. The whole becomes a total unison in harmony. Further, Manṣūr's classic method of colouration and brush strokes serves to create receptacles in depth perspective. His *'Charz-i bor'* [35] in somewhat chiaroscuro effect, for example, produces the illusion of distance and depth most tellingly, notwithstanding the figure's fine projection in relief.

In the miniatures [34, 39, 44] the colour laid in the background does not help to distinguish the planes. It is only the growth of plants and flight of birds which suggests horizontal and vertical planes (Manṣūr's works of the earlier phase also contain the same features). Welch's observation on *'Vīnā*-player' [12] is relevant here: "Although no horizon line is drawn, the clouds and birds imply space and provide the drama of tempting quarry."[7] Though the features 'row of birds shown on the top margin' and 'strips of clouds' can well be seen in the works of other contemporary Mughal painters as well, but in Manṣūr's case they particularly denote aerial perspective and movement in space in the composition.

The vanishing horizon line intended to represent recession of the landscape is emphatically executed in the portrayal of the *sāj* bird [45]. Its rocky landscape with rhythmic hazing away of contours is the main device to bring in the spatial feature in the picture composition, and create the illusion of depth and vastness. Again, the distant bird at the far end is shown comparatively smaller than its counterpart in the middle of the picture, to create depth. These traits draw Manṣūr's art closer to the western style of painting in the sense of scale perspective, though it does not mean that this fact, in any way, brought about a visible change in Manṣūr's essential perception of art. Manṣūr's extraordinary ability to treat the space in accordance with the nature of the subject is observable in its most mature form in the miniature 'Salt water fish' [52]. It is represented in the most rhythmic and powerful shaded strokes in matching with the external contouring of the fish, in the curves of the drawing, in the swift and smooth upward post-dive movement. The movement is further emphasized here by leaving a large space above for aerial perspective, and by composing the figure horizontally from end to end with a slight diagonal bent in posture. It is the most powerfully conceived and realistically painted picture of an aquatic animal, which has no parallel in the whole of the Mughal school.

In general, Manṣūr's drawings exhibit the minimum possible action. Manṣūr adopted for his bird and animal portraits the same contemporary norms and conventions of human portraiture as practised in the Mughal atelier, which featured isolated, single figure in profile dominating the whole composition with a casual landscape and flat background. Consequently, there was hardly any scope for him to create action in his pictures. The action reported in the animal figures executed by Basāwan,[8] Miskīn[9] and Murād (or Mirār)[10] is conspicuously absent in Manṣūr's work. It is, again, a correlated factor necessary for painting natural live objects in their genuine actual forms. The emphasis is not on action but on the form of genus. The birds and animals drawn by Basāwan and Miskīn are meant to illustrate the text related to trapping, hunting, animal fight and expedition scenes. The artists' focus of interest in them is to report the animal's innate character under alarm of fear, danger, or rage. But Manṣūr's studies are concentrated on purely objective reproductions of the calmly and closely observed birds and animals. His study of *'Sāj'* [45] and the 'Salt water fish' [52] are exceptions to the rule. They keep the viewer's eye on the move to a degree. These two examples amply prove that Manṣūr did not lack command over drawing action pictures, but his main aim of painting natural history precluded any such liberty too often. If he could not produce action in his portraits, he substituted it with superb rhythm and lyricism, wherever the opportunity was available to him.

Animal drawings treated in effect as still-life portraits in the most realistic manner met with the desire of the royal connoisseur, whose main interest lay in the historical documentation and record keeping of the objects and events, etc.[11] The Emperor could reasonably expect that his descriptions in the Memoirs would have much greater impact if supported by pictorial illustrations. And thus, the two correspondences — written and illustrated — of the same event could substantiate each other meaningfully. Jahāngīr's own descriptions of birds and animals are long and carefully detailed,[12] and he preferred that his artists draw the illustrations with the same finesse of details.

The repeated occurrence of butterflies, small birds and insects, etc. in Manṣūr's pictures, as subsidiaries to the central figure, to enliven the atmosphere as well as to provide verticality, is yet another typical characteristic of him. Besides, its relevance is felt in the expansion of the central theme by an addition of environmental configuration to meet the demands of his kind of naturalism; of course this is introduced into the composition without sacrificing the intended tranquil atmosphere of the whole. This is Manṣūr's rational mechanics of handling the subjects of his patron's choice.

From the variations observed in the compositions, and the overall treatment of the subjects, it is noticeable that the artist exercises his self-expressiveness though very restrained. The variations do not reveal any uniform linear progression and continual change in style with the passage of time.[13] Further, the variations found are due either to the changes in the artist's mood or his shifts in the application of techniques in handling the space.

During the entire period of his career of three decades (1597-1627), the miniatures that are ascribed to him show his total devotion to painting of bird, animal, or flower portraits, with very minor shifts. Even though in his execution of the portraits he shows superb draughtsmanship, boldness, accuracy and suppleness, as well as certain novelties in compositions through his particular methods of space control and colouration, yet, after a detailed survey of his creations, he does not so much emerge out as an innovator of a school in the modern sense of the word. However, his sole credit and greatest achievement lay in reproducing natural history most objectively, incorporating in it the best aesthetic qualities of the Mughal art.

Manṣūr, thus, through his extremely significant contribution to the Mughal school, gave a special approach to painting natural history, and quite a many tried to adopt his methods, though not with the same success. It resulted in numerous studies of flora and fauna, the best surviving collection of which is preserved in the prestigious Dārā Shukoh Album (IOL). The painters of Dārā Shukoh Album imitated certain compositional aspects of Manṣūr including abandonment of crowded compositions and richly detailed background, in preference to spatial serenity for relief effect.[14] Manṣūr's positive influence is seen in these works, but there is no evidence of any firm commitment to perpetuate his values or style of painting as such. Manṣūr's art, within his sphere of activity, for its sheer perfection, individuality, and charm left no equal in the entire Mughal school. His is the epitome of perfection in that specialized art which had no real predecessor, and left no able follower.

6
COPIES OF MANṢŪR'S ORIGINALS AND FORGED ATTRIBUTIONS

The most enigmatic situation is confronted with regard to the identification of the copies of Manṣūr's originals. The lacunas in the continuity, due to the loss of his large number of paintings pose such a problem of anachronistic nature that it evades all attempts to identify such works by any method other than the internal evidence, or, stylistic devices, notwithstanding the relevance in it of those available few which bear date and signature. Several attempts to ascribe works of dubious originality to Manṣūr seem wanting in proper analysis to be sufficiently convincing. Without meaning any flippancy towards other scholarly opinions, an attempt is further made to scrutinize such works more minutely on the basis of various available facts.

There are many replicas which have no ascriptions, and yet, they have been attributed to Manṣūr. Again some ascriptions are forged. The contribution of Beach is methodical, and rational, as also, a distinguished work on the identification of the late versions of Manṣūr's originals, and the forged ones in Manṣūr's name.[1] However, Beach's observation does not go beyond the paintings preserved at the Freer Gallery of Art, Washington. The need is felt to carry his valuable direction to scrutinize paintings in other collections.

The present study enlists five such bird paintings: 'Himalayan cheer pheasant', 'Indian bustard' (*Charz-i bor*), 'Turkey cock', 'Hornbill', 'King vulture' and 'Himalayan griffon' for closer scrutiny, as each of these has several versions in different collections.

Clarke while referring to 'Turkey cock' [27] says, "When pleased with a work, Jahāngīr usually ordered one or more copies to be prepared for use of gifts."[2] This raises moot points, like: Was it a practice at the royal atelier to make copies of paintings on commission? Was the painter, on such occasions, the copier also, or the copier was some other artist? When were such copies made?

It is true that Jahāngīr ordered to paint the exact likenesses of the objects he found strange for purpose of his *Jahāngīrnāma,*[3] and this may tempt one to take the view that identical replicas of the same subject were made as illustrations for the several other copies of *Jahāngīrnāma* prepared during his reign. Illustration of *Jahāngīrnāma* was in progress in 1618, is evident from Jahāngīr's specific mention of the illustrated frontispiece, namely, the 'Scene of Jahāngīr's accession' painted by Abū'l Ḥasan in 1618.[4] Hardly two months after this event, the first copy of *Jahāngīrnāma* was presented to Shāh Jahān,[5] and a little later, in the same year, two other copies were gifted to I'timādud-Daula and Āṣaf Khān.[6] But there is no specific evidence available to show that the gifted copies of the manuscript contained illustrations.

In addition to the above frontispiece, a few dispersed miniatures, including those preserved at the State Library, Rampur, are suggested by Asok Kumar Das to belong to the royal copy of Emperor's Memoirs.[7] However, Das's identification of these paintings as the illustrated folios of a MS. is not beyond doubt, since none of them contains lines of text set within the picture frame—a characteristic feature of the art of book-illustration of Jahāngīr's reign.[8] The Rampur miniatures very possibly belonged to the tradition of album pictures illustrating major events described in the *Jahāngīrnāma.*

Bird and animal pictures, which are our immediate concerns, do not belong to the category of the manuscript painting, since these are executed on varying formats, and do not contain any text. Detailed notes occurring on some of the paintings in Jahāngīr's handwriting firmly establish that they do not form part of any illustrated manuscript.[9] This is further substantiated by the fact that there is no instance of such autographs on book-illustrations. Thus, Manṣūr's paintings, especially those executed during Jahāngīr's time, and of which duplicates are found, were in all probability either separate individual pieces or album pictures. The question of authenticity of the duplicates has been discussed later.

Das has included only two paintings of Manṣūr, from a large number of them, as possible illustrated folios of the royal copy of Emperor's Memoirs.[10] The number of Manṣūr's portrait studies of animals and birds if corroborated with the corresponding descriptions in the Memoirs, would be fairly large. Das, too, does not deny the existence of a majority of these in the albums or *muraqqa's,*[11] and is also doubtful if the various pictures of exotic birds and animals or notable events, executed by painters while they were in royal entourage, were actually incorporated in the *Jahāngīrnāma.*[12]

So far as we can judge from a comparison of various copies of miniatures or even works with repeated illustration of the same subject or theme, it appears that exact copying was neither in vogue nor was acceptable in the imperial atelier.[13] For example, numerous illustrated copies of the MSS. *Anwār-i Suhailī, Dīwān-i Ḥāfiẓ, Bāburnāma, Akbarnāma,* etc., executed in Mughal atelier are known to contain numerous miniatures representing common themes, but they invariably differ in layout, composition and colouring, and in that, the artist's freedom and individual skill become evident.[14] Considering the tradition of the imperial atelier from earlier on, it seems to be a remote possibility that replicas of the subjects of the Memoirs were allowed in Jahāngīr's atelier, especially, when Jahāngīr was the most astute connoisseur of art among all the Mughals.

In case of album pictures too, identical copies of portraits, etc., are mostly later versions of the originals. For example, an early nineteenth century version of Abū'l Ḥasan's original painting 'Jahāngīr shooting at the head of Malik Ambar' (c. first quarter of seventeenth century),[15] is preserved at Freer Gallery of Art, Washington.[16] Another instance is that of Bichitr's famous painting '*Rubāb* player, his companion and a peasant' (c. first quarter of seventeenth century),[17] which was copied in the early nineteenth century.[18] The interesting thing to note, as a common feature in all such copies, is the absence of copiers' names. Not only this, in some cases, even ascriptions (artist's name, theme, inscription, etc.) given in the originals are copied in the replicas with great exactness. Both the above examples significantly suggest that forged copies were free and many. Sometimes, even lesser artists produced works with forged names of masters.[19] Plagiarism apart, ascribing the copy of one master to another master painter was also not uncommon.[20] From the surviving specimens of replicas it may be inferred that works of master painters were, and are, always in demand, since either an individual collector, or an institution (a more recent phenomenon) would like to take pride in possessing works of great masters. Beach writes that such copies were perhaps made for British purchasers who believed that they were acquiring royal treasures.[21] Rai Krishnadasa and Humayun Kabir say that copies were sometimes made to replace the miniatures which were highly esteemed but got lost; perhaps the *charba*[22] of these were still available, and used for making the duplicates.[23]

Discussing about the copying business, and the rejection of the practice in the imperial atelier, one may be tempted to allege that, after all, Persian miniatures and Western works were often recommended for copying them, why not the original Mughal miniatures. While examples of copying the Persian miniatures are rare and few, more interest was shown towards the Western works in this regard, for their special technical and thematic curiosity. It is significant to note that in most of the copies of Persian miniatures, ascriptions given on them clearly describe them as copies, and record the names of the copiers.[24] Obviously, the approach and intention here is quite different from that of the questionable replicas and forged versions of Manṣūr's miniatures. Of course, in the case of imitation of Western works, pictures/engravings, all of them do not bear the names of the copiers. In all probability, this was due to the fact that both the patron and the painters wished to see how Christian themes and the technique of Western art could be attempted in miniatures. Sometimes, it was also necessary to prepare copies of Western examples to suit the format of the Mug͟hal albums. The monotonous Western engravings were copied very often by the Mug͟hal painters as they had further urge to produce their coloured versions.[24a] Documentation of the Western pictures at the imperial library could be yet another reason for the preparation of the copies, which was considered by the historically conscious Mug͟hal rulers as important. But Western pictures were not generally repeatedly copied, since a single copy sufficed to meet the demand of the patron. Again, when an exhibit of art was brought for a short while by Jesuits, or otherwise, it was copied for the requirements of the royal collection.[24b]

The Western examples prepared at the imperial atelier which bear inscriptions containing the names of the artists who copied them, clearly do not show any intention or pretension to be originals. Could we say, then, that in the imperial atelier mere copying of the originals, just for the sake of copying, was never an objective at all.

Once again, we revert to consider the problem of the genuineness of miniatures in replicas on grounds of style to supplement our factual historical endeavour. Now we shift our parameter of tests to those characteristics of Manṣūr which form his typical individual mode of style and expression. However, some risks are involved in it, since style is an evolving process, and in Manṣūr's case, there are such wide gaps of time among his works that it is difficult to find a steady line of his artistic development, necessary for framing such absolute criteria by which to test the genuinity of pictures of doubtful origin. Under the circumstances, what one can aim at by this method is only to arrive at near approximation and probabilities. But, where, in the process of the whole exercise, the accrued findings are totally negative, the rejection has been free of all doubts.

As we have seen earlier that Manṣūr stands out clearly for his immaculate draughtsmanship in his single figures, and his highly individualized treatment of the background — receding landscape, horizontal patchy sweeps of brush employed for different ends, bird clusters to indicate the skyline and single pigment variations effecting a certain transparency to the background, or deft manipulation of planes and vegetation, etc., it is nearly imperative that we apply these characteristics to test the genuinity of the replicas as well.

The picture of 'Himalayan cheer pheasant' [56], first brought to notice by Asok Kumar Das from the collection of Sawai Man Singh II Museum, Jaipur, which bears an inscription, "*'Amal-i Ustād Manṣūr*" ('Work of *Ustād* Manṣūr'), is identical with the study of this bird in the Wantage Collection [28]. While the latter has very bold sweeping strokes executed so brilliantly in the most Manṣūr-like manner,[25] the Jaipur miniature appears rather constricted. In the Jaipur copy, the brush strokes are slight, hesitant and restricted in movement, and certainly, the frank spontaneity of the Wantage Collection copy is so obviously absent. It is a quite natural result when one tries to run the brush in imitation of another person's hand. And, that puts one in serious doubt about the authenticity of the Jaipur copy. The point is further proved by its puerile brush strokes when juxtaposed with Manṣūr's other established works like 'Indian bustard' [35] and 'Salt water fish' [52].

The ascription given on the Jaipur miniature is exactly identical with that of the Wantage Collection copy both in text and position which may be the likely result of conscious manipulation. The stylistic evidences and the ascriptional aspects, as seen above, put the Jaipur version closer to early nineteenth century — as an imitation work, like many others.

Beach writes emphatically about the version of 'Himalayan cheer pheasant' [57] preserved at Baron Maurice Rothschild Collection, Paris, that it is not by Manṣūr, but is a contemporary copy.[26] Edwin Binney 3rd, while differing with Beach, attributed it to Payāg, a master painter of Shāh Jahān's atelier.[27] However, the Wantage Collection copy should be the original work, as the one under discussion is at obvious variance with it, whether it is the line drawing of the bird or the background of the picture. Deep shading, heavy modelling in the treatment of landscape and well-defined details in the background are things which are strangers to Manṣūr's style, and help buttress only half the truth of Beach's observation, but that it is a 'contemporary copy' is untenable, because in Jahāngīr's atelier such a style and technique of landscaping was not in vogue. Further, Binney's attribution of it to Payāg is also unacceptable on the grounds that there is not a single evidence of painting of a bird or an animal done by Payāg of Shāh Jahān's reign.

The 'Himalayan cheer pheasant' [58] in the collection of Bernard Quartich, Paris, is a reversed figure — right to left — of the original [28]. It seems to have been done at a much later date, possibly in the early nineteenth century. The whole picture is finished with rather rigid linear details, and in thin pigment after the water-colour technique, not to say, its glaring lack of space control, the department in which Manṣūr was an adept. In short, it could neither be attributed to Manṣūr nor to any of his contemporaries of the Mughal atelier.

A copy of the miniature 'Indian bustard' (*Charz-i bor*) [35] painted by Manṣūr in 1619, is preserved in the Dārā Shukoh Album, India Office Library, London [67]. In this, the central figure appears almost identical with Manṣūr's original, but, again, the landscape composition is clearly different.[28] Smith's suggestion that it could be attributed to Manṣūr is unconvincing.[29] The deep shaded strokes seen in the foreground, the swelling and circling clusters of clouds for the sky, modelled heavily with thick shading, are features that associate the style of this piece with the style adopted during early nineteenth century.[30] We should therefore have little hesitation in rejecting it as Manṣūr's work.

An unascribed version of 'Turkey cock' [68] is rather interesting since there appears Jahāngīr's seal on its illustrated margin,[31] which probably suggests that this folio was painted in the imperial atelier itself within close proximity of time of the picture of this bird in the Wantage Collection with the accepted signature of the artist on it [27].[32] The two appear identical at the first sight, but if we accept it as a deliberate duplication, it has to be treated as an exception, since no other definite instance of a contemporary copy of a Mug͟hal miniature is traceable. Rai Krishnadasa and Humayun Kabir have observed that imitations of mounts and *ḥāshiyas* of Jahāngīr's period made during the nineteenth century look like originals.[33] They further say that even the authentic seals of the former Emperors were stamped on such mounts.[34] This copy may thus be an instance of this kind of misrepresentation of the original Manṣūr.

Brown,[35] Havell,[36] Ray,[37] Clarke,[38] and Das[39] have attributed this version to Manṣūr. Though, generally speaking, the main figure looks almost identical with the signed study of this bird [27], but the deviations are sharp and apparent in the treatment of the figure drawing and the background. If we compare closely the two figures, the brush work and the colour textures, especially, on the head portion and lower right plumage of the original,[40] are totally missing in the other one. The reason for this is simple enough to understand; that in a copied version such effects cannot be exactly brought out. If we suppose that Manṣūr made this repetition himself, then, at least, the head studies would have had the same texture of colour, given that the patterning aspect of the plumage could show some small differences in repetition. Evidently, the head study of unascribed version is inferior artistically. The brush strokes, the landscape, the well-defined horizon line with vegetation along the undulated hillocks make the miniature unknown to Manṣūr's art of painting backgrounds. Also the prominently defined contouring of the hillocks and the skyline, absence of bird clusters in high margin, brush lines drawn in deep pigment with water-colour effect to depict the sky, are indeed irreconcilable to Manṣūr's technique.

Another unascribed version known in Maharaja Sawai Man Singh II Museum, Jaipur (No. AG.839), though identical with Manṣūr's original in Wantage Collection [27], shows the landscape background clearly at variance. Here the copier has failed to imitate Manṣūr's method of modelling with the application of defined bold and spontaneous strokes. The puerile brush strokes seen in the version testify it.

An unascribed picture of hornbill from the collection of Geoffrey C.N. Sturt, Painswick, Gloucestershire [71],[41] is almost similar to another picture of this bird preserved in the Metropolitan Museum of Art, New York [26].[42] The latter is ascribed to Manṣūr and bears the stamp of his particular soft spontaneous brush movements in horizontal strokes and along the undulations of the landscape form. The depiction of long and supple tufts of grass and other vegetation too is characteristic of him. A comparison of these two pictures would show that the unascribed version is clearly inferior both in draughtsmanship and colouration. The soft transparency of the pigment with tonal variations, and the minuteness of details of the original, are altogether absent in the Gloucestershire version, which, on the basis of its representational style, may presumably be dated in early nineteenth century, the period which is marked for its wooden treatment of living objects. The chest-bulge line is so flawlessly roundish and linear without any swerve of the soft downs that it has ceased to be in the same natural likeness of the original miniature, which has natural fluffy and furry finish. Again, the rounded ends of wing feathers of the original are distorted into conical and edgy ends, which is more a result of fancy rather than a close objective reproduction of the natural living form. Further, though a minor point, positioning of the talons of the right foot is changed in the copied version.

The separate miniatures 'King vulture' [63] and 'Himalayan griffon' [65], originally preserved in Kevorkian Album, are now dispersed in the Metropolitan Museum of Art, New York[43] and Freer Gallery of Art, Washington,[44] respectively. Though both of them bear ascriptions purporting them as signed works of Manṣūr, yet, they appear conspicuously derived from Manṣūr's signed original miniature 'King vulture and Himalayan griffon' (two birds in a single frame) preserved in the Metropolitan Museum of Art, New York [46].[45] Manṣūr's unique stylistic devices, his superfine draughtsmanship and unobtrusive brush strokes, his softly graded tonal colouration in this miniature, stand out as unchallengeable evidences of its originality, and by contrast, relegate the two copied versions as inferior or imitations. The degree of inferiority of each copied version is of course relative. Another curious fact that has come to light in this particular exercise of imitation is, that it is the only instance of copying in two parts the same miniature, i.e., the king vulture and the Himalayan griffon are bifurcated into two individual miniatures.

An observation of Swietochowski on the border illumination of both the versions, i.e., 'King vulture' and 'Himalayan griffon' is relevant, as it is similar on both, and as such, probably, both the borders were done by the same artist,[46] and besides, the fashioning of it is marked by the early nineteenth century style, as confirmed from the folios of the same period. This fact alone suggests that these copies of Manṣūr's work have common provenance.

The 'King vulture' [63] is undoubtedly a copy of the bird shown in Manṣūr's original, and its ascription "*'Amal-i banda-i dargāh Manṣūr Nādir u'l 'Aṣr Jahāngīr Shāhī*" is forged, as indicated by Welch already. He writes that in the present copy, the brush work is "meticulous" but the copier has failed to capture the "menacing elegance of Manṣūr's superb miniature".[47] It is further important to note that the deep shading employed at the foot of the rock, and rather rough and rugged modelling of its contours in sharp light and dark shades, could not have come from Manṣūr's brush. Manṣūr's specialized style contains, as is evident elsewhere also, a lyrical treatment of the miniature as a whole, and the original miniature 'King vulture and Himalayan griffon' with its rock contours and the horizontal strokes of the foreground in combination manifests that quality truly. In addition to it the fierce menacing posture of the head and the neckline of the original is somewhat dimmed in this version. Therefore, the facts of the style render the miniature as unauthentic.

Again, the controversy does not end yet, as we have two versions of the 'Himalayan griffon' [64-65]. They are in Freer Gallery of Art, Washington and Chester Beatty Library, Dublin, respectively.[48] The comments of some noted authors with regard to it invite a fresh look. Beach has rightly concluded that the picture of Himalayan griffon in the Freer Gallery of Art is a work of early nineteenth century.[49] Therefore, as a logical corollary to this, one may say that both the ascription and Manṣūr's title on the miniature are fake. Beach also talks of several versions of it, but calls the miniature 'King vulture and Himalayan griffon' [46] as the earliest. The stylistic features and Beach's view undoubtedly confirm the authenticity of this particular miniature. According to Welch the miniature 'Himalayan griffon' [64] is a version of the study of this bird preserved in Chester Beatty Library [65], done in the seventeenth century[50] from a lost picture by Manṣūr.[51] But, Welch's view that the FGA version is a copy of the CBL version seems doubtful, for, of the two, the FGA version is closer in drawing and finish to the original one [46] than the CBL version, which is far inferior in artistic qualities. The FGA version, however, lacks the finesse of Manṣūr's brush, and does not conform to Manṣūr's manner of art, especially the way in which the rock contours with the springing sprigs, and vegetation, and heavily shaded foreground are treated in it.

The CBL version is rather of spurious origin, as we have seen, and therefore, it is also difficult to agree with Arnold and Wilkinson who ascribe it to Manṣūr.[52] The CBL copy is notably inferior: the chest-line and the shape of the back, legs and talons, all are disproportionately thick and large, and the folds of the wings are rather crudely patterned. Obviously, it is both a weak drawing and an inaccurate representation of the bird when put side by side with Manṣūr's original [46]. Variations seen in the form of the bird further suggest that the imitator copied the original by looking at it rather than from *charba.* Nowhere can we trace the true characteristics of Manṣūr's style and drawing in it. The probable date of the CBL version could be early nineteenth century, as it shows both decadence of form and colour, such as generally associated with the fall of the Mughal style in this period. These observations on its art form and colouration, as described, are at cross with Welch's contention that it was painted in the seventeenth century, and from a lost work of Manṣūr, and not the miniature [46].

Doubts have been raised on the authenticity of quite a few other miniatures, though they bear ascriptions in support of their being the work of Manṣūr. These doubts can be rejected or accepted only by investigating the internal evidences in terms of style and technique; they could be original pieces or copies. If we take them as copies, then, their originals are not in existence. One may, therefore, venture to categorize them as independent works credited to Manṣūr. The 'Falcon' [55], 'Two deer in landscape' [72], 'Spotted forktail' [73], 'Assembly of pigeons' [74], 'Fantastic bird' [80], 'Jungle fowl' [81] and 'Portrait of Ḥājjī Ḥusain Bukhārī' [82] are the miniatures which are to be enquired into for establishing their genuineness.

The subject of falcon being so common in the Mughal atelier the one in question cannot be traced back to any particular source model, so that by comparison the verity of its originality could be checked. For our purpose it may be expedient to take the case of 'Himalayan cheer pheasant' [56] of the Maharaja Sawai Man Singh II Museum, Jaipur, whose claimed originality has already been rejected by its comparison with Manṣūr's original one in Wantage Collection [28].

Now when we consider the two background treatments of the 'Himalayan cheer pheasant' [56] and the 'Falcon' [55], from the same collection, we see an astonishing similarity of brush strokes. They are slight in execution and very thin in pigment application, almost as in water colour. The grassy ridges also look alike. We know that Manṣūr's repertoire does not include such techniques. Besides, the linear delineation of the drawing of the falcon is so pronounced, very unlike Manṣūr, who would substitute it with his shading techniques, and get out of it even better results. Identical floral margin painting in both the examples, i.e., [55] and [56], confirms that one artist was responsible for the borders of these two later folios, as in the case of the two versions of 'King vulture' [63] and 'Himalayan griffon' [64].

Further, it seems that the inscription "*'Amal-i Nādir u'l 'Aṣr Jahāngīr Shāhī*" minutely placed on the perching stand of 'falcon', though intended to be the artist's signature but it is at clear variance with Manṣūr's identified signatures and his handwriting.[53] Besides, Manṣūr never mentioned his title alone without his name in his signatures.

The miniature 'Two deer in landscape' [72], bearing the ascription "*Kār-i Manṣūr Jahāngīr Shāhī*", is described by Beach, on grounds of its style, as a copy work made much later from an original painting of Manṣūr.[54] Beach has arrived at this conclusion after comparing this painting with the miniature 'Two blue bulls and two hog deer' [2], a folio of *Bāburnāma*. But, Beach does not say anything about which original picture of Manṣūr it was copied from. He observes that "the light and sketchy quality typical of Manṣūr's grasses and vegetation and the overall meticulousness of his draftsmanship are absent" in this miniature.[55] Further scrutiny of the picture will show that the brush strokes are very unlike Manṣūr's. Even the bare drawing of the two animal forms does not rise to Manṣūr's perfection. The landscape in the background with distant ridges of hills and clusters of trees with dense foliage, distinct skyline and overall superimposition of the landscape clearly dissociate it from Manṣūr's mode of expression, and handling of the main object as centrally dominating in the whole composition.

In the context of this miniature Welch's remark is almost invincible: "From top to bottom the miniature oozes green and tan mush, the soil having been turned to mud and the foliage reduced to overcooked spinach."[56] He further observes that such similar pictures were painted at Alwar in Rajasthan by emigre Delhi artists.[57]

Ascribing the picture of the bird 'Spotted forktail' [73] to Manṣūr, appears somewhat far fetched.[58] Actually, the original of this picture is by Abū'l Ḥasan (c. 1615-20),[59] and the one in question was made from the *charba* of this original in reverse (from right to left), in the early nineteenth century. While Abū'l Ḥasan, no less a great contemporary of Manṣūr, puts all the masterly touches in the picture, the copier fails either to catch the thrilling beauty of it, or even to do it in Manṣūr's style and technique. The copy suffers from lack of liveliness, humour, and smooth agility of expression that we observe in the original drawing.[60] Manṣūr could never have missed these refinements had he really rendered this picture with his brush.

Swietochowski spelled out very clearly the marked differences between the two forms of the bird in the original, and in the copy.[61] Further elaboration on the point is not necessary. The difference is also quite noticeable in the layout of the landscape. It lacks the soft soothing quality of the pigment, the chiaroscuro of light and shade emerging through the clouds, and the heavy modelling and shading of the foreground rock formations, of the original. Total omission of clustering birds in the sky as employed by Abū'l Ḥasan, to create an illusion of distance and height in his composition, has further marred the depth perspective of the picture. This miniature, on such evidences and more, is convincingly unattributable to Manṣūr. As we already know, in Manṣūr's pictures the landscape background is in single pigment of variational tones, and the foreground without thick shading of light and dark, which are further strong evidences against associating 'Spotted forktail' [73] with him. Even spelling-wise the inscription in Persian is wrong,[62] which is further indication of its being forged.

Again, the picture 'Assembly of pigeons' [74] is also enigmatic as to its authenticity because of the inscription on it, "*'Amal-i Manṣūr Jahāngīr Shāhī*".[63] The entire composition is indeed very formal and betrays many loose ends to be believed as Manṣūr's work. An arrangement of birds (pigeons) such as seen here in the margin painting is not found in the sixteenth and seventeenth century Mughal paintings. The margin painting and the picture in the middle have been done on two types of paper, which makes it clear that the two were made separately and affixed to each other later. The authenticity of the two pigeons in the middle is palpably dubious also. Falk and Digby's hesitant note that the two middle figures were probably done by Manṣūr, would rather be unconvincing[64] if we just take a close look at the technique and the quality of painting of the border decoration and the picture in the middle itself. They are identical in form and execution. Evidently, all the pigeons seem to have been done by the same hand, and totally lack the soft brush strokes, fine shading and minute details of description which is Manṣūr's forte, and not rare in the works of other master painters among his contemporaries. The toy-like woodenness and opacity in the colouration of the figures and background in this miniature is exactly the reverse of the wonderful lyrical transparency effects in Manṣūr's pictures.

The typical mannerism and stylization in the depiction of the birds, and the layout of the margin illumination in this miniature, conform to the conventions prevalent towards the close of the eighteenth century.

Of the remaining three miniatures, bearing ascriptions attributed to Manṣūr, i.e., 'Fantastic bird' [80], 'Jungle fowl' [81] and 'Portrait of Ḥājjī Ḥusain Bukhārī' [82],[65] the first two are brought to notice by Welch, who calls them as early nineteenth century works forged in Manṣūr's name.[66] Both the birds in the first two pictures show a clear absence of his meticulous draughtsmanship and detailed soft brush strokes, as found in his genuine natural studies. Much more scandalous than the case of 'Jungle fowl' is the ascription of 'Fantastic bird' to Manṣūr who is always emphatically wedded to naturalness and pure objectivity with regard to his subject. He does not deal with birds or animals of imagination. The overall treatment of the figure 'Jungle fowl', its shaded line strokes of the plumage, wings and clumsy drawing, are some of the major points which cannot be ascribed to the master painter Manṣūr. The source of this picture could be another unascribed study of this subject [66] known in G.C. Sturt, Esq. Collection.[67]

The colour scheme of the portrait study 'Ḥājjī Ḥusain Bukhārī' [82], with brilliant splashes of green and reddish hues lavishly used, plus its decorative features in loud colours, is altogether unknown in Manṣūr's art, not to say, in the portraits of Jahāngīr's atelier, as a whole. Needless to say, that Manṣūr always craved for soothing colour harmonies without sacrificing the realism of his main object of painting. Treatment of cypress and the tree laden with flowers further dissociate it from Manṣūr's method of handling vegetation in landscape. And according to Welch, even the figure of cat, in the foreground, cannot be related with Manṣūr's conceptions.[68]

It would not be out of place to mention that the similarity in the arrangement of floral motifs and the method of their execution in the border illumination of the pictures 'Fantastic bird' and 'Portrait of Ḥājjī Ḥusain Bukhārī' would probably suggest the common origin of the illuminations. Swietochowski has observed that the borders are rather better than those of some of the other nineteenth century copies.[69]

The last of the problems is posed when we endeavour to establish the authenticity of the attributions made to Manṣūr with regard to unascribed miniatures, for there can be no sound methodology to arrive at any final conclusion about them which would be reliable for a historical study. We have already encountered this problem in the earlier pages, while discussing the pictures of the 'Dodo' [89], 'Wounded buck' [78] and 'Himalayan cheer pheasant' [57] which Das, Welch, Beach and Brown feel could be by Manṣūr.[70]

In this group of miniatures [55-93], the picture of 'Siberian crane' [88] is of particular significance, since in it an attempt to imitate Manṣūr's typical sweeps of brush is apparent. This isolated figure of the crane is accepted by Das as the work of Manṣūr on the fact of its "very minute brush work and the stamp of distinctiveness expressed in its [bird's] posture".[71] Of course, the striking similarity of brush strokes in the landscape and the flight of birds on the high margin, typical of many of Manṣūr's miniatures, do tempt us into accepting this as his work. But when we closely observe the strokes we see that they are a bit too crowded, and are rather carefully arranged, lacking Manṣūr's spontaneous expressiveness, seeming casualness, and boldness of approach in laying the background. Further, the drawing of the legs (compare with the study of another crane, *Charz-i bor* [35]) is too weak to be accepted as the drawing of the master (*ustād*). Most likely, the miniature 'Siberian crane' is an inspired work of imitation from some original work of Manṣūr, not known to us, and is very likely to have been done in the late eighteenth century.

On the basis of the parameters chosen, including the obvious norms of historical analysis, and clear internal evidences of stylistic devices, certain helpful conclusions could be drawn in order to sift, from among sheafs of forged imitations and copies preserved in different musea of world, the real authentic Manṣūr.

Thus, it may be summed up that, (1) Manṣūr did not leave on record a single instance of copying from his own originals and so, those so-called 'copies' which have been attributed to Manṣūr do not stand any test of authenticity; (2) the 'copies' seem not to have been made at the imperial atelier, because such was not the practice there; (3) such 'copies' and 'duplicates' were certainly the works of later period particularly the early nineteenth century, as has been found from our investigations; (4) the claims about those 'copies' bearing ascriptions apparently similar to the ones on original works of Manṣūr would fall through on grounds of internal stylistic evidences. This category of works does not exclude those extant pictures which are only in single versions, and ascribed to Manṣūr rather faultily, perhaps, as a result of overenthusiasm.

Such conclusions about Manṣūr's work or 'copies' of doubtful origin, if borne in mind while studying the life, style and career of this unique Mughal painter, one may be saved from a lot of pitfalls and distractions.

7
CONCLUSION

The modest little that has been achieved in this present evaluation of Manṣūr's art, has resulted from an attempt, first, to place him in the right frame of reference, followed by an analytical review of his achievements. The journey through the artist's creative process may have been, at times, inadvertently coloured by the obvious modern sensibilities, though very consciously restrained by the historical perspectives, and by an exercise of imagination to relive the heroic times of the great Mughal emperors with their passionate drive for explorations in new areas of activity and all-round achievements. Manṣūr was the product and a faithful representative of this spirited medieval India. He became one of the top luminaries of the Mughal atelier which functioned under the emperor's guidelines or instructions directly. Manṣūr has achieved permanence and relevance both for his creativity and naturalism — a naturalism that could be the pride of zoological museums and art collections with equal grace.

The central focus of this study is on those characteristic traits of Manṣūr which lend him the honour of individuality in his works, and therefore, most other common features of the Mughal school, so well discussed in many books already published, have been excluded.

His art is a fine realization of brilliant draughtsmanship and exquisite colouring of the portraits of birds, animals and flowers in a dominantly serene atmosphere. The figures are at once individual and at the same time representational, achieved through the illumination of life impulses like docility, ferocity, expectation, isolation and gaiety, etc., in their expressions. His '*Vīṇā*-player' [12], a human figure, and done in his early phase, is a beautiful work though it does not concentrate so much on the details of the features, and creates rather a portrait of the mood. Again, the most powerful work of Manṣūr, the 'Salt water fish' [52] with its tremendous vitality, spontaneity of expression, does away with all limitations of linear figure concept, and concentrates on a rhythm, which becomes an expression of the vital-force itself—in the movement of the fish, in the mutually merging spaces of the two elements of nature, the water and the sky.

Purely objective purpose in the portrayals of the rest of his works, necessitated by Jahāngīr's naturalistic curiosities and Manṣūr's uncanny capacity to draw in the exact likeness of the natural form, lead him to austerity in contouring of the organic shapes, but he has the genius to dilute the linear sharpness through his treatment of the bracing background laid with the help of just tonal variations of a single colour, or some other techniques he employed for relief effect.

The true-to-nature figures follow the idiom of profile drawing but the posture is so deftly manipulated that at least three quarters of the body width with all the colour pattern, texture and sinewy flexion appears in exposure, especially in the bird studies. These portraits are generally a little stiff as is required for the true representation of natural history. They are coloured with meticulous care to recreate in pigments the same sheen and softness, or decorativeness and patterning, as found in the natural state. The true model-like pictorial portraits are infused with such expressions that they become captured moments of the eternal flow of life in nature and simultaneously, palimpsests, as it were, of those species of nature, relevant to all times.

However, Manṣūr's real greatness as an artist emerges when these figures are seen in their background landscape. The two seem to co-exist in a state of mutual relationship, and a continuous flow of certain subtle resonances seems to operate between the central objects and the vast spaces of nature with or without any other objects. Manṣūr creates such an integrated movement through the drama of his colouring techniques; he suggests such lyrical nuances and rhythms which quietly acquire a gravity that is present deeper in nature than what appears to the eye. It is here in the layout of the background that Manṣūr wields his brush with mute accents of freedom, never losing on elegance and simplicity, and succeeding, on the whole, in imbuing the pictures with abstractions of moods and very controlled subjectivity proximating expressionistic expression, though never unrelated to his main objective referent: it is all, in effect, a reactive consequence of observing a fact of nature. It is only in the treatment of the background, Manṣūr could get some outlet to his creative emotions that craved freedom of expression. He could break away from the tradition in this aspect so long as he could satisfy Jahāngīr's desire to see portraits of animals and birds done in the very likeness of nature. And thus, he expresses his freedom in his spontaneous horizontal brush sweeps variously employed, to suggest the skyline on the graded monochrome tempera background, in modelling and in creating relief effects.

The earthscape becomes stylized representation of rock and hilly undulations or vegetation, to basically provide space perspective and rhythm, not denying its occasional role of throwing up the central figure in relief. However, it is very deliberately subdued in prominence by the diminution of the size of inanimate components in a slightly deeper grade of the same tone which covers the background. The main portrait always occupies the highlight. Perhaps, when such stylization or distortion of the subsidiary objects of the background fails to satisfy Manṣūr's urge to realize in his pictures the deeper rhythms of life in nature, he asserts his freedom by altogether abandoning this method, and goes on exploring his scope in painting of the background. His success in this regard remains unique for his age. The beauty of it is not lost even today.

Reverting to the presence of vegetation in the composition of the background earthscape, one would notice that it is replete with the richness of details, whether in the individual spread of branches or tufts of grass or in flower petals or in leaf venation. The decorative aspect and the variation of shades not withstanding, it often produces movement in the otherwise pictures of still life, and a depth perspective almost in an artistically concealed manner.

The whole panorama of Manṣūr's portraits set in marvellously and uniquely laid background represents, in his true spirit and characteristics, the very quintessence of nature's endless variety of creation and beauty.

NOTES

1. INTRODUCTION

1. Bābur, *Bāburnāma* or *Tūzuk-i Bāburī*, tr. A.S. Beveridge, London, 1921 pp. 488-515.
2. Jahāngīr, *Jahāngīrnāma* or *Tūzuk-i Jahāngīrī*, ed. S. Ahmad, Ghazipur & Aligarh, 1963-4, pp. 233, 237, 242, 245, 247, tr. A. Rogers, ed. H. Beveridge, London, 1904-14, Vol. II, pp. 16-8, 23-4, 32-3, 39, 42.
3. *Tūzuk-i Jahāngīrī*, ed. text, p. 271, tr. Vol. II, p. 88.
4. Ibid., ed. text, p. 284, tr. Vol. II, p. 114.
5. Percy Brown, *Indian Painting under the Mughals, A.D. 1550-A.D. 1750*, New Delhi, 1981, pl. XXII, Fig. 1.
6. *Tūzuk-i Jahāngīrī*, ed. text, p. 271, tr. Vol. II, pp. 88-9.
7. Pratapaditya Pal, *Court Paintings of India, 16th-19th Centuries*, New York, 1983, p. 51, pl. on p. 156, where it is attributed to Manṣūr.
8. *Tūzuk-i Jahāngīrī*, ed. text, pp. 106-7, tr. Vol. I, pp. 216-7.
9. Ibid., ed. text, p. 117, tr. Vol. I, p. 240, See also pp. 139-40. In 1608, Jahāngīr was presented a white cheeta, which he had never seen earlier. No picture of this animal is known from the Mughal school.
10. *Tūzuk-i Jahāngīrī*, ed. text, p. 54, tr. Vol. I, p. 113.
11. Ibid.
12. A.K. Das, *Mughal Painting During Jahangir's Time*, Calcutta, 1978, p. 142, pl. 59.
13. *Tūzuk-i Jahāngīrī*, ed. text, p. 158, tr. Vol. I, p. 323.
14. Ibid., see Abū'l Faẓl, *Akbarnāma*, ed. Ahmad Ali and Abdur Rahim, Bib. Ind., Calcutta, 1873-87, p. 315, tr. H. Beveridge, Calcutta, 1897-1921, Vol. II, p. 466.
15. Daniel J. Ehnbom, ed. *Indian Miniatures, The Ehrenfeld Collection*, New York, 1985, pl. 22 and text.
16. Ibid.

17. *Tūzuk-i Jahāngīrī,* ed. text, p. 105, tr. Vol. I, p. 215.

18. Douglas Barrett and Basil Gray, *Painting of India,* Lausanne, 1963, p. 81. See also pl. on p. 80.

19. Eletr, M. Raid, "Birds and Animals in Mughal Painting", *BCA*, 1, 1959, p. 16, "But a deviation from the Persian standard may be recognised in colour treatment. We do no longer find horses with such fantastic colours as had been characteristic in Persian art. Rather, the Mughal artists tried to reproduce the natural colours of the horse, but the execution remains flat and one can hardly see the light shadows that distinguish the different parts of the body and impart relief to the representation."

    "A new and naturalistic treatment of birds and animals becomes more and more apparent towards the close of the reign of Akbar and the representations take a more vivid character. They are no longer conventional. The artists appear to have discarded the Persian conventions. The old Indian ideal of naturalistic rendering becomes more and more felt."

20. For example, *Anwār-i Suhailī,* School of Oriental and African Studies, London, dated 1570 (27 miniatures); *Anwār-i Suhailī,* Bharat Kala Bhavan, Varanasi, dated 1596-7 (27 miniatures); *Anwār-i Suhailī,* British Museum, Add. 18579 (29 miniatures); *'Iyār-i Dānish,* Chester Beatty Library, Dublin, c. 1580-1600 (96 miniatures); *'Iyār-i Dānish,* Prince of Wales Museum of Western India, Bombay, c. 1580-1600 (52 miniatures); *'Ajā'ib al Makhlūqāt,* Chester Beatty Library, c. 1600-5 (16 miniatures).

    For their reproductions see John Seyller, "The School of Oriental and African Studies *Anvār-i Suhaylī*: The Illustration of a De Luxe Mughal Manuscript", *Archives of Asian Art,* Vol. 38, New York, 1985, pp. 119-51; S.P. Verma, "*Anwar-ī Suhaili* — an illustrated manuscript of Akbar's court in the collection of Bharat Kala Bhavan, Varanasi", *Roopa-Lekha,* Vol. XLIV (Nos. 1 & 2), New Delhi, 1977, pp. 17-22; J.V.S. Wilkinson, *The Lights of Canopus: Anwar-i Suhaili,* London, 1929; T.W. Arnold and J.V.S. Wilkinson, *A Library of A. Chester Beatty: A Catalogue of the Indian Miniatures,* London, 1936, Vol. I, pp. 12-21, 26-7, Vol. II, pls. 38-47, 50-2; Karl Khandalavala and Moti Chandra, *Miniatures and Sculptures, Collection of Sir Cowasji Jehangir,* Bombay, 1965, p. 17, pl. C.

21. S.K. Saraswati, "Birds in Mughal Art", *Marg,* Vol. 2, 1948, p. 32, fig. 3, "One such picture depicting a study of cranes is worth reproduction here (Fig. 3). A skilful draughtsmanship and a naturalistic rendering of the birds in all their minute details, not barring even their characteristic attitudes, endow the painting with a sense of reality thereby raising it above the category of a mere nature study."

22. Arnold and Wilkinson, op. cit., Vol. I, pp. 26-7, Vol. II, pls. 50-2.

23. For reproductions see Jeremiah P. Losty, *The Art of the Book in India*, London, 1982, No. 58, pp. 87-8, pls. on page 77, where he attributes the drawings of birds and animals executed in the body of the text to Manohar son of the great painter Basawan. He further writes that such drawings towards the end of volume culminate in flocks of 20 large birds per page in vivid shades of green and blue; Arnold and Wilkinson, op. cit., Vol. III, pl. 97 (b, c, d); S.P. Verma, *Art and Material Culture in the Paintings of Akbar's Court,* New Delhi, 1978, p. 35, "Birds are often used as decorative objects on a page of exquisite calligraphy. Figures are drawn in narrow stripes in pairs or groups on the top margin or in the centre of the page."

24. Losty, op. cit., p. 87.

25. For their reproductions see F.R. Martin, *The Miniature Painting and Painters of Persia, India and Turkey,* London, 1912, Vol. II, pls. 178-81; Brown, op. cit., pl. XXXVII; Losty, op. cit., pls. XXI, XXIV; S.C. Welch, "The Emperor Akbar's *Khamsa* of Nizami", *The Journal of Walters Art Gallery,* Vol. XXIII, Baltimore, 1960, Figs. 1-6.

    In these MSS. the margins are illuminated in gold and represent hunting scenes, birds, animals, landscape, etc. In some of the margins these figures are executed in colour.

26. See Lubor Hajek, *Indian Miniatures of the Mughal School,* London, 1960, pp. 76, 78, pls. 20, 28, 31.

27. For the reproductions of the miniatures on these themes see: (1) Hunting scene: Geeti Sen, *Paintings from the Akbarnama,* New Delhi, 1984, pls. 10-11, 20, 39-40, 60; Hamid Suleiman, *Miniatures of Baburnama,* Tashkent, 1970, pls. 42-3, 46, 50, 52; S.P. Verma, *Art and Material Culture, etc.,* op. cit., pls. X-XII. (2) Animal fight: Suleiman, op. cit., pl. 93. (3) Trapping of birds and animals: Suleiman, op. cit., pl. 27; S.C. Welch, *Art of Mughal India,* New York, 1963, pl. 9; M.S. Randhawa, *Paintings of the Baburnama,* New Delhi, 1983, pl. VIII.

28. See Sen, op. cit., Welch, op. cit., p. 28, pl. 11a; Verma, *Art and Material Culture, etc.,* op. cit., p. 36.

29. See Hamid Suleiman, op. cit., pl. 27; S.I. Tyulayev, *Miniatures of Babur Namah,* Moscow, 1960, pl. 21; S.C. Welch, *Art of Mughal India,* op. cit., pl. 9.

30. *Bāburnāma,* tr., pp. 488-575.

    For the reproductions of the *Baburnama* miniatures representing birds and animals see Suleiman, op. cit., pls. 55-75; Tyulayev, op. cit., pls. 37-47; Randhawa, op. cit., pls. on pages 125-131 and colour plate XIX.

31. Verma, *Art and Material Culture, etc.,* op. cit., pp. 34-5, n. 39.

32. R. Grousset, *Civilization of the East: India,* New York, 1931, Vol. II, p. 374. See also S.M. Hasan, "The Mughal School of Zoological Portraiture", *AAL,* No. 37, 1963, pp. 5, 13.
33. E. Kühnel and H. Goetz, *Indian Book Painting,* London, 1926, pp. 6, 56, pl. 10 (colour).
34. E.B. Havell, *Indian Sculpture and Painting,* London, 1908, p. 214, pl. LXI.
35. *Tūzuk-i Jahāngīrī,* ed. text, pp. 280-1, tr. II, p. 108.
36. Ibid., ed. text, pp. 306, tr. II, 157.
37. Ibid., ed. text, p. 300, tr. II, p. 145.
38. Ibid., ed. text, p. 375, tr. II, p. 284.
39. See S.C. Welch, A. Schimmel, M.L. Swietochowski, and W.M. Thackston, *The Emperor's Album, Images of Mughal India,* New York, 1987, pp. 164-5, no. 40, colour plate on p. 166.
40. Salim Ali, "The Mughal Emperors of India as Naturalists and Sportsmen", *JBNHS,* no. 31-2, pp. 53-5, pl. facing p. 53.
41. S.M. Hasan, "The Mughal School of Zoological Portraiture", *AAL,* no. 37, 1963, p. 13.
42. Abū'l Ḥasan, Farrukh Beg, Govardhan, 'Ināyat, Manohar, Manṣūr, Mirār (Murād), Pidārath.
43. *Tūzuk-i Jahāngīrī,* ed. text, p. 235, tr. II, p. 20.
44. H. Goetz, "Indian Miniatures in German Museums and Private Collections", *EAQ,* 2, 1930, p. 143.
45. M.C. Beach, *The Grand Mogul Imperial Painting in India (1600-1660),* Williamstown, Mass., 1978, p. 138, fig. 12.
46. Beach, *The Imperial Image, Paintings for the Mughal Court,* Washington, D.C., 1981, pp. 77-8, Cat. no. 7, reproductions on pages 75-6.
47. Abū'l Fazl, *Akbarnāma,* ed. text, III, p. 570, tr., III, p. 862. See also Verma, S.P., *Art and Material Culture, etc.,* op. cit., pp. xxii-xxiii.
48. Folio 116 bears an inscription which states that it was painted in the forty-second regnal year which is equivalent to 1598. See Rai Krishnadasa and Humayun, Kabir, *Mughal Miniatures,* New Delhi, 1955, text to pl. 2 (colour); Randhawa, M.S., "Paintings of the Baburnama", *Roopa,* 42(1-2), 1975, p. 14.
49. Norah M. Titley, *Miniatures from Persian Manuscripts,* London, 1977, p. 5, Cat. no. 11 (35). This folio represents 'Humāyūn standing on rising ground watching his army in combat with Mīrzā Kāmrān's troops' painted by Khem Karan. It is dated 21 *Sha'bān* 1012 AH/25th January 1604 A.D.

50. *Tūzuk-i Jahāngīrī*, ed. text, pp. 280-1, tr., II, p. 108.
51. Ibid., ed. text, p. 306, tr., II, 157.
52. S.C. Welch and M.C. Beach, *Gods, Thrones and Peacocks*, New York, 1965, pp. 35, 117, pl. 10.
53. S.C. Welch, *A Flower from Every Meadow, Indian Paintings from American Collections*, New York, 1973, no. 61.
54. Brown, op. cit., pl. 54.
55. Beach, *The Grand Mogul Imperial Painting, etc.*, op. cit., p. 171, pl. on p. 173.
56. Ibid., pp. 171-2.

2. HISTORICAL BACKGROUND

1. Abū'l Faẕl, *Ā'īn-i Akbarī*, ed. text, I, 116, tr., I, 113.
2. Ibid., ed. text, I, 118, tr., I, 115.
3. Abū'l Faẕl, *Akbarnāma*, ed. text, III, 434, tr., III, 651 (Daswant), 474, tr., 714 (Farrukh Beg); *Ā'īn-i Akbarī*, ed. text, p. 117, tr., I, 114 (Mīr Sayyid 'Alī, Khwāja 'Abdu'ṣ Ṣamad '*Shīrīnqalam*', Daswant, Basāwan, Kesav, La'l, Miskīn, Mukund, Farrukh the Qalmāq, Mādhav, Jagan, Mahesh, Khem Karan, Tārā, Sānwalā, Haribans and Rām); Qazwīnī, Mullā 'Alā ud Daula, *Nafā'is al Ma'āṣir*, fol. 51b (Mīr Sayyid 'Alī and Khwāja 'Abdu'ṣ Ṣamad); Bayāzīd Bayāt, *Taẕkira-i Humāyūn-o Akbar*, ed. text, pp. 67-9, 117 (Maulānā Dost, Maulānā Darwesh Muḥammad, Maulānā Yūsuf, Mīr Sayyid 'Alī and Khwāja 'Abdu'ṣ Ṣamad); Jahāngīr, *Tūzuk-i Jahāngīrī*, ed. text, p. 7, tr., I, p. 15 ('Abdu'ṣ Ṣamad), 75, tr., I, p. 159 (Farrukh Beg), 235, tr., II, p. 20 (Āqā Riẓā' and Abū'l Ḥasan), 275, tr., II, pp. 116-7 (Bishandās), 235, 281, 299, 306, tr., II, pp. 20, 108, 145, 157 (Manṣūr).
4. Brown, P., *Indian Painting under the Mughals, A.D. 1550 to A.D. 1750*, Oxford, 1924, pp. 195-8 (Appendix A); Arnold, T.W. and Wilkinson, J.V.S., *A Library of A. Chester Beatty: A Catalogue of the Indian Miniatures*, London, 1936, I, pp. xxvi-xxvii; Verma, S.P., *Art and Material Culture in the Paintings of Akbar's Court*, New Delhi, 1978, pp. 124-9.
5. Bābur, *Bāburnāma*, tr., pp. 488-515.
6. See *Bāburnāma* (BM), Or.3714, ff. 378a-407b); *Bāburnāma* (NM, no, 07.271, ff. 267-91) and *Bāburnāma* (MECM, pls. 36-63). For their reproductions, see Suleiman, H., *Miniatures of Baburnama*, Tashkent, 1970, pp. 148-54, pls. 55-86; Randhawa, M.S., *Paintings of the Baburnama*, New

Delhi, 1983, pp. 85-96, pls. on pp. 125-35; Tyulayev, S.I., *Miniatures of Babur Namah,* Moscow, 1956, pls. 25-6, 36-63; Tyulayev, *Indian Art in Soviet Collections,* Moscow, 1956, pls. 10-1.

7. Jauhar, *Tezkereh al Vākiāt,* tr., p. 43.

8. *Ṭūṭīnāma* (CMA). Published: Chandra, P., *The Tutinama of the Cleveland Museum of Art and the Origins of Mughal Painting,* Chicago, 1976; Simsar, A. (tr. and ed.), *The Cleveland Museum of Art's Tutinama, Tales of a Parrot,* Austria, 1978.

   Anwār-i Suhailī (BKB). Published: Verma, S.P., "Miniatures of the *Anwār-i Suhailī*", *Roopa,* 44(1-2), 1977.

   Anwār-i Suhailī (BM, Add.18579). Published: Wilkinson, J.V.S., *The Lights of Canopus: Anwar-i Suhaili,* London, 1929.

   'Iyār-i Dānish (CBL). Published: Arnold and Wilkinson, op. cit.

   'Ajā'ib al Makhlūqāt (CBL). Published: Ibīd.

9. See no. 6 (above). 31 dispersed folios of the *Bāburnāma* (unpublished), preserved in the WAG (W.596), do not represent bird and animal pictures.

10. Bābur, *Bāburnāma,* tr., pp. 488-515.

11. See Appendix, nos. 6-10.

12. Tyulayev, S.I., *Miniatures of Babur Namah,* Moscow, 1960, p. 23, "The same accuracy is also found in the depiction of birds and animals (besides the crocodile, rhinoceroses and especially tapir whom it is difficult to recognize). The miniatures are a vivid testimony to a close observation of nature so that zoologists can easily identify the species of animals and birds they depict"; Verma, *Art and Material Culture, etc.,* pp. 34-5.

13. Barrett, D. and Gray, B., *Painting of India,* Lausanne, 1963, p. 81.

14. Verma, *Art and Material Culture, etc.,* op. cit., p. 35, 41n.

15. Ibid., p. 35, 42n.

16. *Tūzuk-i Jahāngīrī,* ed. text, 105, tr., I, 215.

17. Ibid., ed. text, p. 248, tr., II, pp. 43-4.

    For the portrait 'Dying 'Ināyat Khān', see BLO, MS. Ouseley Add.171; and for its line-drawing, see MFA, no. 14.679. Published: Welch, S.C., *Imperial Mughal Painting,* London, 1978, p. 27, fig. 5, p. 84, pl. 23 (colour); Coomaraswamy, A.K., *Catalogue of Indian Collections in the Museum of Fine Arts, Boston, Pt. VI (Mughal Painting),* Boston, 1930, p. 42, pl. XXXII.

18. *Tūzuk-i Jahāngīrī,* ed. text, p. 275, tr., II, pp. 116-7.

19. Ibid., ed. text, p. 300, tr., II, p. 145.
20. Ibid., ed. text, pp. 305-6, tr., II, p. 57.
21. Ibid., ed. text, p. 275, tr., II, p. 117.
22. Ibid., ed. text, p. 75, tr., I, p. 159.
23. Ibid., ed. text, p. 235, tr., II, p. 20.
24. Pictures of birds and animals ascribed to these painters are as follows:

    (1) Abū'l Ḥasan: Assembly of birds and animals (*Johnson (A),* IOL, v. 67, n. 4), Forktail (*Kevorkian (A),* MMA, no. 55.121.10.15), Squirrels on a chinar tree (*Johnson (A),* IOL, v. 1, f. 30, joint work with Manṣūr), Bird (*Kevorkian (A),* FGA).

    (2) Farrukh Beg: Falcon (CMDu, no. 3.619, N, b).

    (3) Govardhan: Man leading a bear (*Kevorkian (A),* MMA, no. 55.121.10.10r), Lion (Private Collection). See Pinder-Wilson, R.H., *Paintings from the Muslim Courts of India,* London, 1976, no. 123.

    (4) Manohar: Bābur hunting with circle of beaters (*Bābur,* BM, Or.3714, f. 283b), Hunting scene (CHPK, no. 243), Antelope (NM), Black buck (BM), Keeper leading a black buck (CW, VA, IM, no. 134-1921), Falcon on a perch (CGCNS), Horse (*Johnson (A),* IOL, v. 3, no. 1), Birds chivying an owl (CG, MFA, no. 14.662), Partridges (CHV).

    (5) Mirār (Murād): Indian gazelle in open (Staatliche Museum, Berlin), Antelope (CBMR).

    (6) Pidārath: Antelope (*Bābur,* BM, Or.3714, f. 380b), Magpies, wagtails and swallows (*Bābur,* BM, Or.3714, f. 393a), Mountain sheep (Royal Album, CBL, MS. 7, no. 1), Keeper leading the lion (*Kevorkian (A),* MMA, no. 55.121.10.11v), Keeper leading the lion (CW, VA, IM, no. 133-1921).

    (7) 'Ināyat: Himalayan wild goat, *Mārkhor* (CW, VA, IM, no. 138 & A-1921).

    (8) Muḥammad Nādir of Samarqand: Falcon (Album, BM, Add.18801, no. 25, Oriental Antiquities, no. 1920.9.17.013(24)).

25. *Tūzuk-i Jahāngīrī,* ed. text, pp. 280-1, 306, tr., II, pp. 108, 157. See also Appendix, nos. 34 and 45.

3. MANṢŪR

1. Jahāngīr, *Tūzuk-i Jahāngīrī,* ed. text, p. 235, tr., II, p. 20.

2. Ibid., ed. text, p. 105, tr., I, p. 215.
3. Ibid., ed. text, p. 105, tr., I, pp. 215-6, "One of these animals in body is larger than a peahen and smaller than a peacock. When it is in heat and displays itself, it spreads out its feathers like the peacock and dances about. Its beak and legs are like those of a cock. Its head and neck and the part under the throat are very minute of a different colour. When it is in heat it is quite red — one might say it had adorned itself with red coral — and after a while it becomes white in the same places, and looks like cotton. It sometimes looks of a turquoise colour. Like a chameleon it constantly changes colour. Two pieces of flesh it has on its head look like the comb of a cock. A strange thing is this, that when it is in heat the aforesaid piece of flesh hangs down to the length of a span from the top of its head like an elephant's trunk, and again when he raises it up it appears on its head like the horn of a rhinoceros, to the extent of two finger-breadths. Round its eyes it is always of a turquoise colour, and does not change. Its feathers appear to be of various colours, differing from the colours of the peacock's feathers."
4. It may thus be concluded since the above observation (description of turkey cock and Himalayan cheer pheasant) follows: "As these animals appeared to me to be very strange, I both described them and ordered that painters should draw them in the Jahāngīr-nāma, so that the amazement that arose from hearing of them might be increased" (Ibid., ed. text, p. 105, tr., I, p. 215).
5. Ibid., ed. text, pp. 280-1, tr., II, pp. 107-8.
6. Ibid., ed. text, p. 300, tr., II, p. 145.
7. Ibid., ed. text, pp. 305-6, tr., II, p. 157.
8. Ibid., ed. text, p. 327, tr., II, p. 201.
9. Das, A.K., "Ustād Manṣūr", *Lalit*, 17, 1974, p. 37, "Besides these, a large number of drawings of birds and animals are found in museums and collections throughout the world which do not bear any signature or attribution, but on technical and stylistic grounds belong to Ustād Manṣūr's style. In fact, many of them might actually have come from his brush. One of them is a picture of the Dodo, pasted along with smaller details showing a tragopan, a Sumatran Loriquet, ducks and a pair of partridges, on a folio of the 'Leningrad Album'. If it was actually painted by the Ustād it would lead to the conclusion that Ustād Manṣūr lived a few years more than Jahāngīr and continued to paint during the early part of Shāh Jahān's reign."

   See also Verma, S.P., "Mansur, the Master Painter of Jahangir's epoch", *Roopa*, 53(1-2), 1982, p. 11, "Here he attributes this painting to Manṣūr and places the date of the miniature during Shāh Jahān's time to draw the above conclusion, which is uncritical and entirely based on conjecture."

10. For Salim Ali, see "Dodo" in Alvi, M.A. and Rahman, A., *Jahangir the Naturalist,* New Delhi, 1968, p. 17, pl. II (colour). Peter Mundy noticed 'dodos' at Surat in 1628. See Temple, R.C. (ed.), *Travels of Peter Mundy in Europe and Asia, 1608-67,* Hakluyt Society edition, 2nd Series, London, 1914, vol. 3, pt. II, pp. 352-3.
11. Qaisar, Ahsan Jan, *The Indian Response to European Technology and Culture (A.D. 1498-1707),* New Delhi, 1982, p. 153.
12. For Manṣūr, see Appendix, nos. 5, 15 and 30.
13. For Ḥusain *Naqqāsh,* see illuminated folio in *K͟hamsa (K),* WAG, W.624. See Ettinghausen, R., *Paintings of Sultans and Emperors of India in American Collections.* Delhi, 1961, pl. 6 and text. No reproduction.
14. 'Abdu-l Bāqī Nihāwandī, *Ma'āṣir-i Raḥīmī,* ed. text, p. 1688. Cf. Haq, Mahfuzul, "The Khan-i Khanan and his Painters", *ISC,* 5, 1931, p. 627, "He was unrivalled as a calligraphist, gilder, book-binder and gem-cutter. He was much skilled in various arts, and was proficient and unsurpassed in other branches as well. He met and joined the service of His Excellency ('Abdu'r Raḥīm K͟hān-i K͟hānān) in Ahmadnagar in the Deccan. He held the post of a librarian in His Excellency's Library for some time (*muddate*). There are many specimens of his painting, gilding and calligraphy in this library ('School of the Wise')."
15. For which see:
    (1) Āqā Riẓā' in *Gulshan (A),* IL, ff. 16a, 29, 105, 145, 189, 216; MG (see Godard, Y.A. and Gray, B., *Iran: Persian Miniatures, Imperial Library,* New York, 1956, fig. 15).
    (2) Daulat in *Gulshan (A),* IL, f. 44.
    (3) Govardhan in *Jahāngīr (A),* SLB, f. 25b; Sevadijian and Welch Collection, Williams College Museum of Art, no. 76.3 (see Beach, M.C., *The Grand Mogul Imperial Painting in India (1600-1660),* Williamstown, Mass., 1978, pp. 119-20, no. 40.

3.1 Early Phase

1. For his miniatures, see *Dīwān-i Ḥāfiẓ* (SLR), f. 19; *Razmnāma* (SMS) nos. 15, 29-30, 59, 81, 98-9, 115, 121-2; *Tā'rīk͟h-i K͟hāndān-i Timūria* (OPL), f. 30; *Dārābnāma* (BM, Or.4615), f. 67a; *Rāmāyan* (SMS), no. AG 1901, 1911, 1913, 1916, 1950; *'Ajā'ib-al Mak͟hlūqāt* (CBL), nos. 115, 122-5; *Bāburnāma* (FGA), no. 54.29; *Akbarnāma* (VA, IS, 2-

1896, no. 117), pls. 12-3, 57, 64, 97.

See Beach, M.C., *The Imperial Image, Paintings for the Mughal Court,* Washington, D.C., 1981, p. 81.

2. Beach, *The Grand Mogul Imperial Painting in India (1600-1660),* Williamstown, Mass., 1978, p. 138.
3. Beach, *The Imperial Image, etc.,* op. cit., p. 82, Cat. no. 7.
4. For the miniatures ascribed to (a) *Ustād* Bābū, see *Bahāristān,* BLO, Elliot MS. no. 254 (s.v. Ethe, H. and Sachau, E., *Catalogue of Persian, Turkish and Pushtu Manuscripts in the Bodleian Library,* Pt. I, Oxford, 1889, p. 634, no. 963; Brown, P., *Indian Painting under the Mughals, A.D. 1550 to A.D. 1750,* Oxford, 1924, p. 196); (b) *Ustād* Basāwan in a n Album, RLWC, B.20, no. 11a (s.v. Verma, S.P., "Some unnoticed Mughal Miniatures at the Royal Library, Windsor", *Roopa,* 57(1-2), 1985, p. 28); (c) *Ustād* La'l in an Album, RLWC, B.20. no. 3a (s.v. Verma, op. cit., p. 26, pl. on p. 25); (d) *Ustād* Miskīn in *Johnson (A),* IOL, vol. 16, f. 1 (s.v. Falk, Toby and Archer, Mildred, *Indian Miniatures in the India Office Library,* London, 1981, pp. 61-2, Cat. no. 40).
5. Abū'l Fazl, *Ā'īn-i Akbarī,* ed. text, p. 117, tr., I, p. 114.
6. Ettinghausen, R., *Paintings of Sultans and Emperors of India in American Collections,* Delhi, 1961, text facing pl. 6; Beach, *The Grand Mogul Imperial Painting, etc.,* op. cit., p. 140; Losty, J.P., *The Art of the Book in India,* London, 1982, p. 92, no. 66 (unpublished).
7. Losty, op. cit., pp. 92-4, nos. 66, 70, pl. 30 (colour).
8. Illuminated *shamsa* around the seal of the emperor Jahāngīr. Published: *Islamic Art from India* (catalogue of the exhibits put on sale during 24th April-10th May 1980), Spink & Son Ltd., London, 1980, p. 56, no. 62 (frontispiece in colour).
9. *Ā'īn-i Akbarī,* ed. text, p. 118, tr., I, p. 115, "In the same manner as painters are encouraged, employment is held out to ornamental artists, gilders, line-drawers, and pagers."
10. Illuminated folios ascribed to Ḥusain *Naqqāsh,* Khwāja Jān Shirāzī and Luṭfullāh Muzaḥḥib are in *Khamsa (K),* WAG (W.624). Unpublished. See Ettinghausen, op. cit., text to pl. 6; Losty, op. cit., pp. 90-2, nos. 65-6; Beach, *The Imperial Image, etc.,* op. cit., p. 227.
11. See Appendix.
12. For the miniatures ascribed to Ḥusain *Naqqāsh,* see *Tā'rīkh-i Khāndān-i Timūria* (OPL), f. 72a; *Rāmāyan* (SMS), nos. AG1856-7; *Bābur* (BM, Or.3714), f. 386b; *Akb.* (VA, IS, 2-1896, no. 117), pl. 113; miniature in Mme de Behague Collection (see Das, A.K., *Mughal Painting*

During Jahangir's Time, Calcutta, 1978, p. 255, 10n). See also 13n (under Chapter 3 — Manṣūr).

13. Beach, *The Grand Mogul Imperial Painting, etc.*, op. cit., p. 140, 6n.
14. For reproduction, see Brand, Michael and Lowry, Glenn D., *Akbar's India: Art from the Mughal City of Victory,* New York, 1985, p. 140, no. 17, pl. on p. 49.
15. Miniature in *Bahāristān* (BLO), Elliot MS. 254, f. 42. For reproduction, see Barrett, D. and Gray, B., *Painting of India,* Lausanne, 1963, colour pl. facing p. 88; Stchoukine, I., *La Peinture Indienne a l'Epoque des Grand Moghols,* Paris, 1929, pl. 10, where painter's name is given as 'Miskin'; Losty, op. cit., p. 90, no. 64, pl. XXIV (colour).
16. See Appendix, no. 13.
17. Welch, S.C., *The Art of Mughal India: Painting and Precious Objects,* New York, 1963, p. 31, pl. 18.
18. *Ā'īn-i Akbarī,* ed. text, p. 117, tr., I, p. 114.
19. See Appendix, no. 17.
20. This title of the portrait is subject to some doubts.
21. Clarke, C.S., *Victoria and Albert Museum Drawings: Thirty Mogul Paintings from the School of Jahangir (17th century) and four Panels of Calligraphy in the Wantage Bequest,* London, 1922, text to pl. 17.
22. Ibid.

3.2 Specialization

1. Jahāngīr, *Tūzuk-i Jahāngīrī,* ed. text, p. 235, tr., II, p. 20.
2. Ibid., ed. text, pp. 280-1, tr., II, pp. 107-8.
3. Coomaraswamy, A.K., *Catalogue of Indian Collections in the Museum of Fine Arts, Boston, Pt. VI (Mughal Painting),* Boston, 1930, Cat. no. 14.683, p. 51, pl. XLI.
4. Das, A.K., "Some more Manṣūr's drawings", *Lalit,* 18, 1977, p. 28.
5. *Tūzuk-i Jahāngīrī,* ed. text, pp. 305-6, tr., II, p. 157.
6. Ibid., ed. text, p. 300, tr., II, p. 145.
7. Ibid., ed. text, p. 105, tr., I, pp. 215-6.
8. Ibid.
9. Ibid., ed. text, p. 283, tr., II, p. 112.

   For the location of *pargana* Kairana, see Habib, I., *An Atlas of the Mughal Empire, Political and Economic Maps with Detailed Notes, Bibliography and Index,* New Delhi, 1982, 4A, 4B, 29+, 77+.

10. *Tūzuk-i Jahāngīrī*, ed. text, p. 379, tr., II, p. 292.

    It may be quite exciting to note that much before Jahāngīr, his grandfather, Bābur had also noted this difference, as Salim Ali points out. "The florican (*P. charz*) is another. It is rather less than the *tūghdīrī* (*houbara*); the cock's back is like the *tūghdīrī's* and its breast is black. The hen is of one colour" (*Bāburnāma*, tr., p. 498). See Ali, Salim, "The Mughal Emperors of India as Naturalists and Sportsmen", *JBNHS*, vol. 32, pt. I, p. 61. For the likenesses of the cock and the hen, see under Appendix, nos. 35 and 40. For reproduction, see Alvi, M.A. and Rahman, A., *Jahangir the Naturalist*, New Delhi, 1968, pl. XXIV.

11. Smith, V.A., *A History of Fine Art in India and Ceylon*, Oxford, 1911, p. 476, pl. CXX, "The birds in this album, exquisitely drawn and coloured, are worth of Mansur and possibly be from his brush. I admire particularly the picture on folio 8 of a long-legged, brown bird standing by the side of a pool fringed with grass, flowers and bamboos in tolerably good perspective."

12. *Tūzuk-i Jahāngīrī*, ed. text, p. 327, tr., II, p. 201.

13. Ibid., ed. text, p. 105, tr., I, pp. 215-6 (account of the year 1612).

14. Ibid., ed. text, p. 68, tr., I, p. 143.

15. Ibid., ed. text, p. 248, tr., II, pp. 43-4.

16. Ibid., ed. text, p. 375, tr., II, p. 284.

17. See 24n (under Chapter 2 — Historical Background).

18. See reproductions in Suleiman, H., *Miniatures of Baburnama*, Tashkent, 1970, pls. 85-6 (colour); Randhawa, M.S., *Paintings of the Baburnama*, New Delhi, 1983, p. 96, no. 131, pl. on p. 135.

19. See Appendix, nos. 38-42.

20. 'Yellow narcissus and butterfly' (Cowasji Jehangir Collection, PWM), painted by Muḥammad Nādir of Samarqand. Reproduced and described: Khandalavala, K. and Chandra, M., *Miniatures and Sculptures, Collection of Sir Cowasji Jehangir*, Bombay, 1965, pp. 40-1, pl. E (colour).

21. For their reproductions, see Clarke, C.S., *Victoria and Albert Museum Drawings: Thirty Mogul Paintings from the School of Jahangir (17th century) and four Panels of Calligraphy in the Wantage Bequest*, London, 1922, pls. 1, 3-4, 6-8, 13, 16, 18-19, 21; Arnold, T.W. and Wilkinson, J.V.S., *A Library of A. Chester Beatty: A Catalogue of the Indian Miniatures*, London, 1936, III, pls. 59-60, 66-8, 70-1.

22. *Tūzuk-i Jahāngīrī*, ed. text, pp. 299-300, tr., II, pp. 143-5.

23. *Supra*, 20n.

24. For the reproductions of such margin-paintings, see Arnold and Wilkinson, op. cit., III, pls. 59-60; Clarke, op. cit., pls. 8-10, 18, 23-4; Welch, S.C., Schimmel, A., Swietochowski, M.L., and Thackston, W., *The Emperors' Album, Image of Mughal India,* New York, 1987, colour pls. on pp. 105-6, 118, 145, 160, 174-5, 191, 195.

25. Skelton, R., "A Decorative Motif in Mughal Art" in Pal, Pratapaditya, ed., *Aspects of Indian Art,* Leiden, 1972, p. 151, pl. XCb; Rich, V., "Mughal floral paintings and its European sources", *OA,* New Series, XXXIII(2), 1987, p. 186, fig. 8.

26. Skelton, op. cit., p. 151, pl. XCa; Rich, op. cit., p. 186, fig. 7, where the date of the present version is suggested as eighteenth century.

27. Beach, M.C., *The Imperial Image, Paintings for the Mughal Court,* Washington, D.C., 1981, p. 42, Cat. no. 1, pl. in colour on p. 34.

28. Swarup, Shanti, *Flora and Fauna in Mughal Art,* Bombay, 1983, p. 46, "Both the panels are surrounded by a most beautiful and delicate floral ornamentation carved in a very low relief. Among other flowers and plants portrayed one recognises the lily, the almond and the dahlia, all of which are found carved or painted upon Akbar's palace at Fathpur Sikri. Small butterflies and insects are introduced in the panels and are so life-like that they look as if actually flitting from flower to flower." For reproduction, see Smith, op. cit., pl. 136 (B).

29. Welch, S.C., *The Art of Mughal India: Painting and Precious Objects,* New York, 1963, p. 31, pl. 18.

4. ASCRIPTIONS: ARTIST'S SIGNATURES AND EMPEROR'S AUTOGRAPHS

1. For his signatures, see miniatures in *Gulshan* (*A*), IL, f. 145; *Anwār,* BM, Add.18579, ff. 21a, 54b; *Dīwān-i Ḥāfiẕ,* BM, Or.7573, f. 25a.

2. See miniature 'Bullock cart' in Sita Ram Sahu Collection, Varanasi (present location unknown).

3. See miniature 'Jahāngīr preferring a Ṣūfī Shai<u>kh</u> to Kings', FGA, 42.15.

4. See miniatures in *<u>Kh</u>amsa* of Niẕāmī, BM, Or.12208, f. 325b; *Gulshan (A),* IL, ff. 44, 104, 148.

5. See miniatures in BLO, Douce Collection, Or.a.1, f. 41; *Jahāngīr (A),* SLB, ff. 2a, 25a; *Gulshan (A),* IL, f. 99.

6. See Appendix, nos. 36, 38-9, 45-6, 48, 50-1, 53.

7. For this information, I owe to Professor Irfan Habib, Centre of Advanced Study in History, Aligarh Muslim University.
8. See miniatures, 'Young prince conversing with an old mullā', *Gulshan (A),* IL; 'A young man seated on a chair', Völkerkunde Museum, Berlin.
9. See miniatures, 'Celebration on the occasion of Jahāngīr's coronation', *IPM (A),* HL, f. 21; 'Youth holding *surāhī* and a cup of wine', *Gulshan (A),* IL, f. 148.
10. Appendix, nos. 54-5.
11. See miniatures, 'Christ holding a cross' (*CBL (A)*, no. 12); 'Jahāngīr's dream of Shāh 'Abbās's visit' (FGA, no. 45.9); 'Jahāngīr with a picture of Akbar' (MG, no. 3, 676, B); 'Old pilgrim' (CBMR); 'Portrait of 'Abdullā Khān Uzbek' (VA, IM, 20 & A-1925); 'Portrait of 'Abdullā Khān Firoz Jung' (*Minto* (*A*), VA, IM, 16 & A-1925); 'Portrait of Āṣaf Khān' (*IPM* (*A*), HL, f. 5 (top left)); 'Picture of an old woman' (*IPM* (*A*), HL, f. 19 (top left)); 'Spotted forktail' (MMA, no. 55.121.10.15); 'Prince offering wine to a young woman' (WAG, W.668, f. 40).
12. *Tūzuk-i Jahāngīrī,* ed. text, 235, tr., II, 20.
13. See miniature 'Portrait of Prince Khurram (Shāh Jahān)', *Minto* (*A*), VA, IM, 14 & A-1925 (Shāh Jahān's autograph).
14. See miniature 'Shāh Jahān with hands lifted in prayer', *Minto (A),* VA, IM, 17-1925 (Shāh Jahān's autograph).
15. For Jahāngīr's autographs see miniatures, 'Portrait of Rājā Sūraj Singh Rathore', *Jahāngīr (A),* SLB, f. 22b; 'Portrait of Bahādur Khān', *Jahāngīr (A),* SLB, f. 22b; 'Portrait of Khudabandā Mīrzā', *Naṣīruddīn (A),* IL, pl. 51; 'Portrait of Mahārājā Bhīm Kunwar', *Kevorkian (A),* MMA, 55.121.10.2v.
16. See Appendix, nos. 35, 47 and 52.
17. See miniatures, 'Portrait of Rājā Sūraj Mal', IM; 'Camel-fight', *Gulshan (A),* IL; 'Portrait of Ẕū'lfiqār Khān', *Minto (A),* VA, IM, 24 & A-1925.
18. Appendix, nos. 35 and 47.

5. MAJOR CHARACTERISTICS OF MANṢŪR'S ART

1. Picture of 'Hornbill' [26] is not painted in its natural habitat, which is marshy, green and watery, but is shown perched on bare, dry and rocky hump like the birds King vulture and Himalayan griffon [46] which prefer dry and desolate places.

2. Beach, M.C., *The Grand Mogul Imperial Painting in India (1600-1660)*, Williamstown, Mass., 1978, p. 138, where he writes, "The animals are carefully observed and drawn with slow, scientific precision that never allows the line or color to become purely decorative or independently expressive."

3. See Appendix, nos. 27 (Turkey cock) and 28 (Himalayan cheer pheasant).

4. Ray, Niharranjan, *Mughal Court Painting,* Calcutta, 1975, p. 170, pl. 15 (colour).

5. See Appendix, nos. 2, 26, 28, 45, 48 and 50.

6. Beach, M.C., *The Imperial Image, Paintings for the Mughal Court,* Washington, D.C., 1981, p. 178, "Moreover, the light and sketchy quality typical of Mansur's grasses and vegetation and the overall meticulousness of his draftsmanship are absent from the *Kevorkian Album* page."

7. Welch, S.C., *The Art of Mughal India: Painting and Precious Objects,* New York, 1963, p. 31, pl. 18.

8. See miniatures: 'Akbar hunting near Narwar', *Akb.*, VA, IS, 2-1896, no. 117, pls. 17-8 (Published: Sen, Geeti, *Paintings from the Akbarnama,* New Delhi, 1984, pl. 20 (colour)); 'Akbar mounted on an elephant crossing a bridge', *Akb.*, VA, IS, 2-1896, no. 117, pls. 21-2 (Published: Sen, op. cit., pls. 21-2 (colour); Brown, P., *Indian Painting under the Mughals, A.D. 1550 to A.D. 1750,* Oxford, 1924, pl. 39).

9. See miniatures: 'Akbar hunting with a circle of beaters', *Akb.,* VA, IS, 2-1896, no. 117, pls. 55-6 (Published: Sen, op. cit., pls. 39-40 (colour); S.C. Welch, *Imperial Mughal Painting,* London, 1978, p. 68, pl. 14 (colour)); 'Bullocks dragging a siege gun', *Akb.*, VA, IS, 2-1896, no. 117, pl. 72 (Published: Sen, op. cit., pl. 52 (colour)); 'Trained elephants killing followers of Khān Zamān', *Akb.*, VA, IS, 2-1896, no. 117, pl. 90 (Published: Spink, Walter M. and Levine, Deborah, *Akbarnama: Catalogue,* New York, no date, pl. 21; Verma, S.P., "Illustrated Akbarnama of Sixteenth Century Mughal School", *Roopa,* 51(1-2), 1980, p. 51, pl. on p. 48).

10. See miniature: 'Antelopes in the open', Staatliche Museum, Berlin (Published: Kühnel, Ernst, *Miniaturmalerei in Islamischen Orient,* Berlin, 1922, p. 67, pl. on p. 137).

11. *Tūzuk-i Jahāngīrī*, ed. text, p. 105, tr., I, p. 215.

12. For example, see the description on birds and animals: turkey cock, Himalayan cheer pheasant and a monkey (*Tūzuk-i Jahāngīrī,* ed. text, p. 105, tr., I, pp. 215-7), falcon (Ibid., ed. text, pp. 280-1, tr., II, pp. 107-8), zebra (Ibid., ed. text, p. 327, tr., II, p. 201), and *sārus*

crane (Ibid., ed. text, pp. 233, 237, 242, 245, 247, tr., II, pp. 16-8, 23-4, 32-3, 39, 42).

13. Such a surmise is at best tentative in the absence of any foolproof method for chronologically arranging Manṣūr's work, and also, because, scores of his paintings of the middle phase are untraceable.

14. For which see Falk, Toby and Archer, Mildred, *Indian Miniatures in the India Office Library*, London, 1981, Cat. no. 68, ff. 23v, 24, 31v, 32, 41v, 42, 50, 54, 66, reproduced on pp. 384, 390-1 and 397, respectively.

6. COPIES OF MANṢŪR'S ORIGINALS AND FORGED ATTRIBUTIONS

1. Beach, M.C., *The Grand Mogul Imperial Painting in India (1600-1660)*, Williamstown, Mass., 1978, p. 138; Beach, *The Imperial Image, Paintings for the Mughal Court,* Washington, D.C., 1981, pp. 186-88, Cat. nos. 18c and 18e.

2. Clarke, C.S., *Victoria and Albert Museum Drawings: Thirty Mogul Paintings from the School of Jahangir (17th century) and four Panels of Calligraphy in the Wantage Bequest,* London, 1922, text to pl. 16 (no. 24).

3. *Tūzuk-i Jahāngīrī*, ed. text, p. 105, tr., I, 215.

4. Ibid., ed. text, p. 235, tr., II, 20.

5. Ibid., ed. text, p. 239, tr., II, 27.

6. Ibid., ed. text, p. 244, tr., II, 37.

7. Das, A.K., *Mughal Painting During Jahangir's Time,* Calcutta, 1978, pp. 135-52.

8. For example, *Anwār-i Suhailī* (c. 1604-10), BM, Add.18579; *Bostān* of Sa'dī (c. 1605-10), BM, Add.27262; and *Dīwān-i Ḥāfiẓ* (c. 1610), BM, Or.7573.

   For reproductions of some of the miniatures from these MSS., see Wilkinson, J.V.S., *The Lights of Canopus: Anwar-i Suhaili,* London, 1929; Losty, J.P., *The Art of the Book in India,* London, 1982, nos. 74-6, pls. xxvii, xxix and fig. on p. 97; Barrett, D. and Gray, B., *Painting of India,* Lausanne, 1963, pls. on pp. 100-1.

9. See Appendix, nos. 35 (*Charz-i bor*), 47 (Zebra), 52 (Salt water fish).

10. Das, op. cit., pp. 148-9.

11. Ibid., p. 137.

12. Ibid., pp. 136-7.

13. Verma, S.P., "Treatment of similar themes — a study based on the illustrations of *Tuzuk-i Baburi*", *Proceedings of Indian History Congress*, Chandigarh, 1973, pp. 292-97.

14. A double-page illustration wrongly identified by Clarke (op. cit., no. 2, pl. 2) as 'Humāyūn's accession-darbār at Agra in 1530 (c. early seventeenth century)', preserved in the Wantage Collection, VA, IM, nos. 127 & 128-1921, is an early nineteenth century copy of the original in the *Bāburnāma*, BM, Or.3714, ff. 417b-418a, 'Poisoned Bābur feels sick'. For reproduction, see Suleiman, H., *Miniatures of Baburnama*, Tashkent, 1970, pls. 87-8 (colour).

    Wantage version is ascribed to 'Ālam. For another early nineteenth century work ascribed to him, see 'Black partridge' (FGA, no. 39.47b). Published: Beach, *The Imperial Image, etc.*, op. cit., p. 190, fig. 35.

15. Reproduced and described: Arnold, T.W. and Wilkinson, J.V.S., *A Library of A. Chester Beatty: A Catalogue of the Indian Miniatures*, London, 1936, I, p. 31, III, pl. 62.

16. *Kevorkian (A)*, FGA, no. 48.19. Reproduced and described: Beach, *The Imperial Image, etc.*, op. cit., pp. 185-6, Cat. no. 18c.

    Another late version of this study is in the collection of Edwin Binney 3rd.

17. Miniature in *Minto (A)*, VA, IM, no. 27 & A-1925. For reproduction, see Stchoukine, I., *La Peinture Indienne a l'Epoque des Grand Moghols*, Paris, 1929, pl. 44.

18. *Kevorkian (A)*, FGA, no. 48.21a. Reproduced and described: Beach, *The Imperial Image, etc.*, op. cit., p. 191, fig. 38.

    Other examples: (1) 'Jahāngīr holding an orb' in the collection of Shantikumar Morarji, Bombay (Published: Krishnadasa, Rai and Kabir, Humayun, *Mughal Miniatures*, New Delhi, 1955, pl. 10 (colour)). It is a late version of Bichitr's original in *CBL (A)*, no. 5 (Published: Arnold and Wilkinson, op. cit., I, p. 28, III, pl. 57 (colour)). (2) 'Dervish leading a bear', *Kevorkian (A)*, MMA, no. 55.121.10.9r (Published: Welch, S.C., Schimmel, A., Swietochowski, M.L. and Thackston, W., *The Emperors' Album, Images of Mughal India*, New York, 1987, no. 96, colour pl. on p. 276)). It is the late version of Govardhan's original preserved in the same collection (no. 55.121.10.10r). Reproduced: Ibid., no. 76, colour pl. on p. 238.

19. For which see miniature in *Kevorkian (A)*, FGA, no. 39.48, 'Two deer in landscape'. Reproduced and described: Beach, *The Imperial Image,*

etc., op. cit., p. 188. Cat. no. 18e recto. The original from which it is copied, is not known.

See also miniatures in *Kevorkian (A)*, MMA, nos. 55.121.10.26r ('A fantastic bird'), 55.121.10.27r ('Jungle fowl') and 55.121.10.28r ('Portrait of Ḥājjī Ḥusain Bukhārī'). Reproduced and described: Welch, Schimmel, Swietochowski and Thackston, op. cit., nos. 88 (pl. on p. 260), 92 (pl. on p. 268), 94 (pl. on p. 272).

For early nineteenth century works forged in the names of the master painters, namely Bālchand, Bichitr and Farrukh Beg, see miniatures in FGA, no. 48.20b; MMA, no. 55.121.10.26v; FGA, no. 39.47a respectively. For their reproductions, see Welch, Schimmel, Swietochowski and Thackston, op. cit., nos. 83 (pl. on p. 251), 91 (pl. on p. 267), 100 (pl. on p. 284).

20. An early nineteenth century copy of a miniature by Abū'l Ḥasan, 'Spotted forktail' (*Kevorkian (A)*, MMA, no. 55.121.10.15r) forged in the name of Manṣūr is known in *Kevorkian (A)*, FGA, no. 39.46b. For their reproductions, see Alvi, M.A. and Rahman, A., *Jahangir the Naturalist*, New Delhi, 1968, pl. XII; Beach, *The Imperial Image, etc.*, op. cit., p. 189, fig. 33.

    See also 'Shāh Jahān riding a stallion' (*Kevorkian (A)*, MMA, no. 55.121.10.21v), ascribed to Payāg (c. 1627). It is an early nineteenth century copy (FGA, no. 39.46a) forged in the name of Govardhan, a prolific painter of the Mughal school. For their reproductions, see Welch, Schimmel, Swietochowski and Thackston, op. cit., nos. 59 (colour pl. on p. 203), 86 (pl. on p. 256), respectively.

21. Beach, *The Grand Mogul Imperial Painting, etc.*, op. cit., p. 138.

22. *Charba*: a thin transparent sheet of deer skin, used for tracing outline drawings. See Brown, P., *Indian Painting under the Mughals, A.D. 1550 to A.D. 1750*, Oxford, 1924, p. 183.

23. Krishnadasa and Kabir, op. cit., text to pl. 10 (colour).

24. See miniatures: (1) 'Camel-fight' (identical copy of Bihzād's work), *Gulshan (A)*, IL. Published: Binyon, L., Gray, B. and Wilkinson, J.V.S., *Persian Miniature Painting*, London, 1933, pls. 87A (reproduction of Bihzād's original) and 87B (copy made by Nānhā). According to the emperor Jahāngīr's autograph on the version, it was executed by Nānhā in 1608-9 at his command. (2) 'Portrait of Maulānā 'Abdu'r Raḥmān Jāmī', *Gulshan (A)*, IL. Published: Godard, Y.A., "Les marges du Murakka Gulshan", *AEI*, I, 1936, p. 26, fig. 21. According to an inscription near the figure of the poet, this picture was copied by Daulat from an original of Bihzād. See Das, op. cit., p. 127 (no re-

production). (3) 'Masons at work' (copy of Bihzād's work in *Khamsa* of Niẓāmī, BM, Or.6810, f. 154b, dated 1494), *Naṣīruddīn (A)*, IL. Published: Godard, "Un album de portraits des princes Timurides de l'Inde", *AEI*, II, 1937, p. 266, no. 68, fig. 110 (ascribed to Ṣaḥīfa Bānū, a woman painter of Jahāngīr's atelier). For the reproduction of Bihzād's painting, see Gray, B., *Persian Painting*, London, 1961, colour pl. on p. 116. See also Das, op. cit., p. 127, 44-5 ns.

24a. Maclagan, E.D., *The Jesuits and the Great Mogul*, London, 1932, p. 248, "The coloured Mogul picture of a Christian subject was not, as a rule, a copy of a coloured European picture, but was based on some uncoloured European print. In some few cases it is possible that colour was imposed by the Indian artist on the print itself; for Father Jerome Xavier tells us how he once saw one of the King's painters 'illustrating some small pictures by putting on colours and pigments'."

24b. Ibid., p. 236, "As early as 1580 we find Akbar having copies made of the pictures of the Virgin and of Christ which the Fathers had with them, and in 1597 the Prince Salīm is reported to have begged for the loan of the picture of S. Ignatius Loyola that he might have it copied." See also pp. 232-3.

25. Das ("Some more Mansur's drawings", *Lalit*, 18, 1977, p. 30) doubts the authenticity of the inscription given on this miniature. He writes: "Though no scholar has ever doubted the authenticity of the Victoria and Albert Museum's example or questioned the genuineness of Ustād Manṣūr's signature on it, we may point out that the inscription '*amal-e-Ustād Manṣūr* written on the Jaipur example is in fine letters usually found in other authentic Manṣūr works, whereas the inscription on the Victoria and Albert Museum example is in a coarser hand much different from that of the Manṣūr."

Das is mistaken here to accept 'third-person ascription' given on Wantage miniature as artist's signature.

26. Beach, *The Grand Mogul Imperial Painting, etc.*, op. cit., p. 171. Beach may have thought of the 'Himalayan cheer pheasant' in question as a contemporary copy work in the light of his belief: "It was a common practice for Mughal artists to adapt single figures and even whole compositions from the work of their compatriots" (Ibid., p. 172).

While no example of an adaptation of the whole composition is known, and the instances of an adaptation of single figures are rather very rare in contemporary works, Beach's belief perhaps borders on overgeneralization.

27. Edwin Binney 3rd in Beach, *The Grand Mogul Imperial Painting, etc.*, op. cit., p. 172.

28. Compare picture of this bird in IM (no. R.31). Reproduced and described: Ray, Niharranjan, *Mughal Court Painting,* Calcutta, 1975, p. 170, pl. 15 (colour).
29. Smith, V.A., *A History of Fine Art in India and Ceylon,* Oxford, 1911, p. 476, pl. CXX.
30. See also Falk, Toby and Archer, Mildred, *Indian Miniatures in the India Office Library,* London, 1981, p. 74, Cat. no. 68, f. 8, pl. on p. 381, where the date of the present miniature is suggested about 1635. Another late version of this study is noticed in an album, preserved in RLWC, no. A.13, f. 64. Unpublished.
31. Clarke, op. cit., text to pl. 15; Das, *Mughal Painting, etc.,* op. cit., p. 149; Ray, op. cit., p. 164.
32. VA, IM, no. 135 & A-1921. For reproduction, see Clarke, op. cit., no. 23, pl. 15.
33. Krishnadasa and Kabir, op. cit., text to pl. 10 (colour).
34. Ibid.
35. Brown, op. cit., pl. LIII.
36. Havell, E.B., *Indian Sculpture and Painting,* London, 1908, pp. 214-6, pl. LXII (colour), "The painting of a turkey-cock, Plate LXII, is possibly another work of Mansur... There is not much doubt that this splendid little study, which sums up so admirably the arrogant swagger of the turkey-cock and all the characteristics of the plumage, is the original painting ordered by Jahangir."
37. Ray, op. cit., p. 164, pl. XII (colour), "The fine, accurate, sophisticated and minute draughtsmanship, the relief given to the richly coloured bird by the light background and the delicate landscaping leave hardly any doubt that it is a work of a master artist having an insight into the subject he was concerned with; indeed, it is not at all unlikely that the artist was the celebrated bird-painter Manṣūr himself."
38. Clarke, op. cit., no. 23, "Another magnificent portrait of this much lauded bird exists in an unsigned painting, now in the Calcutta Art Gallery. The latter, undoubtedly executed by Mansur, also bears the personal seal of Jahangir on the mount."
39. Das, *Mughal Painting, etc.,* op. cit., p. 149, "Another version of the same bird is preserved in the Indian Museum, Calcutta. Like the Victoria and Albert Museum example it also is mounted on a *muraqqa'* folio with wide *hashiyas* containing fine golden floral designs, and bears the royal seal of Jahangir, but unlike the former it is not signed by Mansur

and there are certain very minute but considerable differences in the minute designs of the feathers. The size of the Indian Museum picture is slightly larger and the floral shrubs in the foreground are replaced by grassy plants. But the drawing is so similar to the signed example that it would not be improbable to ascribe it to the same painter, who may have painted this copy for Khurram at a slightly later date."

Das has further noticed another version of this study in Maharaja Sawai Man Singh II Museum, Jaipur (Ibid., p. 149, 82n). Unpublished.

40. See Appendix, no. 27.

41. See Appendix, no. 71.

42. *Kevorkian (A)*, MMA, no. 55.121.10.14v. For reproduction, see Welch, Schimmel, Swietochowski and Thackston, op. cit., p. 165, no. 41, colour pl. on p. 167.

43. *Kevorkian (A)*, MMA, no 55.121.10.25v. For reproduction, see Welch, Schimmel, Swietochowski and Thackston, op. cit., p. 262, no. 89, pl. on p. 263. See Appendix, no. 63.

44. *Kevorkian (A)*, FGA, no. 48.19a. For reproduction, see Welch, Schimmel, Swietochowski and Thackston, op. cit., p. 249, no. 82, pl. on p. 248. See Appendix, no. 64.

45. *Kevorkian (A)*, MMA, no. 55.121.10.12v. For reproduction, see Welch, Schimmel, Swietochowski and Thackston, op. cit., p. 173, no. 45, colour pl. on p. 175.

46. See Swietochowski in Welch, Schimmel, Swietochowski and Thackston, op. cit., p. 249, no. 82.

47. See Welch in Welch, Schimmel, Swietochowski and Thackston, op. cit., p. 262, no. 89.

48. The CBL version is reproduced and described in Arnold and Wilkinson, op. cit., I, p. 45, III, pl. 80 (colour).

    For another version of this study preserved in FGA, see 44n (*supra*).

49. Beach, *The Imperial Image, etc.*, op. cit., pp. 185-6, Cat. no. 18c (recto), pl. on p. 186.

50. See Welch in Welch, Schimmel, Swietochowski and Thackston, op. cit., p. 249, no. 82.

51. Welch does not quote any evidence for it.

52. Arnold and Wilkinson, op. cit., I, p. 45, III, pl. 80 (colour), "The character of the painting, its delicate and minute workmanship, suggest that this picture is the work of Manṣūr, the famous animal painter who enjoyed the patronage of the Emperor Jahāngīr."

53. For which compare with his signatures in miniatures nos. 27, 33, 45-6 and 48. See Appendix.

54. Beach, *The Imperial Image, etc.*, op. cit., p. 188, Cat. no. 18e, pl. on p. 189, details on p. 179.

55. Ibid., p. 178.

56. See Welch in Welch, Schimmel, Swietochowski and Thackston, op. cit., p. 245, no. 80.

57. Ibid.

58. Reproduced: Beach, *The Imperial Image, etc.*, op. cit., p. 189, fig. 33. For details, see Appendix, no. 73.

59. Picture of 'Spotted forktail', painted by Abū'l Ḥasan is preserved in MMA, no. 55.121.10.15r. For reproduction, see Welch, Schimmel, Swietochowski and Thackston, op. cit., pp. 164-5, no. 49, colour pl. on p. 166.

60. Ibid., p. 254, no. 85, where Welch writes: "All that was lively and lovingly observed in Abu'l Ḥasan's study has become flaccid and weak in this lackluster rehash."

61. Ibid., p. 254, no. 85, where Swietochowski writes: "The nineteenth century artist has added two peculiarities of his own to this copy. Notches appear to have been cut out of the wing feathers just before the tail, the reason for this is unknown. The later artist has also given the bird a slightly hooked bill which in nature it does not possess. The treatment of feathers on the breast and the upper back differs strikingly from that of the earlier painting."

62. The word '*Ustād*' is written as '*Ostād*'.

63. Reproduced and described: Falk, Toby, Digby, Simon and Goedhuis, Michael, *Paintings from Mughal India*, London, no date, p. 48, no. 22, colour pl. on p. 49.

    See Appendix, no. 74.

64. Falk, Digby and Goedhuis, op. cit., p. 48, no. 22.

65. These miniatures are in *Kevorkian (A)*, MMA, nos. 55.121.10.26r, 27r and 28r, respectively. See Appendix, nos. 80-2.

66. See Welch in Welch, Schimmel, Swietochowski and Thackston, op. cit., p. 261 (no. 88), pl. on p. 260, p. 269 (no. 92), pl. on p. 268.

67. Reproduced and described: Wilkinson, *Mughal Painting*, London, 1948, p. 24, colour pl. on p. 3, where it is described as the work of Manṣūr. See also Swietochowski, in Welch, Schimmel, Swietochowski and

Thackston, op. cit., p. 261, no. 88, where he suggests present miniature as Manṣūr's original work.

This particular miniature, described by Wilkinson and Swietochowski as a probable work of Manṣūr, does not bear any testimony either to his style, or drawing, or colouring. This is not a naturalistic study, but a distortion of it as evident from the shapes and exposures of the beak, unnatural growth above and below the beak, talons, the formation of the wings, feathers and plumage, etc. Everything about its form and texture fails to achieve any likeness of the actual bird, which is an immpossible thing to associate with Manṣūr. Besides, there is complete lack of that delicate shading and graded tonality or even that immaculate brush work, for which Manṣūr holds a conspicuous position among his contemporaries. As against Manṣūr's style, it exposes decorative patterning of the feathers and the mannered presentation of the plumage, inaccurate draughtsmanship and ambiguous expression. It could possibly be a work of decadent late eighteenth, or early nineteenth century. A comparison of it with the naturalistic study of this bird [8], executed by Manṣūr in his early phase, further substantiates our observation. For the reproduction of this miniature, see Smith, op. cit., p. 474, fig. 249 on p. 475.

68. See Welch in Welch, Schimmel, Swietochowski and Thackston, op. cit., p. 273, no. 94, pl. on p. 272.

69. See Swietochowski in Welch, Schimmel, Swietochowski and Thackston, op. cit., p. 269, no. 92.

70. Das, "Ustād Manṣūr", *Lalit*, 17, 1974, p. 37.

71. Das, *Mughal Painting, etc.*, op. cit., pp. 197-8, pl. 58. For colour reproduction, see Havell, op. cit., p. 214, pl. LXI.

PART II

NOTES ON PLATES (I-XVIII)

PLATE I

Folio from the *Bāburnāma,* c. 1590-1600
(A) Recto: Two wild buffalo
(B) Verso: The blue bulls and two hog deer
Freer Gallery of Art, Washington, D.C., No. 54.29
Inscription: (on 'A') *"Ṭarḥ-i Kānhā, 'amal-i Manṣūr"* ('Sketch by Kānhā, colouring by Manṣūr'); (on 'B') Same as on 'A'.

Earliest known work of Manṣūr in collaboration with Kānhā. Beach's note on it is relevant:

> "The double-sided folio in the Freer is a superb example of his (Mansur's) early style. The basic characteristics of the design — the simple background, with a few typical plants placed in a way that rhythmically enlivens the surface, or the use of plain, uncolored paper to concentrate attention on the animals — are probably elements contributed here by Kanha, but they continue in Mansur's later natural history works as well. The slow, careful drawing and thinly applied paint, however, seem especially distinctive to Mansur."[1]

An introduction of rows of birds shown on high margin, sweeping horizontal brush strokes for the skyline, or, even the treatment of vegetation with gently curved branches having imparipinnate leaves, seem to be typically Manṣūr's mode of expression in building up the background landscape of his paintings, since these features recur almost constantly in his subsequent works. These, also, lend an exclusive individuality to his handling of the space in his landscapes.

---

1. Beach, M.C., *The Imperial Image, Paintings for the Mughal Court,* Washington, D.C., pp. 77, 81-2, colour pl. on p. 50.

PLATE II

Bābur meets his sister at Qunduz, c. 1598
Bāburnāma, National Museum, New Delhi, No. 50.326, folio 8
Inscription: "*'Amal-i Manṣūr*" ('Work of Manṣūr')

An earliest solo work of Manṣūr, heavily burdened with the characteristics of sixteenth century Mughal art of book-illustration in Akbar's atelier hardly incorporates in it signs of Manṣūr's individuality. Nevertheless, the noticeable thing in this example is the use of deep pigments and contrasts, which was discarded soon by Manṣūr in favour of soothing and calm colours for achieving through their harmonious blends the subdued background and openness in his compositions, which he continues throughout.

Thin shading employed to model Bābur's face shows an attempt to achieve realism. Folds depicted in flowing costumes further show the painter's capability to handle delicate shading, which was a typical virtuosity of the Western technique.

PLATE III

Vīnā-player, c. 1600
Collection of Edward Croft Murray, London
Inscription: "*'Amal-i Manṣūr Naqqāsh*" ('Work of Manṣūr *Naqqāsh*')

A portrait from the early phase of artist's career. A human portrait in three-quarter view along with the crowded composition—a trait of sixteenth century Mughal painting—suggests that Manṣūr was a conventional Mughal painter, but with a difference. Birds fluttering over the blossom, no horizon line, rows of birds on high margin suggesting aerial perspective, are some of the clear major features of Manṣūr's composition, which save him from becoming a stereotype painter. Upward going flowering plants arcading the human figure provide a vertical movement not known elsewhere in portrait styling of the Mughal school, could be attributed to artist's own compositional improvisation to suit the subject of painting. S.C. Welch's observation, "the rhythmic flutter of birds and flowers goes beyond physical description in a successful attempt to interpret music in paint"[1] may be sacrosanct in the context of pure lyricism imparted to the portrait. Here, the musician's reclining head over the *vīnā,* while relates the interaction between

1. Welch, S.C., *The Art of Mughal India: Painting and Precious Objects,* New York, 1963, p. 31.

the ears and the sound emanating from the resonators of the *vīnā*, further makes a rhythmic pattern, it being in harmony with the instrument held diagonally. To capture the musician's feeling in visual form is Manṣūr's real forte, a rare quality in portraiture which only a few Mughal painters, viz., Abū'l Ḥasan, Bichitr, Bishandās, Daulat, Govardhan and Manohar could emulate.

Inscription being partly hidden and written insignificantly on the ground of the picture could possibly be in artist's own hand.

PLATE IV

Akbar while hunting with a circle of beaters, punishes Hamid Bhakkari (second part of double-page illustration), c. 1602-05
Akbarnama, Victoria & Albert Museum, London, I.S. No. 117, pl. 56.
Inscription: *"Ṭarḥ-i Miskīnā, 'amal-i Manṣūr"* ('Sketch by Miskīnā, colouring by Manṣūr')

An illustration from the early phase of artist's career. On this folio Manṣūr has collaborated with Miskīnā, and has done the work of 'colouring' only.

Composition though crowded with clusters of figures, yet each figure is drawn most discriminately to avoid any overlapping — a major characteristic of sixteenth century Mughal school. Modelling of the animal figures has been done with delicate shading of soft tones and thin colour washes; distinguishing each separate species through well-defined features and minute details, shows Manṣūr's uncanny calibre to portray animal life with exceptional accuracy and vividness. Deep shading employed around the figures to provide relief effect — a common practice till late sixteenth century — seems to have been discarded by Manṣūr later with the exception of his zebra (Plate XV). The expression of ferocity, fear and bodily tension imparted in the drawings of animals can be said to have come out most effectively due to a fine coordination between drawing and colouring.

PLATE V

Turkey cock, c. 1612
Wantage Collection, Victoria & Albert Museum, I.M. 135-1921
Inscription: (signature) *"'Amal-i banda-i dargāh Manṣūr Nādir u'l 'Aṣr, Jahāngīr Shāhī"* ('Work of the slave of the court, Manṣūr *Nādir u'l 'Aṣr* ('Unequalled of the Age), [servant] of the King Jahāngīr')

The bird is moderately gaunt and isolated, swelled up in pose, and perched against the plain background, dominates the whole composition. Foreground sprigged with flower plants, and the high margin streaked with typical Manṣūrian spontaneous horizontal strokes to suggest an aerial perspective with a cloud-like effect but without any defined horizon line, are the major characteristics of this composition, which are later repeated in other works as well. In the treatment of landscape the painter exercises a certain liberty of expression, through his horizontal and firm brush strokes, as also he is able to find a distinct character of his own. It testifies to Manṣūr's inherent power of creative articulation while remaining confined to painting the bird in all its natural exactness of details both in the drawing, and colouring.

The panel of calligraphy (quatrains from the *Dīwān* of Ḥāfiẓ)[1] on top and bottom of the miniature, embellished with a margin painting comprising of stylized floral arabesque (a characteristic of seventeenth century album pictures) adds to the decorative effect, as well as, enhances the heaviness in sharp contrast to the bareness of the landscape background. Thus, it brings out in full focus the main figure.

PLATE VI

Himalayan cheer pheasant, c. 1612
Wantage Collection, Victoria & Albert Museum, I.M. 136-1921
Inscription: "*'Amal-i Ustād Manṣūr*" ('Work of *Ustād* Manṣūr')

This bold study of Himalayan cheer pheasant is a profile in isolation, dominating majestically against a landscape subdued in details, is very individual to Manṣūr's expression in the portraits. The technique suited him best for picturization of natural history. Nevertheless, the natural surroundings do create rhythm and proportion, not excluding the suggestive skyline, in the composition. Maximum possible study of details of the main body of the bird comes out prominently in highlight for its contrastive thinly shaded strokes in combination with smoothly curved outline of the form; it gives subsequently the impression of a solid and firm drawing. The still pose of the bird adds tranquillity in atmosphere, not to say, it almost dominates the mood of the form. Such effect of moods and naturalistic exactitude are present in other studies of Manṣūr as well. Bold sweeps of brush strokes em-

1. Clarke, C.S., *Victoria and Albert Museum Drawings: Thirty Mogul Paintings from the School of Jahangir (17th century) and four Panels of Calligraphy in the Wantage Bequest,* London, 1922, No. 23, pl. 15 (right) and text.

ployed to model the landscape further show artist's spontaneous and frank expression commensurate with the overall approach to the form of the bird. It gives an overpowering relief to the central figure also.

Broad margin painting decorated with varied naturalistic flowering plant motifs, executed in gold on indigo blue ground, is a common feature of early seventeenth century album pictures, which was developed as a separate branch of painting. While it aimed at decoration, the studies of plants composed in border-design, however, are the subject of natural history. It is notable that no parallel example of such margin illumination is seen in other contemporary schools of Indian art. The painters who did it largely remain anonymous.

PLATE VII

Himalayan blue-throated barbet, c. 1615-20
Wantage Collection, Victoria & Albert Museum, I.M. 137-1921
Inscription: "*'Amal-i Nādir u'l 'Aṣr Ustād Manṣūr Naqqāsh*" ('Work of *Nādir u'l 'Aṣr Ustād* Manṣūr *Naqqāsh*')

The perching bird on the tree branch, relatively larger in proportions, dominates the composition. Again, Manṣūr's ingenious compositional techique can be seen in the way he subordinates the background to the principal object, and thus, he enhances the effect of the main figure. A stiff pose of the neck and the firm and bold curve of the back tend to somewhat rigidity in the drawing, but it is greatly relieved by the anatomical correctness of the pose, i.e., the bird's searching look below, which also lends it a remarkable living quality and a sense of lyricism. The painter's clarity of vision and spontaneity of expression are notable here in the well-defined form of the bird effected through maximum economy of lines in the drawing.

The background depicted in the varying grades of the same pigment, thinly laid, and yet, making out every detail (Manṣūr's innovation), in combination with the main figure, instills a calm serenity and harmony to the whole composition. Such use of mono-colour scheme imparts in his pictures a rare charm, shows a surprising frugality of colour application as well and sharpens the decorativeness and naturalism of form.

The outer margin embellished in gold with naturalistic flower plant motifs and the inner margin decorated with panels of calligraphy and stylized version of floral motifs/arabesques, offer the convention of the time (characteristic of Jahāngīr's atelier, which formed an integral part of the album pictures, at least, till the mid of seventeenth century). The combination of the two does not simply broaden the margin, but this decorative illumination in its wholeness provides a sharp contrast to the figure in the middle of the folio, separated only by a surrounding space in light wash of graded pale golden yellow, which, in turn, subdues the margin and throws up the figure.

PLATE VIII

Falcon, c. 1619
Museum of Fine Arts, Boston, No. 14.683
Inscription: "*'Amal-i Ustād Manṣūr Nādir u'l 'Aṣr*" ('Work of *Ustād* Manṣūr *Nādir u'l 'Aṣr*')

An isolated figure of falcon shown on its perch, in rigid profile is centrally positioned in the composition. Black markings all over the wings suggest that it is in the likeness of the falcon described by Jahāngīr.[1] Well-defined form of the bird and the high precision of inner details, including the ferocity in the eye and the sharpness of the preying beak, speak of artist's keen perception. Manṣūr's technique of subdued background and slightly stiff figure are visible here also. Plain background in contrast to the slow careful work on the figure, as in other studies also, not only throws the figure in relief to the fore, but provides a background which could be very suitably functional in any objective picture of natural history.

PLATE IX

Indian bustard (*Charz-i bor*), dated 1619
Indian Museum, Calcutta, No. R.31
Inscription: (Emperor Jahāngīr's autograph) *"Shabīh-i charz-i bor. 'Amal-i Nādir u'l 'Aṣrī Ustād Manṣūr hurrarah-i Jahāngīr Akbar Shāh, San 14"* ('Picture of the red bustard. Work of *Nādir u'l 'Aṣri Ustād* Manṣūr. Written by Jahāngīr, son of Emperor Akbar, the 14th [regnal year] = 1619')

The present miniature, an isolated study of the bird, while it retains the usual stiffness, its background is powerfully executed: for it is done boldly and spontaneously in quick horizontal brush strokes in a single pigment, with varied tones. The skyline produces a chiaroscuro effect and distancing which is so enchanting. A close inspection of the brush movement

1. *Tūzuk-i Jahāngīrī*, ed. text, pp. 280-1, trans., II, pp. 107-8.

and tonal variations, blendings and mergings show that while the main figure is drawn on practically dry surface, the background is brought out through a repeated work on wet surface. The aerial perspective, typical of Manṣūr, is highlighted by small strokes remotely suggesting clusters of birds in formation. One noteworthy exception about this painting's composition is the utter lack of any vegetational sprigs in it, common to most of his other works. As a result of it, the entire background has acquired a greater force and vitality and spontaneity. It reflects Manṣūr's greater confidence in his brush and depth of vision. The distribution of the sprigs does supply the artist with a technique to provide receptacles for creating depth perspective but here, his bold strokes serve the same purpose. This peculiarity of the backdrop is hardly surpassed by any other contemporary artist — indeed a remarkable originality for his time. It is his own ingenious touch that through abstraction he creates depth, serenity and relief.

Overall semblance in colour of the background and the bird produces a harmonious affinity between the two. Colouration and the serenity of effects in Manṣūr betray the variations of his moods, though extremely aesthetically restrained. And this highly individualizes and separates him from the other artists of the Mughal school.

PLATE X

Chameleon on a branch, c. 1610-20
Royal Library, Windsor, No. RL.12081
Inscription: *"Ustād Manṣūr"*

We notice in this portrait Manṣūr's abiding concern for details so much so that he did not miss to capture in colour even the granulated roughness of the chameleon's skin texture.

Manṣūr's typical conscious enlargement of the figure in proportion to the space and branches of the tree, and highlighting of details of the main figure to isolate it from the already suppressed background is a masterful technical cunning. It is his special way of according a special dignity to his object of painting. This apart, the naturalistic treatment of the tree's structure, with all the details of knots and bulges, and leaves displaying mid ribs with parallel venation, is thoroughly maintained. The authenticity of the relationship between the chameleon and its environment is projected in a non-conventional manner by somewhat distorting the proportions. The big figure is delicately balanced on a thin twig, which is only a section of a big tree whose major portion is cut out of the focus of vision, but the tree's continuity is suggestively retained beyond the picture frame. One may imagine that the binocular's lens has moved slowly upward and then suddenly got focused on the main object. The composition, in order to give an idea of the natural cycle, does not leave out even the hovering insects, which is food for the animal. While the overall picture is a true natural study, Manṣūr's brilliant manipulation of the main elements in the picture infuses it with an illusion of openness, vastness as well as relief.

One wonders, how Manṣūr, though always engaged in painting natural history, and that too, within the limitations of accepted conventions, could lend such an individuality to the chameleon. The exact details of the figure caught at a particular live moment are integrated with the compact depiction of the close interrelationship between it and its habitat and habit.

Plate XI

The tulip (*Tulipa clusiana*), c. 1620
Maulana Azad Library, Aligarh Muslim University, No. 60-1, *Ba*-3
Inscription: (signature) "*'Amal-i banda-i dargāh Nādir u'l 'Aṣrī Manṣūr Naqqāsh Jahāngīr Shāhī*" ('Work of the slave of the court *Nādir u'l 'Aṣrī* Manṣūr *Naqqāsh* [servant] of the King Jahāngīr')

Manṣūr's extraordinary achievement in floral painting is an evidence in this tulip study. The accuracy of its details in life-like reproduction can be seen under the microscope, such as, the bends of the stems, the drawing of the leaves, the stages of flowering (from bud to full blossom, shown from different angles), a close up of the pollen grains at the ends of the stamens (six in number) and the delicate venation (in few leaves) proceeding towards the margin of the leaf blade in a more or less parallel direction (convergent type) — a characteristic of lanceolate leaves of the plants of the lily family (*liliaceae*). It would seem that the species closest to what Manṣūr was portraying is the *Tulipa clusiana.* The following description by Bailey is relevant:

> "T. Clusiana, DC. Lady Tulip. Tunic brown and leathery, wooly within near apex; lvs. 2-5, somewhat glaucous, sometimes red on edges, sharply folded, the flower 8-10 in. long, 3/8 in. wide; st. glabrous, to 1 ft. high; bud solitary, green, erect; fls. at first campanulate, later almost a flat star; segms. 1.1/2-2 in. long, 5/8 in. wide, acute, white within with basal carmine blotch, backs of

outer segms. red with white margin; stamens less than half as long as segms., purple: midseason."[1]

The butterfly and dragon fly (?) shown hovering above the tulip flowers, are in consonance with Manṣūr's thrust, as ever, toward achieving naturalistic flavour in his studies. Besides, in the selection of the hovering objects, there is an attempt not only to suggest the skyline, but also, to intensify the naturalistic impact of the flower study through an addition of ecological harmony that exists in nature. Very light pale background does help in brightening up in relief the flowering plant as a whole, and also, enhances with ease the vertical movement of it without having to concentrate much on spacing the sky as one might expect otherwise. One may again notice that the clustering of the leaves has been composed with a deliberate purpose and design: at the base, it is denser, which is suggestive of the plant being rooted in the soil, while in its upward growth the leaves have a light openness balanced by a bud, and then, there is a full focus on the flowers showing different folds of petals concerting with various stages of blossoming. There is life not only in their verisimilitude, but they, perhaps, further pulsate with certain variations of mood, at least, in the beholder's consciousness; the final full blossom being in a gay smiling form. At every stage of the drawing, Manṣūr has deftly avoided any monotony creeping in. It is remarkable for all the delicacy one can expect in a realistic flower drawing, as well as, in the control of space.

Margin painting: The inner margin comprising of stylized floral motifs, though highly ornamented, appears subdued enough to throw up the central picture in combination with the background tone. The verses (in the vertical panel) which are well calligraphed bear no relation to the theme of the main painting. This is no more than the contemporary convention associated with album paintings of Jahāngīr's atelier.

On the reverse side of the miniature are verses calligraphed in *nasta'līq* by Mīr 'Alī.

---

1. Bailey, L.H., *The Standard Cyclopedia of Horticulture*, New York, 1947, p. 220; also in his *Manual of Cultivated Plants*, New York, 1947, Vol. III, p. 3402.
   See Verma, S.P., "The Tulip (*ca.* 1621): A Study of Mansur", *Huntia*, Pittsburgh, Vol. 9, No. 1, 1993, pp. 81-87, figs. 1-2. Professor W.T. Stearn erroneously supposes it to be *Tulipa montana*.

PLATE XII

Iris plant with blossom, c. 1620
Imperial Library, Teheran
Inscription: *"Manṣūr Nādir u'l 'Aṣr"*

This study of the iris flower plant, like the tulip study, has with it some common compositional elements, including the hovering of an insect over the blossom, the approaching bird, and caressingly live flowers projecting different facets at different angles. Together they expose the total cross section of the iris flower. While it fully conforms to the rules of naturalistic study, it does not fall short in its essential aesthetic appeal. However, the wonderful perfection of the flower composition so delicately hung in the space of the skyline in an upward movement, suffers from a sudden jerk in the rhythm because of the down inclined but upside down figure of the bird. The emotional state of the excited bird, though adds vitally to the attraction of the flower, but its stiff drawing and contrastive colouration, and a somewhat unproportionate size, arrests the eye a bit oddly, and thereby, hampers the effect of the graceful, proud rise of the flower. Apart from the bird, the exclusive study of the flower shows in all its delicacy of rhythm the finesse of the master's hand, as usual. With prominence to the central theme, the subdued open background, and suggestive perspective of the vertical plane from a denser base to a lighter top, are as perfect here as in the previous study of the tulip (Plate XI). Its gentle bent stems with tilted blossoms and tender petals suggest careful rendering of the pigments, applied thinly. The shading is equally delicate.

PLATE XIII

Dipper (*Sāj*), c. 1620
The Metropolitan Museum of Art, New York, No. 55.120.10.16r
Inscriptions: (1) (in artist's handwriting) *"Jahāngīr Shāhī"* ('[servant] of the King Jahāngīr'); (2) (artist's signature) "*'Amal-i banda-i dargāh Nādir u'l 'Aṣr Manṣūr Naqqāsh*" ('Work of the slave of the court *Nādir u'l 'Aṣr* Manṣūr *Naqqāsh'*)

The dipper is shown in a hilly landscape, with a fast flowing stream in the foreground. It is illustrative of the description given by Jahāngīr in his Memoirs.[1] The main figure of the bird is shown in the middle of the composition, and drawn in still pose with minute details, which are common

1. *Tūzuk-i Jahāngīrī*, ed. text, p. 306, trans., II, p. 157.

to all Manṣūr's portraits of birds and animals. The juxtapositioning of another bird smaller in size and apparently viewed from a distance, and the receding contours of the hills painted in blurred colour, suggest scale perspective besides giving relief to the central figure. Bold sweeps of brush strokes, a familiar technique of Manṣūr, seen here in the modelling of the rocks and the rest of the landscape, are in sharp contrast with the slow and careful work on the bird. As a matter of fact, Manṣūr does not abandon this style in his naturalistic studies till the end of his career.

Depiction of hills with sloping top and simpler contours shows a shift from strict Persian convention. It is Manṣūr's originality that in the treatment of landscape he discards intricate details in favour of suggestive effects of form. He has achieved through broad sweeps of brush strokes a model of landscape which is fully expressive of the purpose—a novel experiment in doing earthscape for the first time perhaps.

The stream shown dividing the picture plane diagonally in concordance with the diagonal axis of the main figure, and by cutting across in the opposite direction of the slant of the vertical hill contours, it creates a balance and a rhythm which is further accentuated by a judicious use of tonal variations of the pigments.

Again, the dotted suggestion of the flock of birds in the sky against the bold sweeps of brush, and below, the typically drawn vegetation, is so common in most of the paintings of Manṣūr.

PLATE XIV

King or black vulture and Himalayan griffon, c. 1620-25
The Metropolitan Museum of Art, New York, No. 55.121.10.12v
Inscriptions: (1) (in artist's handwriting) *"Jahāngīr Shāhī"* ('[servant] of the King Jahāngīr'); (2) (artist's signature) *"'Amal-i banda-i dargāh Manṣūr Nādir u'l 'Aṣr"* ('Work of the slave of the court Manṣūr *Nādir u'l 'Aṣr*')

This is an exceptional work of Manṣūr in the sense that two different figures (here, kinds of vulture) have been put within the same frame embellished with the same prominence of characteristic details, including the differentiating colours, beaks, eyes, claws and plumages, etc. This work testifies to Manṣūr's unequalled capacity for observation, for he is able to capture even the piercing ferocity in the eyes of the birds, and aging features. Both the figures are treated separately on different planes suggesting no optical relationship. These appear as separate illustrations rather than relative components of the same painting. Characteristic features of Manṣūr's art, viz., no defined horizon line, subdued background, isolated figures, flattened top of rock, sweeps of brush strokes employed to model the landscape, are present as much here as elsewhere, in evidence since 1612 (Plate V) to the very last.

Illuminated broad margin-painting with naturalistic floral motifs, and calligraphed text on top and the bottom of the inner margin, is a characteristic conventional practice during Jahāngīr's period.

PLATE XV

Zebra, dated 1621
Victoria & Albert Museum, London, I.M. 32-1925
Inscription: (Emperor Jahāngīr's autograph) "*Astarī ki Rūmiān az Ḥabsha bā hamrāhī-e Mīr Ja'far āwurda būdand. San 1030 Hijrī. Shabīh-i īn rā Nādir u'l 'Aṣrī Ustād Manṣūr kashīdah. San 16*" ('A zebra (lit. mule) which the Turks who came in company with Mīr Ja'far had brought from Abyssinia. Year 1030 of the Hijra [AD 1621]. Painted by *Nādir u'l 'Aṣrī Ustād* Manṣūr. 16th regnal year [1621]')

This study of zebra, well defined in form and accurate in details, is drawn with firm lines. It deserves undoubtedly a place in any album of natural history. Manṣūr's precise vision and eye for details is observable here in the representation of the animal; the isolated figure dominates the composition and a subdued background with a slightly shaded tone around throws up the animal figure in relief. The linear movement, curves, shades and the brush work on the black stripes of the animal give the figure a somewhat three-dimensional effect and muscle formation, in order to capture its natural form. The special quality of Manṣūr is that he never allows the colour to become decorative, has its purpose, that is, not to overshadow the main figure by any interfering visual distraction. The concealed attempt behind the obvious simplicity of the background treatment is to provide an interaction between its tonal quality and the black and white stripes of the zebra, which is at once pleasing to the eye and saves the picture from garishness. The genuinity of the particular shade used in the background is demonstrated amply not only because of its concordance with the exposure of the figure, but also, for creating a serene harmony in the whole picture: a movement of mutually absorbing process without causing any damage to the relief effect. Thus an estimate of Manṣūr as a "draughtsman whose pictures are invariably drawn and tinted rather than conceived and executed more

1. Welch, S.C., *The Imperial Mughal Painting,* London, 1978, p. 93, pl. 27 (colour).

coloristically"[1] appears to be an anomalous judgement.

Margin-painting comprising of stylized floral motifs executed in gay colours and gold outlining, quite unfamiliar to the school of Jahāngīr, seems to have been added to the painting later during Shāh Jahān's reign, when spiralling arabesques of vines with blossoms in delightful colours came in vogue.

PLATE XVI

Goldfinch (*Murgh-i zarīn*), c. 1620-25
National Museum, New Delhi, No. 50.14/27
Inscription: "'*Amal-i Manṣūr Jahāngīr Shāhī*" ('Work of Manṣūr [servant] of the King Jahāngīr')

It is notable here how a gradual mixing of tonal variations through thinly shaded strokes describes the detail of the form. In spite of the usual slight rigidness of the naturalistic figure of the bird in isolation, the technique of colouration and brush work show a kind of deviation from what is generally seen in Manṣūr's other portraits of birds and animals. The features like the high altitude flight of birds on the high margin, landscape with casual growth of plants, and horizontal sweeps of brush strokes on wet surface, associated with Manṣūr, can be seen here also. Similarly, the tonal gradations of a single colour moving upward in the background, manipulated in a way so as to brighten up the details of the central theme, and, though it is kept subdued, it hardly remains an unrelated entity. From the compositional point of view the horizontal dividing line across the middle plane through a casual undulation opposite to the line axis of the bird helps in balancing the space proportions, and besides, it creates the main rhythm of the picture.

PLATE XVII

Pair of Tibetan cranes, c. 1621-25
Wantage Collection, Victoria & Albert Museum, London, I.M. 122a-1921
Inscription: "*Kār-i Ustād Manṣūr Jahāngīr Shāhī*" ('Work of *Ustād* Manṣūr [servant] of the King Jahāngīr')

It is a study quite removed from Manṣūr's general practice of painting birds and animals in isolation. Undoubtedly its beautiful rhythmic quality has the appeal of a captivating lyrical dance.

However, its compositional aspect cannot be readily attributed to Manṣūr's genius in the light of certain evidences. Blunt observes that such vivacious representation is not always to be found in Manṣūr's work, and he considers the present miniature strongly Chinese in form and feeling.[1] He also cites a very similar Chinese painting of two cranes belonging to the Ming period.[2] An identical outline drawing of 'Pair of Tibetan cranes', preserved at the Victoria & Albert Museum (I.M. 42-1925), may have been done at the Mughal atelier, and could be the source used by Manṣūr for this miniature (Fig. 24).[3] The strong evidence of it is observable in the close similarity of outlines of the two.

The visibly charming lyrical forms of coupling cranes, which is obviously a digression from Manṣūr's usual practice of making his figures slightly stiff and very detailed in physical description, and singular in form, could, perhaps, be traced to Jahāngīr's extraordinary zoological curiosity about Indian cranes (*sārus*), and their long graphic accounts in the Memoirs.[4] Manṣūr in order to match it, perhaps, felt drawn to imitate the Chinese model.

Nevertheless, the features of the landscape background with vanishing horizon line in subdued tone, flight of birds on high margin, the delicate brush work and soft colours that are characteristically Manṣūr's can be seen here as well in their unalloyed purity.

---

1. Blunt, W., "The Mughal Painters of Natural History", *BUM*, 90 (529), 1948, pp. 49-50.
2. Otsuka-Kogeisha, *The Pageant of Chinese Painting*, Tokyo, 1936, pl. 475.
3. See Das, A.K., "Mansur" in *Master Artists of the Imperial Mughal Court*, ed. Pratapaditya Pal, Bombay, 1991, p. 47, fig. 8, where he considers it to be a genuine work of Manṣūr.
4. *Tūzuk-i Jahāngīrī*, ed. text, pp. 233, 237, 242, 245, 247, trans., II, pp. 16-8, 23-4, 32-3, 39, 42.

   See also Das, A.K. (*Mughal Painting during Jahangir's Time*, Calcutta, 1978, p. 197), where he writes: "The pair of cranes drawn in a fascinating study now in Victoria and Albert Museum may represent the pair of cranes domesticated and paired by Jahangir and described in so great detail in the *Tuzuk*." But the identification of the birds portrayed in the miniature with Indian crane (*sarus*) as is described by Jahangir, is misleading. The contradiction is self-evident in the light of the few lines from a letter of G.S. Keith of American Museum of Natural History addressed to the Victoria and Albert Museum (Das, op. cit., p. 208, 211n). The lines are:

   "Scientifically it is interesting because these are not in fact the Indian Sarus, *Grus antigone*. They are a rather rare Tibetan crane, *Grus nigricollis*, which nests in Tibet and winters in Yunnan. It does not occur in India at all."

   Keith's factual report is further reinforced by Ambar Habib's (an avid bird watcher) observation on a reproduction of the same miniature exhibited at 'Wild Life in Mughal Painting' (Exhibition) held at the Centre of Advanced Study in History, Aligarh Muslim University, Aligarh, in 1985 (ref.: Catalogue, Exhibit No. 38). Habib did not hesitate to qualify the bird as *Grus nigricollis*. See also, Das, op. cit., p. 242, 124n.

Broad margin-painting embellished with floral arabesques and panel of calligraphy are, as usual, a conventional feature of the time.

PLATE XVIII

Salt-water fish, c. 1621-25
Red Fort Museum, Delhi, No. 40.688
Inscription: (Emperor Jahāngīr's autograph) *"Māhi-Arabi darya-i shor. 'Amal-i Nādir u'l 'Aṣr Ustād Manṣūr"* ('Arabian fish of the sea. Work of *Nādir u'l 'Aṣr Ustād* Manṣūr')

It is undoubtedly an outstanding work of art for its sheer force, vitality and bold spontaneity, hardly surpassed by any other artist of the contemporary period. The entire figure of the fish is in a state of rhythmic movement, as if, it has dived down from above and is about to move up again. Certainly, it has been executed with very sure quick strokes of the brush. The brush work undoubtedly confirms artist's absolute confidence, his maturity, and his expanded sense of freedom. Whereas, in the earlier works he used his free brush strokes only in the construct of the background, here he lets loose his lyrical exuberance, without, of course, flouting the conditions of natural history. The superb handling of the space, that is, the water mass's smooth blending with the sky, has acquired a depth which perhaps Manṣūr has not achieved elsewhere. Obviously, the deep water environs of the fish and the wide open sky merging with it around the isolated fish simply emphasize the unique individuality of this species of nature. Perhaps, the dotted birds, on the high margin, typical tonal variety and spontaneous brush strokes, and close details are sufficient to ascribe this work to Manṣūr, as there was none else in the whole atelier of the imperial Mug͟hals through the sixteenth and seventeenth centuries, who had such a mastery on spontaneous brush strokes, as well as,. an eye for details at the same time, or who could combine the two so marvellously. This work of Manṣūr surely is a work of pure art, so much so, that even the perfect draughtsman in him has gone in concealment in the final composition, and yet, conspicuously enough, it has remained a portrait of natural history.

However, it is a sorry realization that such an all-time masterpiece has been damaged at all the margins and is spotted with moth-eaten holes.

APPENDIX: PAINTINGS BY MANṢŪR

The miniatures ascribed to Manṣūr are arranged (so far as possible) in a chronological order. Each miniature is described with the title and folio number of the manuscript or album it belongs to, and the name of the collections (museum, library and private). The theme of each miniature is given in brief; comments and descriptions of modern scholars are cited, and, where necessary, even reproduced. Transliteration and translation of inscriptions (where they are more than bare ascriptions) found on the paintings and related to the painters are also provided.

The miniatures lacking recorded attributions, but assigned by modern critics to Manṣūr, are also listed here. It is the personal opinion of the author that such attributions are almost always doubtful, and must be disregarded in a study of the style or work of any painter.

(1) Ascribed and Signed Works

1. Two wild buffalo.
   Inscription: *Ṭarḥ-i Kānhā, 'amal-i Manṣūr* (Sketch by Kānhā, colouring by Manṣūr).
   Bābur, FGA, DC, no. 54.29a.
   Reproduced and described: Beach, M.C., *The Imperial Image, Painting for the Mughal Court,* Washington, D.C., 1981, p. 77, Cat. no. 7, pl. on p. 75, colour pl. on p. 50; Das, A.K., "Mansur" in *Master Artists of the Imperial Mughal Court,* ed. Pratapaditya Pal, Bombay, 1991, p. 42, fig. 2; Okada, A., *Imperial Mughal Painters,* Paris, 1992, p. 218, fig. 264. Plate I(A).
2. Two blue bulls and two hog deer.
   Inscription: *Ṭarḥ-i Kānhā, 'amal-i Manṣūr* (Sketch by Kānhā, colouring by Manṣūr).
   Bābur, FGA, DC, no. 655 A.E.
   Reproduced and described: Beach, *The Grand Mogul Imperial Painting*

in India (1600-1660), Williamstown, Mass., 1978, p. 138, fig. 12; Beach, *The Imperial Image, etc.,* op. cit., p. 77, Cat. no. 7, pl. on p. 76; Godden, R., *Gulbadan (Portrait of Rose Princess),* New Delhi, 1980, pl. on p. 105 (colour); Das, op. cit., p. 42, fig. 3.
Plate I(B).

3. Bābur meets his sister at Qunduz.
Inscription: *'Amal-i Manṣūr* (Work of Manṣūr).
Bābur, NM, no. 50.326, f. 8.
Reproduced and described: Krishnadasa, Rai and Kabir, Humayun, *Mughal Miniatures,* New Delhi, 1955, text facing pl. 2; Das, A.K., "Ustād Manṣūr", *Lalit,* 17, 1974, pp. 33, 37, pl. 13, fig. 3; Randhawa, M.S., "Paintings of the Baburnama", *Roopa,* 42 (1-2), 1975, p. 13; Randhawa, *Paintings of the Baburnama,* New Delhi, 1983, p. 62, pl. II (colour); Das, "Mansur", op. cit., p. 42, fig. 4.
Plate II.

4. Episode in battle which Chengiz was obliged to undertake in order to win power.
Inscription: *Ṭarḥ-i Nānhā, 'amal-i Manṣūr, ṣūrat Mādhav* (Sketch by Nānhā, colouring by Manṣūr and figures by Mādhav).
Jami, IL (dated 1596).
Reproduced and described: Godard, Y.A. and Gray, B., *Iran—Persian Miniatures, Imperial Library,* New York, 1956, pl. 30 (colour).

5. Illuminated frontispiece (*'Unwān*).
Painted by Manṣūr (inscription not published).
Khamsa (*K*), WAG, W.624 (dated 1597-8).
Described: Losty, J.P., *The Art of the Book in India,* London, 1982, p. 92, no. 66; Beach, *The Grand Mogul Imperial Painting, etc.,* op. cit., p. 140, where it is suggested that Manṣūr may have been responsible for many of the floral borders found in Shāh Jahān's Album. See Ettinghausen, R., *Paintings of Sultans and Emperors of India in American Collections,* Delhi, 1961, text facing pl. 6 (colour).

6. Partridge.
Inscription: *'Amal-i Manṣūr Naqqāsh* (Work of Manṣūr *Naqqāsh*).
Bābur, BM, Or.3714, f. 387a.
Described: Titley, Norah M., *Miniatures from Persian Manuscripts,* London, 1977, p. 124.

7. Birds of Kaujal and Pulpaikar species.
Inscription: *'Amal-i Manṣūr Naqqāsh.*
Bābur, BM, Or. 3714, f. 387b.
Reproduced and described: Suleiman, H., *Miniatures of Baburnama,* Tashkent, 1970, p. 150, pl. 64 (colour); Titley, op. cit., p. 124.

8. Jungle fowl and partridge.
Inscription: *'Amal-i Manṣūr Naqqāsh.*
Bābur, BM, Or. 3714, f. 388a.
Reproduced and described: Smith, V.A., *A History of Fine Art in India and Ceylon,* p. 474, fig. 249; Titley, op. cit., p. 124; Okada, op. cit., p. 218, fig. 263.

9. Quails.
Inscription: *'Amal-i Manṣūr* (Work of Manṣūr).
Bābur, BM, Or.3714, f. 388b.
Reproduced and described: Smith, op. cit., p. 474, fig. 250; Titley, op. cit., p. 124.

10. *Kharchal* and *Charz* (Indian bustard).
Inscription: *'Amal-i Manṣūr.*
Bābur, BM, Or.3714, f. 389a.
Reproduced and described: Suleiman, op. cit., p. 150, pl. 65 (colour); Titley, op. cit., p. 124; Titley, *Persian Miniature Painting and its influences on the art of Turkey and India,* London, 1984, pl. 36 (colour); Okada, op. cit., p. 218, fig. 262.

11. Painting executed by Manṣūr in BM, MS. Stove Or.16.
Mentioned: Brown, P., *Indian Painting under the Mughals, A.D. 1550 to A.D. 1750,* Oxford, 1924, p. 196.

12. *Vīṇā*-player.
Inscription: *'Amal-i Manṣūr Naqqāsh* (Work of Manṣūr *Naqqāsh*). CECM.
Reproduced and described: Das, "Ustād Manṣūr", op. cit., pp. 33, 37, pl. 13, fig. 4; Das, *Mughal Painting during Jahangir's Time,* Calcutta, 1978, p. 196, pl. 52; Rogers, J.M., *Mughal Miniatures,* London, 1993, p. 62, fig. 38 (colour).
Exhibited at Asia House Academy of Arts, London (1947-8). See Ashton, Sir Leigh, ed., *The Art of India and Pakistan,* London, 1948, pp. 98, 159, no. 717.
Exhibited at Asia House Gallery, New York (1964). See Welch, S.C., *The Art of Mughal India, Painting and Precious Objects,* New York, 1963, pp. 164-5, pl. 18.
Exhibited at BM (1961). See *Exhibition of Islamic Art in India of the Sixteenth and Seventeenth Centuries,* London, 1961, no. 44.
Exhibited at World of Islam Festival (1976) at Prints and Drawings Gallery, BM. See Pinder-Wilson, R.H., *Paintings from the Muslim Courts of India,* London, 1976, pp. 60-1, no. 85.
A version of the present miniature is in J. Goldschmidt Collection, Berlin. Reproduced and described: Goetz, H., "Indian Miniatures in German Museums and Private Collections", *EAQ,* 2, 1930, p. 151, pl. 92,

fig. 5, where it is described as the portrait of Parśurām, *bīnkār-i Jahāngīr Shāhī* (a *vīnā*-player [servant] of King Jahāngīr). See also Okada, op. cit., p. 219, where a similar archaic and conventional portrait of a 'Prince with Falcon', attributed to Manṣūr, is noticed in the Musée Guimet, Paris (no reproduction).
Plate III.

13. Akbar, while hunting with a circle of beaters, punishes Ḥamīd Bhakkarī (second part of double-page illustration).
Inscription: *Ṭarḥ-i Miskīnā, 'amal-i Manṣūr* (Sketch by Miskīnā, colouring by Manṣūr).
Akb., VA, IS, 2-1896, no. 117, pl. 56.
Reproduced and described: Spink, Walter M. and Levine, Deborah, *Akbarnama: Catalogue,* New York, no date, pl. 11 and text; Hendley, T.H., "Sport in Indian Art", *JIAI,* 17, 1916, pl. 6(A); Irwin, J., "Treasures of Indian Art at the Victoria and Albert Museum", *Marg,* 1977, pl. 34; Goetz, *Bilderatlas zur Kulturgeschichte Indiens in der Grossmoghul-Ziet,* Berlin, no date, pl. 13, fig. 39; Zebrowski, Mark, "Three Indian Exhibitions", *OA,* 28 (3), 1982, p. 300, fig. 13; Sen, G., *Paintings from the Akbarnama,* New Delhi, 1984, pp. 99-103, pl. 39 (colour); Welch, *Imperial Mughal Painting,* New York, 1978, p. 68, pl. 14 (colour); Wellesz, E., *Akbar's Religious Thought Reflected in Mughal Painting,* Oxford, 1952, fig. 20.
Exhibited at Royal Academy of Arts, London (1947-8). See *Exhibition of Art chiefly from the Dominions India and Pakistan (2400 B.C. to 1947 A.D.),* London, 1947-8, no. 886, where the name of Sarwan is added to that of Manṣūr.
Exhibited at VA (1982). See Topsfield, A., "Paintings and the Arts of the Book" in *The Indian Heritage (Court Life and Arts under Mughal Rule),* London, 1982, p. 34, no. 32. See also Verma, *The Reign of Akbar: An Illustrated History,* Aligarh, 1991, p. 29, nos. 112-3.
Plate IV.

14. Ḥusain Qulī Khān Jahān presenting his prisoners to Akbar at Agra in 1573 (first part of double-page illustration).
Inscription: *Ṭarḥ-i Basāwan, 'amal-i Manṣūr.*
Akb., VA, IS, 2-1896, no. 117, pl. 112.
Reproduced and described; Staude, W., "Contribution á l'étude de Basawan", *RAA,* 8 (1), 1934, pl. 12, fig. 17; Staude, *Moghul Maler der Akbar Zeit,* Wien, 1935, fig. 33; Goetz, *Bilderatlas zur, etc.,* op. cit., pl. 27, fig. 74; Sen, op. cit., pp. 148-9, pl. 65 (colour); Das, "Mansur", op. cit., pp. 44-5, fig. l. See also Verma, *The Reign of Akbar, etc.,* op. cit., p. 42, no. 181.
Exhibited at World of Islam Festival (1976) at Prints and Drawings Gallery, BM. See Pinder-Wilson, op. cit., p. 47, no. 46.

15. Illumination of *sar-i lauḥ*.
Akb., BM, Or.12988, ff. 1b and 2.
Painted by Manṣūr (inscription not clear in the reproduction).
Reproduced and described: Losty, op. cit., pp. 93-4, pl. XXX (colour).

16. Timūr granting an audience.
Inscription: *'Amal-i Manṣūr Naqqāsh* (Work of Manṣūr *Naqqāsh*).
Akb., BM, Or.12988, f. 35b.
Mentioned: Titley, *Miniatures, etc.*, op. cit., p. 4; Verma, "Aspects of Paintings in the British Museum Manuscript of Akbarnama", *Lalit*, No. 27, 1993, p. 27. See also Verma, *The Reign of Akbar, etc.*, op. cit., p. 7, no. 18.

17. Capture of a fort by Humāyūn.
Inscription: *Ustād Manṣūr, chihra nāmī Narsing[h]* (Painted by *Ustād* Manṣūr, august portrait by Narsing[h]).
Akb., BM, Or.12988, f. 110a.
Mentioned: Titley, *Miniatures, etc.*, op. cit., p. 4; Verma, "Aspects of Paintings in the British Museum Manuscript of Akbarnama", op. cit., p. 28. See also Verma, *The Reign of Akbar, etc.*, op. cit., pp. 10-1, no. 27.

18. Humāyūn granting an audience.
Inscription: *Ustād Manṣūr.*
Akb., BM, Or.12988, f. 110b.
Reproduced and described: Brand, M. and Lowry, G.D., *Akbar's India: Art from the Mughal City of Victory*, New York, 1985, p. 141, no. 17, pl. on p. 49; Titley, *Miniatures, etc.*, op. cit., p. 4; Verma, "Aspects of Paintings in the British Museum Manuscript of Akbarnama", op. cit., p. 28. See also Verma, *The Reign of Akbar, etc.*, op. cit., p. 11, no. 28.
Exhibited at The Asia Society Galleries, New York (1985-6); Harvard University Art Museum, Cambridge (1986); Museum of Fine Arts, Boston (1986). See Brand and Lowry, op. cit., p. 140, no. 17.

19. Young Akbar presented to Humāyūn.
Inscription: *Manṣūr.*
Akb., BM, Or.12988, f. 112a.
Mentioned: Titley, *Miniatures, etc.*, op. cit., p. 4; Verma, "Aspects of Paintings in the British Museum Manuscript of Akbarnama", op. cit., p. 28. See also Verma, *The Reign of Akbar, etc.*, op. cit., p. 11, no. 29.

20. Coronation (?) portrait of Jahāngīr.
Painted by Manṣūr and Manohar (inscription not published).
IPM (A), OIUSSR, f. 3.
Reproduced and described: Ivanova, A.A., Akimushkin, O.F., Grek, T.V. and Gyuzalyana, P.L.T., *Albom Indiyskikh i Pyersidskikh Miniatyar XVI-XVIIIvv*, Moscow, 1962, Eng. text, p. 8, pl. 17; Wolf, R.E., *Islam and*

Muslim Art (trans. from French), London, 1960, fig. 558; Das, "Ustād Manṣūr", op. cit., p. 34; Das, *Mughal Painting, etc.*, op. cit., p. 196, 200n.

21. A red parrot.
Inscription: *Manṣūr.*
CMDu, MduL, no. 3.619, M.c.
Described: Stchoukine, I., *Les Miniatures Indiennes de l'Epoque des Grand Moghols du Musée du Louvre,* Paris, 1929, pp. 19-20, no. 19.

22. Two young partridges.
Inscription: *Manṣūr.*
CMDu, MduL, no. 3.619, P.a.
Described: Stchoukine, op. cit., p. 20, no. 22.

23 Two birds.
Inscription: *Manṣūr.*
CMDu, MduL, no. 3.619, Q.b.
Described: Stchoukine, op. cit., pp. 21-2, no. 25.

24. Youth clad in red dress.
Inscription: *Manṣūr.*
CMDu, MduL, no. 3.619.
Described: Stchoukine, op. cit., pp. 25-6, no. 35.

25. Pair of Indian *maināṣ.*
Inscription: *Manṣūr Naqqāsh* (partly erased).
SMS, no. AG1272.
Reproduced and described: Das, "Some more Manṣūr's drawings", *Lalit,* 18, 1977, p. 27, pl. 12, fig. 1; Das, "Mansur", op. cit., p. 49, fig. 14.
On the reverse, a painting ascribed to Mushfiq, dated A.H. 1012 (A.D. 1604).

26 Hornbill.
Inscription: *Kār-i Ustād Manṣūr* (Work of *Ustād* Manṣūr).
Kevorkian (A), MMA, no. 55.121.10.14v.
Reproduced and described: Dimand, M.S., *Indian Miniature Painting,* Milan, no date, pl. on p. 226; Dimand, *A Handbook of Muhammadan Art,* New York, 1944, pl. on p. 100 (top); Welch, S.C., Schimmel, A., Swietochowski, M.L. and Thackston, W., *The Emperors' Album, Images of Mughal India,* New York, 1987, p. 165, no. 41, colour pl. on p. 167; Das, *Mughal Painting, etc.*, op. cit., p. 198, pl. 61; Das, "Mansur", op. cit., p. 49, fig. 11; Okada, op. cit., fig. 254.
Exhibited at Asia Gallery, New York (1964). See Welch, op. cit., p. 168, no. 37, pl. 37.
Exhibited at MMA (1981). See *The Art of Islam,* New York, 1981, p. 296, no. 126, colour pl. on p. 297.

Margin-illumination is characteristic of Shāh Jahān's reign. For similar margin-paintings, see nos. 47 and 48 (below).
For a late version of this miniature, see no. 71 (below).
Fig. 9.

27. Turkey cock.
Inscription: (signature) *'Amal-i banda-i dargāh Manṣūr Nādir u'l 'Aṣr Jāhāngīr Shāhī* (Work of the slave of the court Manṣūr *Nādir u'l 'Aṣr* (Unequalled of the Age), [servant] of King Jahāngīr).
CW, VA, IM, no. 135 & A-1921.
Reproduced and described: Clarke, C.S., *Victoria and Albert Museum Drawings: Thirty Mogul Paintings from the School of Jahangir (17th century) and four Panels of Calligraphy in the Wantage Bequest,* London, 1922, no. 23, pl. 15; Alvi, M.A. and Rahman, A., *Jahangir the Naturalist,* New Delhi, 1968, pp. 63-4, pl. 12 (middle), where the painting is wrongly credited to Hermitage, Leningrad; Lawrence, G., *L'Art Des Indes, Miniatures Mogholes,* Paris, 1963, pl. 10 (colour); Rawson, Philip S., *Indian Painting,* London, 1961, p. 111, colour pl. on p. 115; Eletr, M. Raid, "Birds and Animals in Mughal Painting", *BCA,* I, 1959, p. 17, fig. 8; Swarup, Shanti, *The Arts and Crafts of India and Pakistan,* Bombay, 1957, pl. 71 (left); Swarup, *Flora and Fauna in Mughal Art,* Bombay, 1983, fig. 82; Hambly, G., *Cities of Mughal India (Delhi, Agra and Fatehpur Sikri),* Delhi, 1968, pl. 95 (colour); Gascoigne, B., *The Great Moghuls,* London, 1971, pl. on p. 132; Das, *Mughal Painting, etc.,* op. cit., pp. 148-9, pl. 57; Das, *Splendour of Mughal Painting,* Bombay, 1968, 34, pl. VII (colour); Topsfield, A., *An Introduction to Indian Court Painting,* p. 18, fig. 9; Jones, D. (ed.), *A Mirror of Princes, The Mughals and The Medici,* Bombay, 1987, p. 18, fig. 14 (colour); Okada, op. cit., p. 222, fig. 257.
Exhibited at World of Islam Festival (1976) at Prints and Drawings Gallery, BM. See Pinder-Wilson, op. cit., p. 64, no. 19.
Unascribed pictures of this bird are in SMS (no. 839) and Fitzwilliam Museum, Cambridge. Cf. Das, "Some more Manṣūr's drawings", op. cit., p. 31, 34n; also in his "The Turkey in Mughal and Amber-Jaipur Painting", *JIM,* 30-1, 1974-5, p. 65, where paintings are illustrated (figs. 3-5).
For a version of this study, see below no. 68.
Jahāngīr gives a description of this bird (*Tūzuk-i Jahāngīrī,* ed. text, p. 105, trans., I, p. 216).
Plate V.

28. Himalayan cheer pheasant.
Inscription: *'Amal-i Ustād Manṣūr* (Work of *Ustād* Manṣūr).
CW, VA, IM, no. 136 & A-1921.
Reproduced and described: Clarke, op. cit., no. 24, pl. 16; Alvi and Rahman, op. cit., pl. 14; Swarup, *The Arts and Crafts, etc.,* op. cit.,

pl. 66; Swarup, *Flora and Fauna, etc.*, fig. 84; Das, *Mughal Painting, etc.*, p. 149; Welch, *Indian Drawings and Painted Sketches (16th through 19th centuries)*, New York, 1976, p. 45, no. 14; Verma, S.P., "Mansur, the Master Painter of Jahangir's Epoch", *Roopa*, 53 (1-2), 1982, p. 8, pl. on p. 7; Okada, op. cit., p. 222, fig. 256.
Exhibited at Royal Academy of Arts, London (1947-8). See *Exhibition of Art, etc.*, op. cit., no. 1110.
A description of the pheasant is given in *Tūzuk-i Jahāngīrī*, ed. text, p. 105, trans., I, 216.
Almost identical pictures of this bird are in miniatures nos. 56, 57 and 58 (below).
Plate VI.

29. Elephant.
Painted by Manṣūr (inscription not published).
Folio of an unidentified album, KFM.
Described: Goetz, *Indian Miniatures, etc.*, op. cit., p. 153.

30. Illuminated *shamsa,* around the central seal of the Emperor Jahāngīr.
Opening page of a *Dīwān* of Anwarī.
Painted by Manṣūr *Naqqāsh* (inscription on the reverse is not published). Also bears autographs of Jahāngīr (AH 1026/AD 1617) and Shāh Jahān (AH 1037/AD 1628). Not published.
Dīwān (A), location not known.
Reproduced and described: See *Islamic Art from India,* London, 1980, p. 36, no. 62, frontispiece (colour); Losty, op. cit., p. 92.

31. Himalayan blue-throated barbet.
Inscription: *'Amal-i Nādir u'l 'Aṣr Ustād Manṣūr Naqqāsh* (Work of *Nādir u'l 'Aṣr Ustād* Manṣūr *Naqqāsh*).
CW, VA, IM, no. 137 & A-1921.
Reproduced and described: Clarke, op. cit., no. 22, pl. 15; Alvi and Rahman, op. cit., pl. 20; Gascoigne, op. cit., colour pl. on p. 62; Kübmaul, F., *Indische Kunst,* Hamburg, 1966, no. 227, pl. 58; Swarup, *Flora and Fauna, etc.*, op. cit., fig. 91.
Plate VII.

32. Picture of a prince.
Painted by Manṣūr (inscription not published).
CCJ.
Reproduced and described: See *Catalogue of the Loan Section of Indian Art,* Bombay, 1939, no. 33, pl. on p. 20.
See also Tandon, R.K., *Indian Miniature Painting, 16th through 19th Centuries,* Bangalore, 1981, p. 52, pl. 7 (colour), where a similar picture 'Prince smelling flower' is noticed. Also see Das, "Mansur", op. cit., p. 45, fig. 5, where he writes that present work is not quite as suc-

cessful: "The lines do not have the wiry vigour and the face is devoid of liveliness. But the mellow colour scheme, the presence of meticulously drawn flowering plants are typical of Mansur's style."

33. Portrait of Khwāja Kalān Beg, *wazīr.*
Inscription: (signature) *Shabīh-i Khwāja Kalān Beg Wazīr, kār-i banda-i dargāh Manṣūr* (Portrait of Khwāja Kalān Beg, *Wazīr,* work of the slave of the court, Manṣūr).
CW, VA, IM, no. 125-1925.
Reproduced and described: Clarke, op. cit., no. 25, pl. 17.
This noble remains unidentified. Clarke is of the opinion that this person may possibly be the Khwāja Kalān Beg who was defeated by Shāh Ṭahmāsp I of Persia (1524-76) at Qandahar, about 1539. See Moti Chandra, *The Technique of Mughal Painting,* Lucknow, 1946, p. 81, where it is described as a late work forged in the name of Manṣūr.

34. Falcon on its perch.
Inscription: *'Amal-i Ustād Manṣūr, Nādir u'l 'Aṣr* (Work of *Ustād* Manṣūr, *Nādir u'l 'Aṣr*).
CG, MFA, no. 14.683.
Reproduced and described: Coomaraswamy, A.K., "Mughal Paintings (Schools of Akbar and Jahangir)", *BMFA,* 16 (93), 1918, pl. on p. 2; Coomaraswamy, *Portfolio of Indian Art,* Boston, 1923, pl. 93; Coomaraswamy, "Les Miniatures Orientales de la collection Goloubew au Museum of Fine Arts de Boston", *AA,* 13, 1929; p. 84, pl. 77, fig. 132; Coomaraswamy, *Catalogue of Indian Collections in the Museum of Fine Arts, Boston, Pt. VI (Mughal Painting),* Boston, 1930, p. 51, pl. 41; Marteau, G. and Vever, H., *Miniatures Persanes exposees au Musée des Arts Decoratifs,* Paris, 1912, II, pl. 176; Gascoigne, op. cit., pl. on p. 133.
Jahāngīr gives a description of this bird. See *Tūzuk-i Jahāngīrī,* ed. text, pp. 280-l, trans., II, p. 108.
Plate VIII.

35. Indian bustard (*Charz-i bor*).
Inscription: (Jahāngīr's autograph) *Shabīh-i charz-i bor. 'Amal-i Nādir u'l 'Aṣrī Ustād Manṣūr hurrarah-i Jahāngīr Akbar Shāh. San 14* (Picture of the red bustard. Work of *Nādir u'l 'Aṣrī Ustād* Manṣūr. Written by Jahāngīr, son of Emperor Akbar, the 14th Regnal year/1619).
IM, no. R.31.
Reproduced and described: Ray, Niharranjan, *Mughal Court Painting,* Calcutta, 1975, pl. 15 (colour) and text; Das, "Ustād Manṣūr", op. cit., p. 36, pl. XII, fig. 2; Das, "Mughal Painting" in *History and Culture of the Indian People, VII: The Mughal Empire,* ed. R.C. Majumdar, Bombay, 1974, p. 815, pl. 64; Das, *Mughal Painting, etc.,* p. 197, pl. 56; Das, "Manṣūr", op. cit., p. 49, fig. 13.

For a late version of it, see miniature no. 67 (below).
Plate IX.

36 Black buck.
Inscription: *'Amal-i Ustād Manṣūr Jahāngīr Shāhī* (Work of *Ustād* Manṣūr [servant] of King Jahāngīr).
SML, n. 21.138.
Described: Patel, Seema, *Jahangir kala men prakartik itihas par bane laghu chitron ka vishleshanatmak addhayan* (in Hindi), Ph.D. thesis, Agra University, 1984 (unpublished), fig. 43 (colour).

37. Chameleon on a branch.
Inscription: *Ustād Manṣūr.*
RLWC, R.A. 967.
Reproduced and described: Blunt, W., "The Mughal painters of Natural history", *BUM,* 90 (529), 1948, p. 49, fig. 29; Welch, *Indian Drawings, etc.,* op. cit., p. 46, no. 15, frontispiece; Visser, H.F.E. "Tentoonstelling der kunst van India te Londen", *Phoenix,* 3 (1), 1948, p. 16, fig. 10; Okada, op. cit., p. 219, fig. 261.
Exhibited at Royal Academy of Arts, London (1947-8). See Ashton, op. cit., p. 160, no. 724, where the miniature is illustrated on pl. 135; *Exhibition of Art, etc.,* op. cit., no. 967.
Exhibited at MMA (India Festival Programme, 1985). See Welch, *Art and Culture (1300-1900),* New York, 1985, no. 143, colour pl. on p. 217, where it is observed that 'Mansur knew no rival — not even Abu'l Hasan — as a painter of wildlife'.

38. Tulip and butterfly.
Inscription: (signature) *'Amal-i banda-i dargāh Nādir u'l 'Aṣrī Manṣūr Naqqāsh Jahāngīr Shāhī* (Work of the slave of the court, *Nādir u'l 'Aṣrī* Manṣūr *Naqqāsh,* [servant] of King Jahāngīr). The *dāl* and *rā* of *Nādir u'l 'Aṣrī* and the *nūn* of *Naqqāsh* have been lost by overpainting.
MAU (Habibganj Collection), no. 60-l *Bā*(3).
Reproduced and described: Mehta, N.C., "Red lilies, a newly discovered Mansur", *Rupam,* 19-20, 1924, pp. 117-9, colour pl. facing p. 118; Mehta, *Studies in Indian Painting,* pp. 80-l, pl. 31; Dickinson, E.C., "The treatment of nature in Moghul paintings", *PQ,* 1951, p. 46, pl. on p. 43; Swarup, *5000 Years of Arts and Crafts in India and Pakistan,* Bombay, 1957, Pl. C (colour); Swarup, *Flora and Fauna, etc.,* op. cit., pp. 51-2, fig. 67; Skelton, R., "A Decorative Motif in Mughal Art" in Pal, Pratapaditya, ed., *Aspects of Indian Art,* Leiden, 1972, p. 151, 25n, fig. 90a, where he identifies the flower with Western Asiatic Tulip (*Tulipa montana*); Das, *Mughal Painting, etc.,* op. cit., p. 199, pl. 66; Verma, "Mansur, etc.", op. cit., p. 10; Rich, V., "Mughal floral paintings and its European sources", *OA,* XXXIII(2), 1987, p. 183; Koch, "Pietre Dure and other artistic contacts between the court of the

Mughals and that of the Medici", in Jones, op. cit., p. 49, fig. 29 (colour).

It would seem that the species of what Manṣūr was portraying is the *Tulipa clusiana.* For a description of *Tulipa clusiana,* see Bailey, L.H., *The Standard Cyclopedia of Horticulture,* New York, 1947, III, p. 3402; Bailey, *Manual of Cultivated Plants,* New York, 1947, p. 220. See Verma, "The Tulip (*ca.* 1621): A study of Mansur", *Huntia,* Pittsburgh, Vol. 9, No. 1, 1993, pp. 81-87, figs. 1-2.

The date of the illuminated panel as given by Mehta and also Swarup, as being AD 1544 seems unjustified. On the reverse of the miniature are the verses calligraphed in *nasta'līq,* signed by Mīr 'Alī.

Exhibited at MMA (India Festival Programme, 1985). See Welch, *Art and Culture, etc.,* op. cit., p. 220, no. 145, colour pl. on p. 220.

Plate XI.

39. Seven varieties of flowers.
Inscription: *'Amal-i Manṣūr Jahāngīr Shāhī* (Work of Manṣūr [servant] of King Jahāngīr).
Gulshan (A), IL, f. 103.
Reproduced and described: Atabai, Badri, *Fehrist-i Muraqqat-i Kitab Khana-i Saltanti,* Teheran, s. 1353, p. 355, colour pl. facing p. 354. See Gray, B. and Wilkinson, J.V.S., "Indian Paintings in a Persian Museum", *BUM,* 66, 1935, p. 177, where this miniature is referred to f. 53; Beach, "The Mughal painter Abu'l Hasan and some English sources for his style", *JWAG,* XXXVIII, 1975, p. 140.
Fig. 2.

40. Floricans with plant of pea family.
Inscription: *Manṣūr.*
IPM (A), OIUSSR, f. 81.
Reproduced and described: Ivanova, Akimushkin, Grek and Gyuzalyana, op. cit., p. 12, pl. 45; Alvi and Rahman, op. cit., pl. 24, where two other unascribed miniatures "Decorative spike" and "Spike of nerium with red poppy" from the same collection are attributed to Manṣūr (pls. 15-6); Swarup, *Flora and Fauna, etc.,* op. cit., fig. 93.

41. Branch of flowers with leaves.
Inscription: *Ustād Manṣūr Nādir u'l 'Aṣr.*
Naṣīruddīn (A), IL, pl. 80.
Described: Godard, Y.A., "Les marges du murakka Gulshan", *AEI,* I, 1936, p. 274.

42. Iris plant with a bird.
Inscription: *Manṣūr Nādir u'l 'Aṣr.*
Naṣīruddīn (A), IL, pl. 81.

Reproduced and described: Godard, op. cit., p. 274, fig. 113.
Plate XII.

43. Black bird.
Painted by Manṣūr (inscription not published).
Present location unknown.
Described: Beach, *The Grand Mogul Imperial Painting, etc.*, op. cit., p. 143.

44. *Mayanā* (a bird).
Painted by Manṣūr (inscription not published).
PWM.
Reproduced and described: Swarup, *Flora and Fauna, etc.*, op. cit., p. 59, fig. 86.

45. Dipper (*Sāj*).
Inscription: (signature) *'Amal-i banda-i dargāh Nādir u'l 'Aṣrī Manṣūr Naqqāsh Jahāngīr Shāhī* (Work of the slave of the court *Nādir u'l 'Aṣr* Manṣūr *Naqqāsh* [servant] of King Jahāngīr).
Kevorkian (A), MMA, 55.121.10.16r.
Reproduced and described: Alvi and Rahman, op. cit., pp. 78-9, pl. 16; Verma, "Mansur, etc.", op. cit., p. 8, pl. on p. 7; Beach, *The Grand Mogul Imperial Painting, etc.*, op. cit., p. 76; Swarup, *Flora and Fauna, etc.*, op. cit., fig. 88; Welch, Schimmel, Swietochowski and Thackston, op. cit., p. 172, no. 44, colour pl. on p. 174; Das, "Mansur", op. cit., pp. 45-6, fig. 7; Okada, op. cit., p. 222, fig. 255. See also, Ali, Salim, "The Mughal Emperors of India as Naturalists and Sportsmen", *JBNHS*, 32, Part I, 1927, pp. 43-4.
Jahāngīr gives a graphic description of this bird (*Tūzuk-i Jahāngīrī*, ed. text, p. 306, trans., II, p. 157).
Plate XIII.

46. King or Black vulture and Himalayan griffon.
Inscription: (signature) *'Amal-i banda-i dargāh Manṣūr Nādir u'l 'Aṣr Jahāngīr Shāhī* (Work of the slave of the court, Manṣūr *Nādir u'l 'Aṣr* [servant] of King Jahāngīr).
Kevorkian (A), MMA, 55.121.10.12v.
Reproduced and described: *Sotheby's Sale Catalogue*, 12 December 1929, lot 144; Alvi and Rahman, op. cit., pl. 19; Beach, *The Grand Mogul Imperial Painting, etc.*, op. cit., p. 76; Beach, *The Imperial Image, etc.*, op. cit., p. 186, fig. 31; Ettinghausen, R., *Islamic Painting (Indian)*, New York, no date, p. 40, pl. on p. 41; Das, *Mughal Painting, etc.*, op. cit., p. 198; Swarup, *Flora and Fauna, etc.*, op. cit., fig. 96; Welch, Schimmel, Swietochowski and Thackston, op. cit., p. 173, no. 45, colour pl. on p. 175; Okada, op. cit., p. 222, fig. 258.

For later versions of early nineteenth century, see below, nos. 63-5.
Plate XIV.

47. Zebra.
Inscription: (Jahāngīr's autograph) *Astarī ki Rūmiān az Ḥabsha bā hamrāhī-e Mīr Ja'far āwurda būdand. San 1030 Hijrī. Shabīh-i īn rā Nādir u'l 'Aṣrī Ustād Manṣūr kashīdah. San 16* (A zebra (lit. mule) which the Turks who came in company with Mīr Ja'far had brought from Abyssinia. Year 1030 of the Hijra (AD 1621). Painted by *Nādir u'l 'Aṣr Ustād* Manṣūr. 16th Regnal Year/1621).
Minto (A), VA, IM, no. 23-1925.
Reproduced and described: Archer, W.G., *Indian Miniatures,* Greenwich, 1960, pl. 26 and text; Stchoukine, *La Peinture Indienne a l'Epoque des Grand Moghols,* Paris, 1929, pl. 27; Eletr, op. cit., p. 17, fig. 11; Lee, Sharman, *A History of Far Eastern Art,* London, 1964, p. 217, pl. 272; Lawrence, G., *L'Art Des Indes, Miniatures Mogholes,* Paris, 1963, pl. 11 (colour); Alvi and Rahman, op. cit., pp. 34-6, pl. 6; Anand, Mulk Raj, *Album of Indian Painting,* New Delhi, 1973, pl. on p. 104; Du Ry, *Art of Islam,* New York, 1972, pl. on p. 250 (colour); Welch, *Imperial Mughal Painting,* op. cit., p. 93, pl. 27 (colour); Das, "Ustad Mansur", op. cit., p. 35; Das, *Mughal Painting, etc.,* op. cit., p. 197, pl. 60; Das, "Mansur", op. cit., p. 49, fig. 9; Okada, op. cit., pp. 219-22, fig. 260; Swarup, *Flora and Fauna, etc.,* op. cit., fig. 99; Jones, op. cit., p. 18, fig. 13 (colour); Verma, "Mansur, etc.", op. cit., p. 8, pl. on p. 5. See also Ali, op. cit., Part II, p. 273.
Jahāngīr gives a graphic description of this animal (*Tūzuk-i Jahāngīrī,* ed. text, p. 327, trans., II, p. 201).
Plate XV.

48. *Nīlgāi* (Blue-bull).
Inscription: (signature) *'Amal-i banda-i dargāh Manṣūr Nādir u'l 'Aṣr Jahāngīr Shāhī* (Work of the slave of the court, Manṣūr *Nādir u'l 'Aṣr* [servant] of King Jahāngīr).
Kevorkian (A), MMA, no. 55.121.10.13v.
Reproduced and described: Das, "Ustād Manṣūr", op. cit., p. 38, pl. 13, fig. 5; Beach, *The Grand Mogul Imperial Painting, etc.,* op. cit., p. 76; Welch, Schimmel, Swietochowski and Thackston, op. cit., pp. 178-81, no. 47, colour pl. on p. 179, where it has been pointed out that its border is similar to that of 'Zebra' (no. 47 above) and that it must have been painted by the same artist; and that both the miniatures *'Nīlgāi'* and 'Zebra' were probably once part of the same album; Das, "Mansur", op. cit., p. 49, fig. 10; Okada, op. cit., p. 222, fig. 259. An unascribed version of this painting is in CPCM. See no. 85 (below).

Exhibited at MMA (India Festival Programme, 1985). See Welch, *Art and Culture, etc.*, op. cit., pp. 216-7, no. 142, colour pl. on p. 214, where he notices, "Mansur's crystal-clear image of the calmly appealing animal emerges from an infinitude of fine brushstrokes, rarely covering the paper underneath and never failing to define bony structure, musculature, or textures. Flexibility of ears, wrinkled at the base; luster of eyes; hardness of horn and skull, felt through the short hairs covering the bridge of the nose; brushlike bristles of mane; and softness of tail—all are faithfully and knowingly conveyed."

49. Picture of a deer.
Painted by Manṣūr (inscription not published).
Kevorkian (A), MMA.
Reproduced and described: *Sotheby's Sale Catalogue,* 12 December 1929, lot 143; Das, "Ustad Mansur", op. cit., p. 35, 42n.

50. Goldfinch (*Murgh-i zarīn*).
Inscription: *'Amal-i Manṣūr Jahāngīr Shāhī* (Work of Manṣūr [servant] of King Jahāngīr).
NM, no. 50.14/27.
Reproduced and described: Alvi and Rahman, op. cit., pp. 83-4 pl. 17(A) (colour); Swarup, *Flora and Fauna, etc.,* op. cit., fig. 92; Brunel, Francis, *Splendour of Indian Miniatures,* New York, no date, no. 100, pl. 100.
Exhibited at NM (1981). See Khandalavala, K., *Islamic Heritage of India,* Delhi, 1981, p. 34, no. 160.
Plate XVI.

51. Pair of Tibetan cranes.
Inscription: *Kār-i Ustād Manṣūr Jahāngīr Shāhī* (Work of *Ustād* Manṣūr [servant] of King Jahāngīr).
CW, VA, IM, no. 122a-1921.
Reproduced and described: Clarke, op. cit., no. 20, pl. 14; Eletr, op. cit., p. 17, fig. 9; Havell, *The Art Heritage of India,* Bombay, 1964, p. 91, pl. 59; Saraswati, S.K., "Birds in Mughal Art", *Marg,* 2, 1948, fig. 4; Das, "Ustad Mansur", op. cit., p. 34; Das, *Mughal Painting, etc.,* op. cit., pp. 197, 242; Blunt, op. cit., fig. 27. He considers the painting to be "strongly Chinese in feeling", and "showing a vivacity not always to be found in his (Manṣūr's) work". He cites a very similar Ming painting of two cranes, reproduced in *The Pageant of Chinese Painting* (Otsuka-Kogeisha), Tokyo, 1936, pl. 475.
Identical line drawing of 'Pair of Tibetan cranes', preserved at VA (IM, no. 42-1925), would probably suggest that present drawing (figures of birds) is derived from Chinese example. For reproduction, see Das, "Mansur", op. cit., p. 47, fig. 8.

Exhibited at Royal Academy of Arts, London (1947-8). See Ashton, op. cit., p. 158, no. 714, where illustrated on pl. G (colour); *Exhibition of Art, etc.,* op. cit., no. 1095.
On the reverse of this painting is the portrait of 'Ināyat Khān, painted by Daulat *Kalān* (the Elder). Published: Clarke, op. cit., no. 26, pl. 17.
Plate XVII and Fig. 24.

52. Salt-water fish.
Inscription: (Jahāngīr's autograph) *Māhī-i 'Arabī, daryā-i shor. 'Amal-i Nādir u'l 'Aṣr Ustād Manṣūr* (Arabian fish of the sea. Work of *Nādir u'l 'Aṣr Ustād* Manṣūr).
RFM, no. 40.688.
Reproduced and described: Das, "Ustad Mansur", op. cit., pp. 34, 36, pl. 12, fig. 1; Verma, "Mansur, etc.", op. cit., pp. 8-9, pl. on p. 6.
Plate XVIII.

53. White-eye (a bird).
Inscription: (signature) *'Amal-i banda-i Ma(nṣūr) Jahāngīr Shāhī* (Work of the slave Ma(nṣūr), [servant] of King Jahāngīr). The words *"Jahāngīr Shāhī"* are written separately within the picture. Inscription is partly damaged.
CE, FMC.
Reproduced and described: Martin, F.R., *The Miniature Painting and Painters of Persia, India and Turkey,* London, 1912, II, pl. 219; *Sotheby's Sale Catalogue,* February, 1949, pl. 18; Beach, *The Grand Mogul Imperial Painting, etc.,* op. cit., p. 143; Das, "Ustad Mansur", op. cit., p. 38, no. 17; Das, "Mansur", op. cit., p. 49, fig. 12.
Another miniature (unascribed) mounted with it shows a buck (Martin, op. cit., II, pl. 217).
Exhibited at Royal Academy of Arts, London (1947-8). See Ashton, op. cit., p. 159, no. 176 ("fine animal drawing").

54. Squirrels on a chinar tree.
Inscriptions on the reverse side: (i) *Nādir uz Zamān* (i.e., Abū'l Ḥasan); (ii) *Nādir u'l 'Aṣr* (i.e., Manṣūr). It may thus be a joint work of Abū'l Ḥasan and Manṣūr
Johnson (A), IOL, f. 30.
Reproduced and described: Brown, op. cit., pl. 15; Wilkinson, *Mughal Painting,* London, pl. 6 (colour) and text; Archer, op. cit., pl. 25 (colour) and text; Chaitanya, K., *A History of Indian Painting: Manuscript, Moghul and Deccani Traditions,* New Delhi, 1979, fig. 54; Heath, L., *Examples of Indian Art at the British Empire Exhibition, 1924,* London, 1925, frontispiece; Dickinson, E.C., "The treatment of nature in Moghul paintings", *PQ,* August 1951, pl. on p. 49; Smith, op. cit.,

pl. 152; Blunt, op. cit., p. 50; Das, "Ustad Mansur", op. cit., p. 39, no. 17; Das, *Mughal Painting, etc.,* op. cit., p. 199, pl. 67, where attributed to Manṣūr; Das, "Mansur", op. cit., pp. 46-7, where he observes the attribution doubtful; Beach, *The Grand Mogul Imperial Painting, etc.,* op. cit., p. 90; Beach, "The Mughal painter Abu'l Hasan, etc.", op. cit., p. 27, fig. 25; Godden, R., *Gulbadan (Portrait of Rose Princess),* New York, 1980, pl. on p. 147 (colour); Swarup, *Flora and Fauna, etc.,* op. cit., fig. 77; Welch, *Imperial Mughal Painting,* op. cit., p. 88, pl. 25 (colour).

For a detailed description, see Falk, Toby and Archer, Mildred, *Indian Miniatures in the India Office Library,* London, 1981, pp. 59-60, no. 34, pl. on p. 369, colour pl. no. 4. They write, "...the present picture was built up from European sources which have not been identified. The hunter himself is not an Indian figure, but would be quite at home in a sixteenth century engraving by Pieter Brueghel the Elder, or a hunting scene by Phillip Galle after J. vander Straat."

Falk and Archer think that the inscription refers to Abū'l Ḥasan only, here *'Nādir uz Zamān'* with the supporting honorific *'Nādir u'l 'Aṣr'*.

Inscription being recorded on the reverse side is of doubtful genuineness. See Khandalavala, "Mughal Painting: Considerations and Reconsiderations", *Lalit,* No. 27, 1993, pp. 50-1, where he disregards the opinions of Das, Falk and Archer, and considers it a work of Manṣūr.

Exhibited at Royal Academy of Arts, London (1947-8). See Ashton, op. cit., p. 163, no. 737, where Gray names Abū'l Ḥasan only as the artist; *Exhibition of Art, etc.,* op. cit., no. 971.

Exhibited at BM (1961). See *Exhibition of Islamic Art, etc.,* op. cit., no. 43.

Exhibited at Asia House Gallery, New York (1964). See Welch, *The Art of Mughal India, etc.,* op. cit., p. 74, pl. 35 (colour).

Exhibited at World of Islam Festival (1976) at Prints and Drawings Gallery, BM. See Pinder-Wilson, op. cit., p. 65, no. 100, where the inscription given on the reverse side of the miniature is inaccurately represented (Abū'l Ḥasan, Nādir u'l 'Aṣr).

Exhibited at MMA (India Festival Programme, 1985). See Welch, *Art and Culture, etc.,* op. cit., p. 215, no. 141.

(2) Suggested Attributions and Forged Miniatures

55. Falcon on perch.

Inscription: (signature [?]) *'Amal-i Nādir u'l 'Aṣr, Jahāngīr Shāhī* (Work of *Nādir u'l 'Aṣr* [servant] of King Jahāngīr). The words are inscribed on the bird-stand. The *nasta'līq* characters are not of high quality.

Other inscriptions in Rajasthani (Devanagri character): *Jahāngīr Pātshāh*

(Emperor Jahāngīr); *Baharī* (Falcon); *Utam* (Good) were apparently written over the painting later.
SMS, no. AG824.
Reproduced and described: Das, "Some more Manṣūr's drawings", *Lalit,* 18, 1977, pp. 27-8, pl. 12, fig. 2; Das, *Treasures of Indian Art,* Series 4, pl. 4 (colour); Das, "Mansur", op. cit., p. 45, pl. on p. 39.
On the reverse there is an unascribed miniature: "Reception of Jahāngīr and Shāh Jahān by Nūr Jahān [?]". Das takes Nūr Jahān's portrait to be authentic ("Some more Manṣūr's drawings", op. cit., p. 29, 18n). Unpublished.
Fig. 3.

56. Himalayan cheer pheasant.
Inscription: *'Amal-i Ustād Manṣūr* (Work of *Ustād* Manṣūr).
SMS, no. AG834.
Reproduced and described: Das, "Some more Manṣūr's drawings", op. cit., pp. 29-30, pl. 13, fig. 3; Das, "Mansur", op. cit., p. 51, fig. 15.
Note: An early nineteenth century copy of Manṣūr's original in Wantage Collection. See miniature no. 28 (above). On the reverse, there is a miniature "Shaikh Salīm Chistī seated with a *faqīr",* ascribed to Manohar. Unpublished.
Fig. 4.

57. Himalayan cheer pheasant.
No inscription.
CMBR.
Reproduced and described: Brown, op. cit., pl. 54, where attributed to Manṣūr. See Beach, *The Grand Mogul Imperial Painting, etc.,* op. cit., p. 171, pl. on p. 173, where Edwin Binney 3rd suggests its attribution to Payāg and the period is suggested as early Shāh Jahān's reign (1630-40). Other reproductions: Ali, op. cit., pp. 53-4, pl. facing p. 53; Saraswati, op. cit., fig. 5; Swarup, *Flora and Fauna, etc.,* op. cit., fig. 85; Das, *Mughal Painting, etc.,* op. cit., pp. 149-50 (no reproduction); Das, *Splendour of Mughal Painting,* op. cit., p. 50, pl. XVI (colour).
Exhibited at Colnaghi, London (1976). See Robinson, B.W., ed., *Persian and Mughal Art,* London, 1976, p. 184, no. 100, where miniature is reproduced on p. 210.
Note: A late version of Manṣūr's miniature no. 28 (above).
Fig. 5.

58. Himalayan cheer pheasant.
No inscription.
CBQ.
Reproduced and described: Martin, op. cit., II, p. 12, pl. 220, where attributed to Manṣūr.

Note: An early nineteenth century version of Manṣūr's miniature no. 28 (above).
Fig. 6.

59. Indian red-wattled lapwing.
Inscription: (signature [?]) *'Amal-i banda-i dargāh Āqā Sāhibuzzaman* (Work of the slave of the court, Āqā Sāhibuzzamān (or, the court of the Lord, Master of the Age).
CW, VA, IM, no. 126a-1921.
Reproduced and described: Clarke, op. cit., no. 21, pl. 14; Swarup, *Flora and Fauna, etc.,* op. cit., fig. 94; Das, *Mughal Painting, etc.,* op. cit., p. 198 (no reproduction).
Clarke's identification of the painter with Manṣūr is very dubious.
On the reverse, a picture by Farrukh Beg: "Accident in the life of Khwāja Jahān Dost Muḥammad". Reproduced: Clarke, op. cit., no. 5, pl. 4. An early nineteenth century copy of Āqā Riẓā's miniature in *Kevorkian (A),* MMA, no. 55.121.10.20v. See Welch, Schimmel, Swietochowski and Thackston, op. cit., pp. 190-3, no. 53 & 2n, colour pl. on p. 191.

60. Picture of a falconer.
No inscription.
CANH.
Reproduced and described: Das, "Ustad Mansur", op. cit., pp. 33-4, where attributed to Manṣūr; Das, *Mughal Painting, etc.,* op. cit., p. 197; Khandalavala, "Some problems of Mughal painting", *Lalit,* 11, 1965, p. 12, fig. E. Khandalavala thinks it a copy prepared at Delhi in late nineteenth century. See also Pratapaditya Pal, *Indian Painting, A Catalogue of the Los Angeles County Museum of Art Collection,* California, 1993, p. 244, no. 64, where the present work is suggested to have been a most probable work of Abū'l Ḥasan or Manṣūr.
Exhibited at Asia House Gallery, New York (1964). See Welch, *The Art of Mughal India, etc.,* op. cit., p. 31, pl. 19.
Exhibited at VA (1982). Topsfield, "Paintings and the Arts of the Book" in *The Indian Heritage (Court Life and Arts under Mughal Rule),* London, 1982, p. 35, no. 34.

61. Bird with long feet.
No inscription.
Naṣīruddīn (A), IL, pl. 76.
Reproduced and described: Godard, op. cit., p. 271, fig. 112, where it is suggested to have been a work of Manṣūr.

62. *Simurgh* and the army of the birds.
No inscription.
Anwār, BM, Add.18579, no. 12.
Reproduced and described: Wilkinson, J.V.S., *Lights of Canopus:*

Anwar-i Suhaili, London, 1929, p. 16, pl. 12 (colour), where attributed to Manṣūr. Other miniatures (nos. 11 and 36) in the same MS. are also attributed to Manṣūr.

63. King vulture.
Inscription: (signature [?]) *'Amal-i banda-i dargāh Manṣūr Nādir u'l 'Aṣr Jahāngīr Shāhī* (Work of the slave of the court Manṣūr *Nādir u'l 'Aṣr* [servant] of King Jahāngīr).
Kevorkian (A), MMA, no. 55.121.10.25v.
Reproduced and described: Welch, Schimmel, Swietochowski and Thackston, op. cit., p. 262, no. 89, pl. on p. 263, where it is described as an early nineteenth century copy of Manṣūr's original with forged signature of the artist. See miniature no. 46 (above).
Fig. 11.

64. Himalayan griffon.
Inscription: (signature [?]) *Kār-i banda-i dargāh Manṣūr Jahāngīr Shāhī* (Work of the slave of the court Manṣūr [servant] of King Jahāngīr).
Kevorkian (A), FGA, no. 48.19a.
Reproduced and described: Alvi and Rahman, op. cit., pl. 18; Beach, *The Grand Mogul Imperial Painting, etc.,* op. cit., p. 76; Beach, *The Imperial Image, etc.,* op. cit., p. 186, where date of the miniature is given early nineteenth century; Welch, Schimmel, Swietochowski and Thackston, op. cit., p. 249, no. 82, pl. on p. 248, where it is described to have been copied from a picture of this bird in CBL (see below no. 65).
Present miniature is identical with Manṣūr's original (miniature no. 46 (above), bird 'Himalayan griffon depicted on top right) with a slight variation in the details of wings.
Fig. 13.

65. Himalayan griffon perched on rock.
No inscription.
CBL (A), no. 10.
Reproduced and described: Arnold and Wilkinson, op. cit., I, p. 45, III, pl. 80 (colour), where attributed to Manṣūr; Blunt, op. cit., p. 49, fig. 28; Saraswati, op. cit., fig. 6; Swarup, *Flora and Fauna, etc.,* op. cit., fig. 95; Irwin, J., "The Heritage of Art in India: (3) The Mughal Period", *Studio,* 135, 1948, p. 42, pl. 9.
Exhibited at Royal Academy of Arts, London (1947-8). See Ashton, op. cit., p. 160, no. 723(961); *Exhibition of Art, etc.,* op. cit., no. 961.
Note: An early nineteenth century copy. Compare with miniatures nos. 46 and 64 (above).
Fig. 14.

66. Jungle fowl.
No inscription.
G.C. Sturt, Esq. Collection.
Reproduced and described: Wilkinson, *Mughal Painting,* London, 1948, p. 24, colour pl. on p. 3, where it is described as the work of Manṣūr. See also Welch, Schimmel, Swietochowski and Thackston, op. cit., p. 261, no. 88; Rogers, op. cit., fig. 63, p. 97. See below, no. 81.
Fig. 20.

67. Indian bustard (*Charz-i bor*).
No inscription.
Dārā Shukoh (A), IOL, no. 68, f. 8.
Reproduced and described: Falk and Archer, op. cit., p. 74, no. 68, f. 8, pl. on p. 381; Smith, op. cit., p. 476, pl. 120, where it is tentatively attributed to Manṣūr.
Note: Early nineteenth century version of Manṣūr's miniature no. 35, above.
Fig. 7.

68. Turkey cock.
No inscription.
IM, no. R.210.
Reproduced and described: Ashton, op. cit., pp. 159-60, no. 722, where Gray attributes it to Manṣūr. Other reproductions: Havell, *Indian Sculpture and Painting,* London, 1908, p. 214, pl. 60 (colour); Havell, *The Art Heritage, etc.,* op. cit., pp. 90-1, pl. 85(A); Brown, op. cit., p. 139, pl. 53; Ray, op. cit., pl. 12 (colour); Dickinson, op. cit., p. 46, pl. on p. 47 (below, right); Swarup, *Flora and Fauna, etc.,* op. cit., fig. 83; Das, "The Turkey in Mughal and Amber-Jaipur Painting", op. cit., p. 65; Das, *Mughal Painting, etc.,* op. cit., p. 149 (no reproduction); Anand, op. cit., pl. on p. 104.
Another unascribed copy of this miniature is noticed by Das in SMS, no. AG839. See Das, "The Turkey in Mughal and Amber-Jaipur Painting", op. cit., p. 31, no. 34, where he writes: "The copy is made by some competent artist whose name is not written. With the exception of the minute inscription written in the Victoria and Albert Museum original one can hardly find any difference in the two versions of Jaipur (SMS, no. AG839) and Calcutta"; Das, *Splendour of Mughal Painting,* p. 34; also in his "Mansur", op. cit., p. 51, fig. 16.
Fig. 23.
Exhibited at Royal Academy of Arts, London (1947-8). See Ashton, op. cit., pp. 159-60, no. 722(1197).
Exhibited at NM (1981). See Khandalavala, K., *Islamic Heritage of India,* Delhi, 1981, p. 34, no. 163.
Note: A late copy of Manṣūr's miniature no. 27, above.

69. Two ducks.
No inscription.
MFA (Ross Collection), no. 17.2654.
Reproduced and described: Coomaraswamy, *Portfolio of Indian Art,* op. cit., pl. 95, where attributed to Manṣūr; Coomaraswamy, *Catalogue of Indian Collections, etc.,* op. cit., p. 52, pl. 43.

70. Flower painting.
No inscription.
CGCNS.
Described: Beach, *The Grand Mogul Imperial Painting, etc.,* op. cit., p. 143, where included in the list of Manṣūr's work.
Exhibited at Royal Academy of Arts, London (1947-8). See Ashton, op. cit., p. 155, no. 696(924); *Exhibition of Art, etc.,* op. cit., no. 924.

71. Hornbill.
No inscription.
CGCNS.
Reproduced: Alvi and Rahman, op. cit., pl. XVIIB (colour); Swarup, *Flora and Fauna, etc.,* op. cit., fig. 90. Here the present miniature is wrongly referred to MMA. See Rogers, J.M., *Mughal Miniatures,* London, 1993, fig. 6.
Exhibited at Royal Academy of Arts, London (1947-8). See Ashton, op. cit., p. 159, no. 718(911); *Exhibition of Art, etc.,* op. cit., no. 911.
Exhibited at BM (1980). See *Princely Paintings from Mughal India,* London, 1980, p. 17, no. 47, pl. facing p. 17 and frontispiece (colour), where its attribution is suggested to Manṣūr.
Note: An early nineteenth century copy. Compare with miniature no. 26 (above).
Fig. 10.

72. Two deer in landscape.
Inscription: *Kār-i Manṣūr Jahāngīr Shāhī* (Work of Manṣūr [servant] of King Jahāngīr).
Kevorkian (A), FGA, no. 39.48a.
Reproduced and described: Beach, *The Grand Mogul Imperial Painting, etc.,* op. cit., p. 76; Beach, *The Imperial Image, etc.,* op. cit., p. 188, Cat. no. 18e recto, pl. on p. 189, detail on p. 179, where date of the miniature is given early nineteenth century. He describes it as a late version of a painting by Manṣūr. See also Welch, Schimmel, Swietochowski and Thackston, op. cit., p. 245, no. 80, pl. on p. 244, where it is observed that similar pictures were painted at Alwar (Rajasthan) during the early nineteenth century by emigre Delhi artists. Here the inscription is misread as "Work (*Kar*) of Mansur-i Jahangiri".
Fig. 12.

73. Spotted forktail.
Inscription: (signature [?]) *Taswīr-i jānwa[r] abalaq, banda-i dargāh O[U]stād Manṣūr Jahāngīr Shāhī* (Picture of a piebald bird. Slave of the court *Ustād* Manṣūr [servant] of King Jahāngīr).
Kevorkian (A), FGA, no. 39.46b.
Reproduced and described: Beach, *The Grand Mogul Imperial Painting, etc.,* op. cit., p. 92; Beach, *The Imperial Image, etc.,* op. cit., p. 189, fig. 33, where it is described as an early nineteenth century copy; Welch, Schimmel, Swietochowski and Thackston, op. cit., p. 254, no. 85, pl. on p. 255, where it is observed: "All that was lively and lovingly observed in Abu'l Hasan's study has become flaccid and weak in this lackluster rehash."
Note: An early nineteenth century copy with faulty inscription with forged signature of Manṣūr.
Compare with the picture of this bird (c. 1620), painted by Abū'l Ḥasan (*Kevorkian (A),* MMA, 55.121.10.15r). Published: Alvi and Rahman, op. cit., pl. 22; Welch, Schimmel, Swietochowski and Thackston, op. cit., pp. 164-5, no. 40, colour pl. on p. 166. See Fig. 15.
On the reverse of this miniature there is a painting 'Shāh Jahān riding on a horse' (FGA, no. 39.46a) ascribed to Govardhan (an early nineteenth century copy of Payāg's work in *Kevorkian (A),* MMA, 55.221.10.21v). See Welch, Schimmel, Swietochowski and Thackston, op. cit., p. 202, no. 59, pl. on p. 203, and no. 86, pl. on p. 256.
Fig. 16.

74. Assembly of pigeons round a dovecote.
Inscription: *'Amal-i Manṣūr Naqqāsh* (Work of Manṣūr *Naqqāsh*).
Private Collection.
Reproduced and described: Falk, Toby, Digby, Simon and Goedhuis, Michael, *Paintings from Mughal India,* London, no date, p. 48, no. 22, colour pl. on p. 49, where attribution is accepted as doubtful.
Note: A late eighteenth century painting forged in the name of Manṣūr.
Fig. 17.

75. Peafowl.
No inscription.
CMBR.
Reproduced and described: Brown, op. cit., pl. 23; Saraswati, op. cit., fig. 8; Dickinson, op. cit., pl. on p. 48 (below, left); Ali, op. cit., pp. 51-3, pl. facing p. 52; Swarup, *Flora and Fauna, etc.,* op. cit., fig. 97; Koch, op. cit., p. 49, fig. 28 (colour); Welch, *Imperial Mughal Painting,* op. cit., p. 91, pl. 26 (colour); Beach, *The Grand Mogul Imperial*

Painting, etc., op. cit., p. 140, pl. on p. 141, where attributed to Manṣūr. Exhibited at Colnaghi, London (1976). See Robinson, op. cit., p. 184, no. 99, where miniature is reproduced on p. 185 (colour plate). Exhibited at MMA (India Festival Programme, 1985). See Welch, *Art and Culture, etc.,* op. cit., no. 144, colour pl. on p. 218, detail on p. 219. Welch writes: "The peacock's forward rush and the peahen's split-second turn are recorded with lightning speed. The unnervingly palpable bone, muscle, and sinew of their legs are accelerated by smoky grays scumbled over Mansur's corrected underdrawing."

76. Zebra.
No inscription.
CG, MFA, no. 14.659.
Reproduced and described: Marteau and Vever, op. cit., II, no. 256, pl. 177; Coomaraswamy, "Mughal Painting (Schools of Akbar and Jahangir)", *BMFA,* 16(93), 1918, pl. on p. 7; Coomaraswamy, *Portfolio of Indian Art,* op. cit., pl. 94(A), where attributed to Manṣūr; Coomaraswamy, "Les Miniatures Orientales de la collection Goloubew au Museum of Fine Arts de Boston", *AA,* 13, 1929, p. 84, pl. 78, fig. 133; Coomaraswamy, *Catalogue of Indian Collections, etc.,* op. cit., p. 51, pl. 42. See also *Islamic Art from India,* London, 1980, p. 37, no. 70, pl. on p. 47.

77. Ram.
No inscription.
CRC, MFA, no. 17.3104.
Reproduced and described: Coomaraswamy, *Portfolio of Indian Art,* op. cit., pl. 94(B), where attributed to Manṣūr; Coomaraswamy, *Catalogue of Indian Collections, etc.,* op. cit., p. 51, pl. 42.

78. Wounded buck.
No inscription.
FAM.
Reproduced and described: Welch and Beach, *Gods, Thrones and Peacocks,* New York, 1965, pp. 35, 117, pl. 10, where attributed to Manṣūr; Welch, "Mughal and Deccani miniature paintings from a Private Collection", *AOS,* 5, 1963, p. 228, no. 14, fig. 15; Beach, *The Grand Mogul Imperial Painting, etc.,* op. cit., p. 143; Welch, *A Flower from Every Meadow, Indian Paintings from American Collections,* New York, 1973, no. 61, now attributing it to Abū'l Ḥasan.

79. A pair of Rosy Pastors.
No inscription.
Jahāngīr (A), SLB, f. 17b.
Reproduced and described: Kühnel, E. and Goetz, H., *Indian Book Painting,* London, 1926, pp. 6, 56, pl. 10 (colour), where attributed to

Manṣūr; Goetz, "Indian miniatures in German Museums and Private Collections", *EAQ*, 2, 1930, p. 151; Dimand, M.S., *A Guide to an Exhibition of Islamic Miniature Painting and Book Illumination,* New York, 1933-4, frontispiece (colour); Dimand, "An exhibition of Islamic and Indian Painting", *BMMA,* 14, 1955, p. 18, pl. 5; Swarup, *Flora and Fauna, etc.,* op. cit., fig. 34; Das, "Ustad Mansur", op. cit., p. 39, where the birds are described as "Rosy Pastors"; Chaitanya, op. cit., fig. 55. See also Dickinson, op. cit., pl. on p. 43 (above), where the miniature is wrongly traced to *Dārā Shukoh Album* (IOL).
Margin-painting: flower sprays, painted in gold, interspersed with cross-shaped medallions in each of which is a bird (Kühnel and Goetz, op. cit., p. 6, no reproduction).

80. A fantastic bird.
Inscription: (signature [?]) *"Īn murgh rā būqalamūn mī goyand. Kār-i banda-i dargāh Manṣūr Jahāngīr Shāhī"* ('This bird is called *būqalamūn* [?]. Work of the slave of the court Manṣūr [servant] of King Jahāngīr').
Kevorkian (A), MMA, no. 55.121.10.26r.
Reproduced and described: Beach, *The Grand Mogul Imperial Painting, etc.,* op. cit., p. 76; Welch, Schimmel, Swietochowski and Thackston, p. 269, no. 92, pl. on p. 268, where it is observed that this bird is unknown to ornithologists, and the present miniature is an early nineteenth century work with forged signature of Manṣūr.
Fig. 18.

81. Jungle fowl.
Inscription: (signature [?]) *"Banda-i dargāh Ustād Manṣūr Nādir u'l 'Aṣr Jahāngīr Shāhī"* ('Slave of the court *Ustād* Manṣūr *Nādir u'l 'Aṣr* [servant] of King Jahāngīr').
Kevorkian (A), MMA, no. 55.121.10.27r.
Reproduced and described: Welch, Schimmel, Swietochowski and Thackston, op. cit., p. 261, no. 88, p. 260, where it is described as an early nineteenth century work with forged signature of Manṣūr. Compare with no. 66 (above).
Fig. 19.

82. Portrait of Ḥājjī Ḥusain Bukhārī.
Inscription: *Shabīh-i Ḥājjī Ḥusain Bukhārī, 'amal-i Ustād Manṣūr* (Portrait of Ḥājjī Ḥusain Bukhārī, work of *Ustād* Manṣūr).
Kevorkian (A), MMA, no. 55.121.10.28r.
Reproduced and described: Dimand, "An Exhibition of Islamic and Indian Painting", op. cit., pl. on p. 98; Beach, *The Grand Mogul Imperial Painting, etc.,* op. cit., p. 76; Welch, Schimmel, Swietochowski and Thackston, op. cit., p. 273, no. 94, pl. on p. 272, where it is described as an early nineteenth century work, forged in the name of Manṣūr.

83. Falcon on perch.
Inscription: *'Amal-i Ustād* (Work of *Ustād*).
PWM, no. 15.302.
Reproduced and described: Krishnadasa and Kabir, op. cit., pl. 4 and text, where it is said to be the work of Manṣūr. Other reproductions: Chandra, M., *Indian Art,* Bombay, 1964, pl. 35 (colour); Chandra, M., *A Handbook of the Indian Art Collection in the Prince of Wales Museum of Western India, Bombay,* Bombay, no date, fig. 11; Ali, op. cit., pl. between pages 52-3; Gorakshkar, S. (ed.), *Animal in Indian Art,* Bombay, 1979, p. 41, no. 331, fig. 331.

84. Black buck.
No inscription.
SMS, no. 1303.
Reproduced and described: Das, "Some more Manṣūr's drawings", op. cit., pp. 30-1, pl. 13, fig. 4, where attributed to Manṣūr.

85. *Nīlgāi* (Blue-bull).
No inscription.
CPCM.
Reproduced and described: Ashton, op. cit., p. 159, no. 719, pl. on p. 139, where attributed to Manṣūr. Other reproductions: Michell, G., *In the Image of Man (The Indian Perception of Universe through 200 years of Painting and Sculpture),* Delhi, 1982, no. 38, fig. on p. 105; Leach, L., "Painting" in Doshi, S. (ed.), *Pageant of Indian Art,* Bombay, 1983, fig. 21.
Exhibited at Royal Academy of Arts, London (1947-8). See Ashton, op. cit., p. 159, no. 719(964).

86. Black buck.
No inscription.
Kevorkian (A), MMA, no. 55.121.10.17r.
Reproduced and described: Alvi and Rahman, op. cit., pl. 4, where attributed to Manṣūr. See Welch, Schimmel, Swietochowski and Thackston, op. cit., p. 185, no. 50, colour pl. on p. 184, where its attribution is suggested to Manohar.

87. Flamingoes.
No inscription.
CCJ.
Reproduced and described: Khandalavala, K. and Chandra, M., *Miniatures and Sculptures, Collection of Sir Cowasji Jehangir,* Bombay, 1965, p. 18, no. 20, fig. 20; Alvi and Rahman, op. cit., pl. 15 (colour); Das, "Ustad Mansur", op. cit., p. 39, where attributed to Manṣūr.

88. Siberian crane.
No inscription.
IM, no. R.32.
Reproduced and described: Smith, op. cit., p. 475; Havell, *Indian Sculpture and Painting,* op. cit., pl. 61; Das, *Mughal Painting, etc.,* op. cit., pp. 197-8, pl. 58, where attributed to Manṣūr.

89. Pictures of the dodo, tragopan, Sumatran loriquet, ducks and partridges.
IPM (A), OIUSSR, f. 80.
Reproduced and described: Ivanova, Akimushkin, Grek and Gyuzalyana, op. cit., p. 12, pl. 47 (colour); Alvi and Rahman, op. cit., pp. 15-7, pl. 2 (colour); Swarup, *Flora and Fauna, etc.,* op. cit., fig. 98; Das, "Ustad Mansur", op. cit., p. 37, where attributed to Manṣūr and the period is suggested as early Shāh Jahān's reign.
Fig. 1.

90. Study of mountain goats.
No inscription.
Private Collection.
Reproduced and described: Pal, Pratapaditya, *Court Painting of India, 16th-19th Centuries,* New York, 1983, p. 51, pl. on p. 156, where attributed to Manṣūr.

91. A pair of wild fowls.
No inscription.
Private Collection.
Reproduced and described: Pal, op. cit., p. 52, pl. on p. 158, where attributed to Manṣūr.

92. Partridges.
No inscription.
CHV.
Reproduced and described: Marteau and Vever, op. cit., II, no. 257, pl. 177, where attributed to Manṣūr.

93. Partridge.
No inscription.
CHV.
Reproduced and described: Marteau and Vever, op. cit., II, no. 259, pl. 178, where attributed to Manṣūr.

94. Falcon on its perch.
Inscription: *"Jahāngīr Shāhī, 'amal-i banda-i dargāh Nādir u'l 'Aṣr Manṣūr"* ('Work of the slave of court *Nādir u'l 'Aṣr* Manṣūr [servant] of King Jahāngīr').
BM, 1969.3-17.02.

Reproduced and described: Rogers, J.M., *Mughal Miniatures,* London, 1993, fig. 70, pp. 102-3, where it is described as a later copy of Manṣūr's original.

95. Hen and chicks (painting on cloth).
BM, 1953.2-104.02.
Reproduced and described: Pinder-Wilson, op. cit., no. 99, p. 65, colour plate facing p. 52, where an artist's name is not noticed. However, Rogers, op. cit., p. 97, no. 65, notices an inscription (not clear in the colour reproduction) on it which reads *"Manṣūr Nādir u'l 'Aṣr".*

GLOSSARY

'Amal	: Work, (especially) execution of painting, colouring.
Banda	: Slave, servant; used by painters in their signatures.
Banda-i dargāh	: Slave of the court (person in service of the Emperor); used by painters in their signatures.
Charba	: Thin transparent sheet used for tracing, drawing.
Chihra	: Face, portrait.
Chihra nāmī	: Illustrious face; portrait of Emperor or prince; august portrait.
Dārogha	: Superintendent.
Darwesh	: A mystic, a member of a sufic order, whence English 'dervish'.
Ḥājjī	: One who has performed the pilgrimage to Mecca (*ḥajj*).
Ḥāshiya	: Border, margin.
Jahāngīr Shāhī	: (Noble, court-servant) of King Jahāngīr.
Kār	: Work (interchangeable with '*amal*).
Manṣab	: Rank in the Mughal service.
Manṣabdār	: Holder of a rank (*manṣab*) in the Mughal service.
Muraqqa'	: Album (containing miniatures and specimens of calligraphy).
Muṣauwir	: Painter; artist.
Muẕaḥḥib	: Gilder.
Naqqāsh	: Carver; sculptor; engraver; gilder; limner, painter.
Nasta'līq	: Style of Persian writing, with rounded letters.
Pargana	: A division of a province.
Qalam	: Pen; style of writing or painting.
Rangāmezī	: Colouring; colour-mixing.
Rubāb	: Stringed musical instrument, played with a spectrum.
Sar-i lauḥ	: (Lit.) upper side of tablet. Illuminated heading or title page.

Shabīh : Likeness; portrait; representation; figure.

Shamsa : (In modern usage) illuminated heading, sometimes containing the initial invocation.

Ṣūrat : Figure; face; portrait-painting.

Ṭarḥ : Sketch; outline; drawing.

Umarā : (Plural of *amīr* (noble), commander). Holders of high rank in Mughal service.

'Unwān : Heading; portion of title-page generally gilded and highly ornamented.

Ustād : Teacher; master-painter.

Vīnā : Indian stringed musical instrument with gourds.

Wazīr : Minister; (in the Mughal Empire) the principal minister, who was also the minister controlling finance.

SELECT BIBLIOGRAPHY

Abdu-l Bāqī Nihāwandī, *Ma'āṣir-i Raḥīmī* (1616), ed., H. Hosain, Bib. Ind., Calcutta, 1910-31.

Abū'l Fazl, *Akbarnāma* (1601), ed., Ahmad Ali and Abdur Rahim, Bib. Ind., Calcutta, 1873-87, trans. H. Beveridge, RAS, Calcutta, 1897-1921.

Abū'l Fazl, *Ā'īn-i Akbarī* (1595). ed., H. Blochmann, Bib. Ind., Calcutta, 1867-77, trans. in 3 vols., I by H. Blochmann (1868), II & III by H.S. Jarrett (1894). Revised by D.C. Phillott (I, 1927, 1939), J. Sarkar (II and III, 1949).

Ahmad, T., "Nādiru'l 'Aṣr Manṣūr", *INI*, 25, 1972.

Ali, Salim, "The Mughal Emperors of India as Naturalists and Sportsmen", *JBNHS*, Vols. 31, Part IV (1926) and 32, Parts I & II (1927).

Alvi, M.A. and Rahman, A., *Jahangir the Naturalist*, New Delhi, 1968.

Anand, Mulk Raj, *Album of Indian Painting*, New Delhi, 1973.

Archer, W.G., *Indian Miniatures*, Greenwich, 1960.

Arnold, T.W. and Wilkinson, J.V.S., *A Library of A. Chester Beatty: A Catalogue of the Indian Miniatures*, 3 Vols., London, 1936.

Ashton, Sir Leigh, ed. *The Art of India and Pakistan* (A Commemorative Catalogue of the Exhibition held at the Royal Academy of Arts, 1947-48, London), London, 1948.

Atabai, Badri, *Fehrist-i Muraqqa't-i Kitāb Khānā-i Sultanatī*, Teheran, s. 1353.

Babur, *Bāburnāma* or *Tūzuk-i Bāburī* (1530), Turki text, ed., A.S. Beveridge, Leiden & London, 1905, Persian trans. by 'Abdu'r Raḥīm Kh̲ān-i Kh̲ānān (1590), B.M. Or.3714; Eng. tr., J. Leyden and W. Erskine, revised L. King, Oxford, 1921; and A.S. Beveridge, London, 1921.

Bailey, L.H., *The Standard Cyclopedia of Horticulture*, New York, 1947.

Bailey, L.H., *Manual of Cultivated Plants*, New York, 1947.

Barrett, D. and Gray, B., *Painting of India*, Lausanne, 1963.

Bayazid Bayat, *Tazkira-i Humāyūn-o Akbar* (1585), ed., M. Hidayat Hosain, Bib. Ind., Calcutta, 1941.

Beach, M.C., *The Grand Mogul Imperial Painting in India (1600-1660)*, Williamstown, Mass., 1978.

Beach, M.C., *The Imperial Image, Paintings for the Mughal Court,* Freer Gallery of Art, Washington, D.C., 1981.

Beach, M.C., "The Mughal painter Abu'l Hasan and some English sources for his style", *JWAG,* XXXVIII, 1975.

Beach, M.C., "The Mughal Painter Kesu Das", *AAA,* 30, 1976-7.

Beach, M.C., "*The New Cambridge History of India: Mughal and Rajput Painting,* Cambridge, 1990.

Binney, Edwin 3rd, *Indian Miniature Painting from the Collection of Edwin Binney 3rd. The Mughal and Deccan Schools with some related Sultanate Material* (exhibition catalogue: Portland Art Museum, 1 December 1973 to 20 January 1974), Portland, 1973.

Binyon, L., Gray, B. and Wilkinson, J.V.S., *Persian Miniature Painting,* London, 1933.

Blunt, W., "The Mughal Painters of Natural History", *BUM,* 90 (529), 1948.

Brand, Michael and Lowry, Glenn D., *Akbar's India: Art from the Mughal City of Victory,* New York, 1985.

Brown, Percy, *Indian Painting under the Mughals, A.D. 1550 to A.D. 1750,* Oxford, 1924.

Brunell, Francis, *Splendour of Indian Miniatures,* New York, no date.

Catalogue of the Loan Section, Catalogue of the Loan Section of Indian Art (Golden Jubilee Exhibition held at Town Hall, Bombay, 20 January to 5 February 1939). Bombay, 1939.

Chaitanya, Krishna, *A History of Indian Painting: Manuscript, Moghul and Deccani Traditions,* New Delhi, 1979.

Chandra, Moti, *The Technique of Mughal Painting,* Lucknow, 1946.

Chandra, Moti, *Indian Art,* Prince of Wales Museum, Bombay, 1964.

Chandra, Moti, *A Handbook of the Indian Art Collection in the Prince of Wales Museum of Western India, Bombay,* Bombay, no date.

Chandra, Pramod, *The Tutinama of the Cleveland Museum of Art and the Origins of Mughal Painting,* Chicago, 1976.

Clarke, C.S., *Victoria and Albert Museum Drawings: Thirty Mogul Paintings from the School of Jahangir (17th century) and four Panels of Calligraphy in the Wantage Bequest,* London, 1922.

Coomaraswamy, A.K., "Mughal Paintings (schools of Akbar and Jahangir)", *BMFA,* 16 (93), 1918.

Coomaraswamy, A.K., *Portfolio of Indian Art* (objects selected from the collection of the Museum of Fine Arts, Boston), Boston, 1923.

Coomaraswamy, A.K., "Les Miniatures Orientales de la collection Goloubew au Museum of Fine Arts de Boston", *AA,* 13, 1929.

Coomaraswamy, A.K., *Catalogue of Indian Collections in the Museum of Fine Arts, Boston, Pt. VI (Mughal Painting),* Boston, 1930.

Das, A.K., "Ustad Mansur", *Lalit,* 17, 1974.

Das, A.K., "Mughal Painting" in *History and Culture of the Indian People, VII: The Mughal Empire,* ed., R.C. Majumdar, Bombay, 1974.

Das, A.K., "Some more Mansur's drawings", *Lalit,* 18, 1977.

Das, A.K., "The Turkey in Mughal and Amber-Jaipur Painting", *JIM,* 30-1, 1974-5 (published in 1977).

Das, A.K., *Mughal Painting during Jahangir's Time,* Calcutta, 1978.

Das, A.K., *Treasures of Indian Painting,* Series 1, Jaipur, 1976; Series 2, Jaipur, 1978; Series 3, Jaipur, 1982; Series 4, Jaipur, 1983.

Das, A.K., *Splendour of Mughal Painting,* Bombay, 1986.

Das, A.K., "Mansur" in *Master Artists of the Imperial Mughal Court,* ed. Pratapaditya Pal, Bombay, 1991.

Dickinson, E.C., "The Treatment of Nature in Moghul Paintings", *PQ,* Special Issue, August 1951.

Dimand, M.S., *A Guide to an Exhibition of Islamic Miniature Painting and Book Illumination,* New York, 1933-4.

Dimand, M.S., *Indian Miniature Painting,* Milan, no date.

Dimand, M.S., *A Handbook of Muhammadan Art,* 2nd edition, New York, 1944.

Dimand, M.S., "An Exhibition of Islamic and Indian Painting", *BMMA,* 14, 1955.

Du Ry, J. Carl, *Art of Islam,* New York, 1972.

Ehnbom, Daniel J., ed., *Indian Miniatures, The Ehrenfeld Collection,* New York, 1985.

Eletr, M. Raid, "Birds and Animals in Mughal Painting", *BCA,* 1, 1959.

Ethe, H. and Sachau, E., *Catalogue of the Persian, Turkish and Pushtu Manuscripts in the Bodleian Library,* Pt. I, Oxford, 1889.

Ettinghausen, R., *Paintings of Sultans and Emperors of India in American Collections,* Delhi, 1961.

Ettinghausen, R., *Islamic Painting (Indian)* (Reprint from The Metropolitan Museum of Art Bulletin, 1978), New York, no date.

Exhibition of Art, Exhibition of Art chiefly from the Dominions India and Pakistan (2400 B.C. to 1947 A.D.), catalogue of the exhibition held at Royal Academy of Arts, London, 1947-8.

Exhibition of Islamic Art, Exhibition of Islamic Art in India of the Sixteenth and Seventeenth Centuries (Catalogue of the exhibition held at British Museum, London, November 1961), London, 1961.

Falk, Toby and Archer, Mildred, *Indian Miniatures in the India Office Library,* London, 1981.

Falk, Toby, Digby, Simon and Goedhuis, Michael, *Paintings from Mughal India,* Colnaghi, London, no date.

Gascoigne, B., *The Great Moghuls,* London, 1971.

Godard, Y.A., "Les marges du Murakka Gulshan", *AEI,* I, 1936.

Godard, Y.A., "Un album de portraits des princes Timurides de l'Inde", *AEI,* II, 1937.

Godard, Y.A. and Gray, B., *Iran-Persian Miniatures, Imperial Library,* New York, 1956.

Godden, R., *Gulbadan (Portrait of Rose Princess),* New York, 1980.

Goetz, H., "Indian Miniatures in German Museums and Private Collections", *EAQ,* 2, 1930.

Goetz, H., *Bilderatlas zur Kulturgeschichte Indiens in der Grossmoghul-Ziet,* Berlin, no date.

Goetz, H., "The Early Muraqqas of the Mughal Emperor Jahangir", *EW,* 8 (2), 1957; also published in *Marg,* 11 (4), 1958.

Gorakshkar, Sadashiv, ed. *Animal in Indian Art* (Catalogue of the exhibition held at Prince of Wales Museum of Western India, Bombay from 30th September to 21st October 1977), Bombay, 1979.

Gray, B., *Persian Painting,* London, 1961.

Gray, B. and Wilkinson, J.V.S., "Indian Paintings in a Persian Museum", *BUM,* 66, 1935.

Grousset, R., *Civilization of the East: India,* New York, 1931.

Habib, Irfan, *An Atlas of the Mughal Empire, Political and Economic Maps with Detailed Notes, Bibliography and Index,* New Delhi, 1982.

Hambly, G., *Cities of Mughal India (Delhi, Agra and Fatehpur Sikri),* Delhi, 1968.

Haq, M. Mahfuzul, "The Khan-i Khanan and his Painters", *ISC,* 5, 1931.

Hasan, S.M., "The Mughal School of Zoological Portraiture", *AAL,* 37, 1963.

Havell, E.B., *Indian Sculpture and Painting,* London, 1908.

Havell, E.B., *The Art Heritage of India,* Bombay, 1964.

Heath, L., *Examples of Indian Art at the British Empire Exhibition,* 1924, London, 1925.

Hendley, T.H., "Sport in Indian Art", *JIAI,* 17, 1916.

Irwin, J., "The heritage of art in India: (3) The Mughal period", *Studio,* 135, 1948.

Irwin, J., "Treasures of Indian Art at the Victoria and Albert Museum", *Marg,* 1977.

Islamic Art, Islamic Art from India (catalogue of the exhibits put on sale during 24th April-10th May 1980), Spink & Son Ltd., London, 1980.

Ivanova, A.A., Akimushkin, O.F., Grek, T.V. and Gyuzalyana, P.L.T., *Albom Indiyskikh i Pyersidskikh Miniatyar XVI-XVIIIvv,* Moscow, 1962 (Russian text with English resume).

Jahāngīr, *Tūzuk-i Jahāngīrī (1624)*, ed., S. Ahmad Ghazipur & Aligarh, 1963-4, trans. A. Rogers, ed., H. Beveridge, London, 1904-14.

James, David, *Islamic Masterpieces of the Chester Beatty Library* (catalogue of an exhibition held at Leighton House, London, 1981), London, 1981.

Jauhar, *Tezkereh al Vakiat, tr.,* C. Stewart, *Private Memoirs of the Moghul Emperor Humayun,* London, 1832.

Jones, Dalu, ed. *A Mirror of Princes, The Mughals and The Medici,* Bombay, 1987.

Khandalavala, K., "Some problems of Mughal painting", *Lalit,* 11, 1965.

Khandalavala, K., *Islamic Heritage of India,* Delhi, 1981.

Khandalavala, K., "Mughal Painting: Considerations and Reconsiderations", *Lalit,* No. 27, 1993.

Khandalavala, K. and Chandra, Moti, *Miniatures and Sculptures, Collection of Sir Cowasji Jehangir,* Bombay, 1965.

Koch, Ebba, "Pietre Dure and other artistic contacts between the Court of the Mughals and that of the Medici", in Jones, D., ed.

Krishnadasa, Rai and Kabir, Humayun, *Mughal Miniatures,* New Delhi, 1955.

Krishna, Kalyan, "Problem of a Portrait of Jahangir in the Musee Guimet, Paris", Krishna Anand (ed.), *Chhavi* (Golden Jubilee Volume), Benaras, 1971.

Kübmaul, F., *Indische Kunst* (exhibition catalogue), Hamburg, 1966.

Kühnel, Ernst, *Islamische Miniaturmalerei,* Berlin, 1922.

Kühnel, Ernst, *Miniaturmalerei in Islamischen Orient,* Berlin, 1922.

Kühnel, Ernst and Goetz, H., *Indian Book Painting,* London, 1926.

Lawrence, G., *Art Des Indes, Miniatures Mogholes,* Paris, 1963. English text: *Indian Art, Mughal Miniatures,* London, 1963.

Leach, Linda, "Painting" in Doshi, Saryu (ed.), *Pageant of Indian Art,* Bombay, 1983.

Lee, Sharman, *A History of Far Eastern Art,* London, 1964.

Losty, J.P., *The Art of the Book in India* (catalogue of an exhibition mounted at British Library from 16 April to 1 August 1982), British Library, London, 1982.

Maclagan, E.D., *The Jesuits and the Great Mogul,* London, 1932.

Marteau, G. and Vever, H., *Miniatures Persanes exposees au Musee des Arts Decoratifs,* Paris, 1912.

Martin, F.R., *The Miniature Painting and Painters of Persia, India and Turkey,* London, 1912.

Mehta, N.C., "Red lilies, a newly discovered Mansur", *Rupam,* 19-20, 1924.

Mehta, N.C., *Studies in Indian Painting,* Bombay, 1926.

Michell, George, ed. *In the Image of Man (The Indian Perception of Universe through 200 years of Painting and Sculpture),* catalogue of the Festival of India held at Hayward Gallery, London (25 March-13 June 1982), New Delhi, 1982.

Okada, Amina, *Imperial Mughal Painters (Indian Miniatures from the Sixteenth and Seventeenth Centuries),* Paris, 1992.

Otsuka-Kogeisha, *The Pageant of Chinese Painting,* Tokyo, 1936.

Pal, Pratapaditya, *Court Paintings of India, 16th-19th Centuries,* New York, 1983.

Pal, Pratapaditya, ed. *Master Artists of the Imperial Mughal Court,* Bombay, 1991.

Pal, Pratapaditya, *Indian Painting, A Catalogue of the Los Angeles County Museum of Art Collection,* California, 1993.

Patel, Seema, *Jahangir kala men prakartik itihas par bane laghu chitron ka vishleshanatmak addhayan* (in Hindi), Ph.D. thesis, Agra University, 1984 (unpublished).

Pinder-Wilson, R.H., *Paintings from the Muslim Courts of India* (catalogue of the exhibition of the World of Islam Festival, 1976, held at Prints and Drawings Gallery, British Museum from 13th April to 11th July 1976), London, 1976.

Princely Paintings, Princely Paintings from Mughal India, British Museum, London, 1980.

Qaisar, Ahsan Jan, *The Indian Response to European Technology and Culture (A.D. 1498-1707),* Delhi, 1982.

Qaisar, Ahsan Jan and Som Prakash Verma, ed. *Art and Culture, Endeavours in Interpretation,* New Delhi, 1996.

Qazwini, Mulla 'Ala ud Daula, *Nafais-al Maasir,* dated 1573, MS. in Maulana Azad Library, Aligarh Muslim University, Aligarh.

Randhawa, M.S., "Paintings of the Baburnama", *Roopa,* 42 (1-2), 1975.

Randhawa, M.S., *Paintings of the Baburnama,* National Museum, New Delhi, 1983.

Rawson, Philip S., *Indian Painting,* London, 1961.

Ray, Niharranjan, *Mughal Court Painting,* Calcutta, 1975.

Rich, Vivian, "Mughal floral paintings and its European sources", *OA,* New Series, XXXIII (2), 1987.

Robinson, B.W., ed. *Persian and Mughal Art* (catalogue of the exhibition of Persian and Mughal Art held at Colnaghi, London, from 7th April to 22nd May 1976), London, 1976.

Rogers, J.M., *Mughal Miniatures,* London, 1993.

Saraswati, S.K., "Birds in Mughal Art", *Marg,* 2, 1948.

Sen, Geeti, *Paintings from the Akbarnama,* New Delhi, 1984.

Seyller, John, "The School of Oriental and African Studies *Anvār-i Suhaylī*: The Illustration of a De Luxe Mughal Manuscript", *Archives of Asian Art,* vol. 38, New York, 1985.

Simsar, A., trans. & ed. *The Cleveland Museum of Art's Tutinama, Tales of a Parrot,* Austria, 1978.

Skelton, Robert, "A Decorative Motif in Mughal Art" in Pal, Pratapaditya, ed. *Aspects of Indian Art,* Leiden, 1972.

Smith, V.A., *A History of Fine Art in India and Ceylon,* Oxford, 1911.

Spink, Walter M. and Levine, Deborah, *Akbarnama: Catalogue,* New York, no date.

Staude, W., "Contribution a l'etude de Basawan", *RAA,* 8 (1), 1934.

Staude, W., *Moghul Maler der Akbar Zeit,* Wien, 1935.

Stchoukine, I., *La Peinture Indienne a l'Epoque des Grand Moghols,* Paris, 1929.

Stchoukine, I, *Les Miniatures Indiennes de l'Epoque des Grand Moghols du Musee du Louvre,* Paris, 1929.

Suleiman, H., *Miniatures of Baburnama,* Tashkent, 1970.

Swarup, Shanti, *The Arts and Crafts of India and Pakistan,* Bombay, 1957.

Swarup, Shanti, *5000 Years of Arts and Crafts in India and Pakistan,* Bombay, 1963.

Swarup, Shanti, *Flora and Fauna in Mughal Art,* Bombay, 1983.

Tandon, R.K., *Indian Miniature Painting, 16th through 19th Centuries,* Bangalore, 1981.

Temple, R.C., ed. *Travels of Peter Mundy in Europe and Asia, 1608-67,* Hakluyt Society edition, 2nd series, London, 1914, (vol. V, reprint, 1967).

The Art of Islam, The Art of Islam (Masterpieces from The Metropolitan Museum of Art, New York), Catalogue of the exhibition of Islamic Art held at the Museum from 20-6-81 to 23-8-81, New York, 1981.

Titley, Norah M., *Miniatures from Persian Manuscripts* (a catalogue and subject index of paintings from Persia, India and Turkey in the British Library and the British Museum), London, 1977.

Titley, Norah M., *Persian Miniature Painting and its influence on the art of Turkey and India (The British Library Collection),* London, 1984.

Topsfield, Andrew, "Paintings and the Arts of the Book" in *The Indian Heritage (Court Life and Arts under Mughal Rule),* catalogue of the exhibition held at Victoria and Albert Museum from 21 April to 22 August 1982, Festival of India, London, 1982.

Topsfield, Andrew, *An Introduction to Indian Court Painting,* London, 1984.

Tyulayev, S.I., *Indian Art in Soviet Collections,* Moscow, 1956.

Tyulayev, S.I., *Miniatures of Babur Namah,* Moscow, 1960.

Verma, S.P., "Treatment of similar themes — a study based on the illustrations of Tuzuk-i Baburi", *Proceedings of Indian History Congress,* Chandigarh, 1973.

Verma, S.P., "Miniatures of the Anwar-i Suhaili", *Roopa,* 44 (1-2), 1977.

Verma, S.P., *Art and Material Culture in the Paintings of Akbar's Court,* New Delhi, 1978.

Verma, S.P., "Illustrated Akbarnama of Sixteenth Century Mughal School", *Roopa,* 51 (1-2), 1980.

Verma, S.P., "Mansur, the Master Painter of Jahangir's Epoch", *Roopa,* 53 (1-2), 1982.

Verma, S.P., "Artists' Signatures in Miniatures of the Mughal School", *IHR,* 10 (1-2), 1983-4.

Verma. S.P., "Some Unnoticed Mughal Miniatures at the Royal Library, Windsor", *Roopa,* 57 (1-2), 1985.

Verma, S.P., *Wild Life in Mughal Painting, A Catalogue of the Exhibition held at Aligarh Muslim University,* November 5-10, 1985 (mimeograph).

Verma, S.P., *The Reign of Akbar: An Illustrated History, A Catalogue of the Exhibition held at Aligarh Muslim University,* October 9-12,1991 (mimeograph).

Verma, S.P., "Aspects of Paintings in the British Museum Manuscript of Akbarnama", *Lalit,* No. 27, 1993.

Verma, S.P., "The Tulip (*ca.* 1621): A Study of Mansur", *Huntia,* Pittsburgh, Vol. 9, No. 1, 1993.

Verma, S.P., *Mughal Painters and Their Work, A Biographical Survey and Comprehensive Catalogue,* New Delhi, 1994.

Visser, H.F.E., "Tentoonstelling der kunst van India te Londen", *Phoenix,* 3 (1), February, 1948.

Welch, S.C., "The Emperor Akbar's *Khamsa* of Nizami", *Journal of Walters Art Gallery,* Vol. XXIII, Baltimore, 1960.

Welch, S.C., *The Art of Mughal India: Painting and Precious Objects* (catalogue of an exhibition shown in the galleries of Asia House, New York, 1964), New York, 1963.

Welch, S.C., "Mughal and Deccani Miniature Paintings from a Private Collection", *AOS,* 5, 1963.

Welch, S.C., *A Flower from Every Meadow, Indian Paintings from American Collections (*catalogue of an exhibition shown in the galleries of Asia House, New York, 1973), New York, 1973.

Welch, S.C., *Indian Drawings and Painted Sketches (16th Through 19th Centuries),* New York, 1976.

Welch, S.C., *Imperial Mughal Painting,* London, 1978.

Welch, S.C., *Art and Culture (1300-1900),* catalogue of the exhibition "India" held at The Metropolitan Museum of Art from September 14, 1985 to January 5, 1986, New York, 1985.

Welch, S.C. and Beach, M.C., *Gods, Thrones and Peacocks* (catalogue of an exhibition held in Asia House Gallery, New York, 23rd September to 12th December 1965; Baltimore Museum of Art, 18th January to 27th February 1966 and Munson-Williams-Proctor Institute, Utica, New York, 3rd April to 15th May 1966), New York, 1965.

Welch, S.C., Schimmel, A., Swietochowski, M.L. and Thackston, W., *The Emperors' Album, Images of Mughal India,* New York, 1987.

Wellesz, Emmy, *Akbar's Religious Thought Reflected in Mughal Painting,* Oxford, 1952.

Wilkinson, J.V.S., *The Lights of Canopus: Anwar-i Suhaili,* London, 1929.

Wilkinson, J.V.S., *Mughal Painting,* London, 1948.

Wolf, R.E., *Islam and Muslim Art* (tr. from French), London, 1960.

Zebrowski, Mark, "Three Indian Exhibitions", *OA,* 28 (3), 1982.

Index